SOCIAL AND CULTURAL HISTORY OF THE PUNJAB

Social and Cultural History of the Punjab

Prehistoric, Ancient and Early Medieval

J.S. GREWAL

MANOHAR
2026

First published 2004

Reprinted 2026

ISBN 978-81-7304-565-3

Published by
Ajay Kumar Jain *for*
Manohar Publishers & Distributors
4753/23 Ansari Road, Daryaganj
New Delhi 110 002

Printed at
Replika Press Pvt. Ltd.

Contents

Preface

I agreed to write a book on the socio-cultural history of the Punjab for the National Book Trust of India in 1992. My familiarity with the history of the region after AD 1000 encouraged me to think that such a book could be easily written. However, when I turned to the works dealing with the history of the region before AD 1000 I experienced difficulties. Neither the period nor the region as a whole was covered by all the published work put together, and there was more information on political than on social and cultural history. A clear focus on the region and use of original sources became necessary. As the work proceeded it became more and more interesting. Consequently, instead of producing a short book for the general reader under the banner of the National Book Trust of India, I prepared the present volume for a serious student of history, covering the period only up to AD 1000.

Certain matters related to this volume were discussed from time to time with Professors R.S. Sharma, Romila Thapar, D.N. Jha, Suvira Jaiswal, and B.D. Chattopadhyaya. Their own work, though not focused on the region, has been very helpful, and I feel grateful to them personally and professionally. After the original draft was prepared, Professor G.S. Mann of Santa Barbara, California, invited me to give lectures to a small group of researchers from North America and Western Europe, which obliged me to rethink and to clarify certain issues. The recent publication of Shereen Ratnagar's *Understanding Harappa: Civilization in the Greater Indus Valley* served as the final incentive for revising the original draft.

This work would not have been possible without help from younger colleagues. I may particularly mention Professors Indu Banga and Karuna Goswamy, Dr Reeta Grewal, Dr Veena Sachdeva, and Ms Sheena Pall from the Panjab University, Chandigarh, and Professors Radha Sharma and Harish C. Sharma from Guru Nanak Dev University, Amritsar. Indu Banga has read the manuscript and given valuable suggestions.

I am thankful to Shri Ramesh Jain and Shri Ajay Jain for their readiness to publish this volume. Since the original proposal came from the National Book Trust of India, I feel happy to dedicate this volume to the Trust, still hoping that I would write the book they invited me to write.

7 September 2003 J.S. GREWAL

Introduction

Generally, historians have written on the 'Punjab' without defining the region consciously. Before venturing on its social and cultural history we may define the region.

In the *Akbarnama* of Abu al-Fazl, the Punjab stands equated with the Mughal province of Lahore.[1] This is the province described in his *Ain-i Akbari* too. It covered two kinds of territory: the areas administered directly by governors (*nazims*) appointed by the emperor, and the areas administered by hereditary rulers (*rajas*) who were politically subordinate to the emperor. This Punjab did not cover the lower *doabs* between the Satlej and the Indus, but it did cover a large area in the hills as well as the upper portions of all the five *doabs*. The unit was formed for politico-administrative purposes by the Emperor Akbar.[2] If there were any geographical considerations in his mind, Abu al-Fazl was not concerned with those. So too was the case with Sujan Rai Bhandari who wrote his *Khulasa ut-Tawarikh* in the reign of Aurangzeb. Both of them simply accepted the existence of the province of Lahore as a politico-administrative unit equated with the Punjab.

Abu al-Fazl and Sujan Rai wrote as historians, but not as historians of the Punjab. The first historian to write on 'the Punjab' was Ganesh Das, the author of the *Char Bagh-i Panjab*, at the beginning of British rule in the Punjab in 1849. For his description of the region he equates the Punjab with the former Mughal province of Lahore without the hill areas under the vassal chiefs. But there is also another connotation of the Punjab in the *Char Bagh*: the dominions of Ranjit Singh and his successors, which made this 'Punjab' larger than the former Mughal province because it included Kashmir and a large portion of the former Mughal province of Multan. For the first connotation, Ganesh Das was guided by the usage of the Persian historians and for the second, by the existence of a state with the former Mughal province of Lahore as its core area. In both cases the connotation was politico-administrative.

The Punjab province created by the British was larger than the dominions of Ranjit Singh. From the very beginning it did not include Jammu and Kashmir, and after 1901 the areas covered by the North-

Western Frontier Province, but it included the entire plain between the Indus and the Jamuna and a large part of the hills between these two rivers. Like the Mughal province of Lahore, the British province of the Punjab incorporated a number of princely states for politico-administrative purposes. The British administrators began to equate 'the Punjab' with the British Punjab. This is the connotation, for instance, in S.S. Thorburn's *Punjab in Peace and War.* A few like H.K. Trevaskis in his *Land of the Five Rivers: An Economic History of the Punjab*, used 'the land of the five rivers' for the British Punjab. There cannot be any doubt that their 'land of the five rivers' was nothing more and nothing less than the British Punjab.[3] Like the Persian historians before them, the British accepted an existing politico-administrative unit as their unit of study.

It is interesting that historians have tended to project into the past their own connotation of the Punjab. The history of the Punjab in the *Char Bagh* starts with the mythical past and comes down to the time of the author. Throughout this narrative, his 'Punjab' remains essentially the former province of Lahore. Similarly, B.S. Nijjar projects the British Punjab into the past for writing three books on the region under the Sultans, the Great Mughals, and the Later Mughals. In G.L. Chopra's *Punjab as a Sovereign State*, the region stands equated with the dominions of Ranjit Singh and his successors. Similarly, in B.R. Chopra's *Kingdom of the Punjab*, the region is equated with the dominions of Ranjit Singh's successors. The criterion in all these cases remains politico-administrative.

This, however, is not true of all historians of the Punjab. Buddha Prakash, for instance, points out that the region for his *Political and Social Movements in Ancient Punjab* is not conterminus with either the contemporary Punjab or the Punjab of the British period. Parts of Afghanistan and Sind were included in his 'Punjab', his criterion being socio-cultural. In his view, socio-cultural development in 'the ancient Punjab' transcended political and geographical boundaries. We need not accept his interpretation, but what is relevant is his criterion for defining the region. Again, in Veena Sachdeva's *Polity and Economy of the Punjab During the Late Eighteenth Century*, the Punjab is not equated with any known politico-administrative unit, but consists of the plains between the Indus and the Satlej and the lower ranges of the Himalayas between these two rivers. Again, we may not find this definition of the region entirely satisfactory, but the criterion adopted in her work is pronouncedly geographical.

However, the Geographers do not necessarily agree in defining the Punjab. O.H.K Spate's 'Punjab' does not include the Salt Range and the Pothohar, not even the Jalandhar Doab; it contains the plains beyond the Indus, around Dera Ghazi Khan and Dera Ismail Khan, and the plains beyond the Satlej, around Bahawalpur. He is actually concerned with 'the Punjab plain'. He looks upon the Indo-Gangetic Divide as a transitional 'region' between the Punjab and the Ganges plains. This divide covers the whole of the Jalandhar Doab, the submontane belt between the Satlej and Jamuna, the plain up to the ridges of the Aravali near Delhi, and the dry bed of the Ghaggar above the Thar Desert. In a collection of articles entitled *India: A Regional Geography* (edited by R.L. Singh), the Punjab covers the Indian states of Haryana and Punjab, and the Union Territories of Delhi and Chandigarh. This Punjab is more or less the same as Spate's Indo-Gangetic Divide.

The most remarkable feature of the north-west of the Indian subcontinent is the Indus river system. It links the plains with the lower Himalayas in the north and the north-west. The Aravali and the Thar Desert mark the southern boundary. The Jamuna becomes an important feature because it belongs to a different river system and serves as the extremity of 'the east'. Thus, if we are looking for a broad geographical region, it appears to lie between the Himalayas, the Jamuna, the Aravalis, and the Thar. It is interesting to note that the Punjab of all definitions is either contained in or overlaps with this geographical region. It may serve as our starting point.

However, even in terms of physical environment this region is not, and never was, homogeneous. It was marked by sub-regional differences. All the sub-regions did not have the same kind of political, economic or cultural development at one and the same time. One subregion could develop more in one set of circumstances; and another sub-region could develop differently in another set of circumstances. The possibilities of sub-regional variations have to be kept in mind by the historian of social and cultural development. Equally important is the possibility of interaction between the sub-regions. A major part of the history of the Punjab involves the study of interaction between its sub-regions.

Further, a region is never isolated from the rest of the world. Its contacts with the outside world may be violent or peaceful, extensive or piecemeal. Within the parameters of intra-regional and inter-regional interaction, the socio-cultural history of the Punjab may actually be the history of some of its sub-regions. Conversely, we cannot take it for granted that what we observe in the case of one sub-region was also true of the others at any point of time. Therefore, it is necessary to remember not only the question 'when' but also the question 'where' even in the context of the region. Furthermore, an important concern of the historian is with regional articulation and its consciousness among an increasing number of people, leading to an awareness of regional identity.[4]

A large volume of literature related to the Punjab is available to the student of its history in the form of books, monographs and articles. However, all of it is not focused on the Punjab, and it is uneven in terms of quantity, relevance, and quality. Much of this literature ignores the question 'where'. Consequently, it is not possible to write a socio-cultural history of the Punjab simply on the basis of published work. A lot of spadework has to be done by a number of scholars before a good general history of the region can be attempted. It is necessary, therefore, to consult original sources. The variety and the mass of these sources are truly formidable, so that only the most important and the most relevant could be used.

NOTES

1. It must be pointed out that the term 'Panjab' came into currency in the reign of Akbar. Whereas Abu al-Fazl uses it quite frequently, the word does not occur in the *Tuzk-i Baburi* though Babur refers to the two river systems of the subcontinent and to the politico-administrative units in existence between Kabul and Delhi, including the province of Lahore.
2. Akbar reorganized the province of Lahore to include all the five *doabs* in the new province. This was the only province in his empire with five *doabs*. He gave a name to each of these, which has come down to the present day. It appears that he gave the name 'Panjab' to the new province of Lahore because it contained five *doabs*. In any case, if we drop two letters from *panj-doab* (five *doabs*), namely the Persian letters *dal* (d) and *wao* (o), we are left with *Panjab*, which was meant to stand for the province of five *doabs*.
3. If we take the word '*panjab*' literally as the 'land of five rivers' we fail to understand which five and why. A land of five rivers could have only four *doabs*. To take a metaphor literally is to create confusion rather than clarity.

4. Consciousness of Punjabi identity was to emerge clearly before the end of the eighteenth century with reference to a language and a people. This identity was more openly expressed and espoused in the early nineteenth century. It was not a creation of the period of colonial rule. If anything, colonial rule pushed this regional identity into the background and brought others to the fore. No identity is exclusive, and regional identity is not an exception in this respect.

1

Rise and Decline of Civilization

FOOD GATHERING AND HUNTING

According to the geologists, the Himalayas arose from a continuous process of uplift due to the impact of the continental block of peninsular India on the Asian block in the north. A process of refolding resulted in the rise of the Shiwalik hills about 45,00,000 years ago. The discovery of a jaw at Pilbeam in the Pothohar Plateau suggests the existence of 'humans' in this part of the region prior to 4,00,000 years. Fourteen artefacts, including two hand axes, discovered at Jalal Shah in the Jhelam district, are said to be about 4,00,000 years old. Stone tools consisting largely of cores and flakes have been discovered at many other sites in the Pothohar Plateau, particularly in the valley of the river Soan which has given its name to the stone age cultures discovered in the Punjab.

Life in the Stone Age in the Punjab can be surmised from what is thought of the Stone Age communities the world over. D.D. Kosambi has underlined the importance of food gathering in the Indian context. This should be true of the Punjab, but without the implication that hunting or fishing was not known. Sharp chips could be set in handles of wood, horn or bone to make javelins, arrows, knives and harpoons. Pointed flakes could be used as needles or awls for stitching hides. Much before the appearance of pottery, leather bags could be used for storing food. Not to let the food rot when in plenty, group feasts could be held on special occasions. The rudiments of social life could thus emerge at this primitive stage. Among the hunting communities, dance could emerge as a ritual as well as a sort of drill in the techniques of hunting in which some would imitate the animals and others would imitate the hunters. A kind of specialization could emerge when the food-sharing units concentrated on a particular type of food. In due course this particular item could become the totem. The need of exchange could bring different units together, leading eventually to marriage between members of different totem groups. Exchange would lead to a better diet through a wider range of foods, and to improved techniques of tool making. The language of the combined groups would also get enriched.

Incipient agriculture appears to have emerged towards the end of the Stone Age. Microlithic tools have been discovered at a number of places in the Pothohar Plateau and elsewhere in the Punjab. A full range of microlithic industry has come to light at the site known as Khanpur Cave near Taxila. Microliths have been discovered also at a place called Rehman Dheri in the district of Dera Ismail Khan. A number of sites in the valleys of the Beas and the Satlej, and their tributaries, have yielded stone tools, broadly comparable to the Soan industries. Refined microlithic tools have been found at places like Dera Gopipur on the Beas and Pinjore near Chandigarh. The neolithic community at Ror on the river Banganga near Haripur-Guler in the Kangra district appears to have separated the workshops from the hearths. Important among its neolithic tools were axes, axe-hammers, chisels, picks, celts and ring stones. It is possible that the neolithic people of this area used their tools for digging roots and tubers. However, the neolithic axe could be used for clearing small patches of land for seed plantation by means of a digging stick. Possibly, the stage of 'incipient agriculture' and domestication of animals was reached.

RISE OF AGRICULTURAL COMMUNITIES

The domestication of animals and agriculture marked a decisive step in social evolution in the Punjab, as elsewhere in the world. For an early village community in the Punjab we may turn first to Sarai Khola (Sarai Kala) in the Pothohar Plateau, about 3 kilometres to the south-west of Taxila. The oldest period of this settlement is regarded as neolithic on the basis of its ground stone axes, stone blades, bone points and unpainted burnished pottery which was handmade or shaped on a simple turntable. There is no evidence of the use of metal, or of structural remains. It has been surmised that this settlement came into existence between 5000 and 3500 BC.

What is more important, a second phase has been noticed at this site. Stone microliths, celts and chisels continue to appear, but there are also copper tools as well as copper bangles, pins, rings and rods. The pottery is wheel-made and bears motifs such as the *pipal* leaf and the arrow. Apart from large jars, there are bowls, flat dishes, ladles, knobbed pot lids and dishes-on-stand. There are terracotta figurines, including humped bulls and cows, and toy carts with solid wheels. There are stone beads (carnelian and agate) and a lapis lazuli; there are beads also of steatite paste. There are some ceramic balls too. The post holes discovered at the site are suggestive of habitational structures of rather insubstantial nature, and there is evidence of prepared clay floors and a stone wall. It is extremely important to note that there is evidence of contact between Sarai Khola and Kot Diji in Sind during this phase.

The earliest settlement at Jalilpur on the left of the river Ravi, close to its confluence with the Chenab, was 'neolithic': there was no copper or bronze, or any other metal in use. The stone blade industry and bone points show similarity with the earliest period at Sarai Khola. There are no clear structural remains, but there are prepared floors and doubtful evidence of the use of mudbrick. The most interesting artefact is the net-sinker, showing the importance of fishing. Some of the animal remains at the site are those of sheep, goat, cattle and gazelle. The pottery was handmade, with a coating of slurry made up of clay mixed with fragments of crushed pottery. This feature of the pottery is an equivalent to the granular sand roughening of the pottery during the first period at Sarai Khola. The globular jar with a short neck was the characteristic vessel of Jalilpur. Beads of terracotta were also found at the site.

There was a second phase at Jalilpur when the pottery was wheel-made, and bowls, dishes-on-stand and knobbed pot lids were added to the globular jar with a short neck. This pottery presents parallels with the pottery of the second phase at Sarai Khola. The pottery at Jalilpur bore bichrome decorations, black on red, or black and white on red; it also bore animal and geometric motifs. As at Sarai Khola during the second phase, there were female figurines and humped bulls and cows in terracotta at Jalilpur. Apart from beads, there were toy cart frames. Several lapis lazulis were found at the site. Above all, there were copper or bronze rods, and a definite use of mud bricks.

A large number of sites have been discovered in Cholistan, on the Pakistan stretch of the Ghaggar (called Hakra). Thirty-two of these sites, concentrated around Derawar fort and towards its south-west, are regarded as Jalilpur-related and placed in the fourth millennium BC. Pottery from these sites, called Hakra ware, was mostly handmade red and with a series of multiple incised lines, wavy, oblique and vertical. Forty-one sites are regarded as Kot Diji-related and date to the third millennium.

About 200 kilometres to the south-east of Harappa, there was an important settlement at Kalibangan on the left bank of the river Ghaggar which formed either a part of the Indus river system or of an independent system between the Beas and the Ganges. Even in its earliest phase this settlement was fortified, forming a rough parallelogram of 250 × 180 metres. Constructed of mudbricks of a standard size, its walls were plastered. The entrance in the north-west corner, which was actually curved so that it could be defended from either side of the flanking wall, gave access to the river, and it was wide enough for vehicular traffic. The settlement had well laid out houses. An average house consisted of a courtyard and a few rooms along its margin. Ovens, similar to the present day oven (*tandur*), were a common feature of the houses. Pits plastered with lime suggest that they were meant for storing grain. Remains of a field with furrow marks in both east-west and north-south directions suggest mixed cropping. The tools used were mostly of stone, including serrated blades which could be used for cutting crops. The use of copper was known and, apart from bangles, a few copper axes have been found at the site. Agriculture was supplemented by fishing and hunting, adding meat and fish to cereals for diet. The banana plant painted on pottery suggests that this fruit was grown.

The pottery of the earliest culture of Kalibangan was essentially monochrome, turned rather indifferently on the wheel. It consisted of large globular jars meant presumably for storing water, bowls, basins, dishes-on-stand, knobbed pot lids, and a tall cylindrical vessel. Flora and fauna designs were painted on the pottery, like the sunflower, the stag, the bull, the duck, the scorpion, and the fish. Bangles of shell and terracotta as well as copper were in use, and so were beads of terracotta, carnelian, agate, shell and copper. Terracotta bull-figurines and solid cart-wheels have been found at the site. There are some graffiti on the pottery, but their significance is not clear. The period suggested for this culture is 3000-2750 BC.

In the valley of the Ghaggar and its tributary, the Chautang (Drishadvati), many sites have been discovered where pottery is identical to the pottery of Kalibangan. Among many other sites which indicate the existence of an early rural culture in the eastern Punjab, the most interesting is the excavated site at Banawali on the right bank of the dried up Ghaggar. Its earliest period bears striking similarities to the earliest period at Kalibangan so far as ceramic ware and other artefacts are concerned. Copper is rather poorly represented. Among the other sites which show similarities with the earliest phase of Kalibangan are Siswal, Rakhigarhi and Mitathal in Haryana. Similarly at Ropar, on the left bank of the Satlej, pottery analogous to that of the early period at Kalibangan has been discovered. Close to Ropar, artefacts have been found at Bara.

The pottery recovered from the excavated sites is generally red, with a small quantity of grey ware. There are quite a few vessel forms: hemispherical and angular-walled bowls, globular jars, small S-shaped jars, dishes-on-stand, and pedestal-footed vessels. Black paint and incised lines are used for decoration, and motifs are confined to geometric patterns. The most distinguishing feature of the painted pottery is the use of white paint to fill in some of the geometric patterns.

Archaeological evidence, thus, gives a clear indication of settlements based on agriculture in different parts of the Punjab, between the Indus and the Jamuna. The number of villages appears to have increased enormously from 3300 to 2600 BC. Even more important is the indication of interaction between local or regional cultures. It has been noticed that Kot Dijian pottery was widely distributed during this period from Kot Diji to Sarai Khola and Manda (near Akhnur) in the north and to Makran in the west.

The transitional phase at Harappa, where the earliest Indus stratum is also in evidence, is very significant in this context. It was marked by an expansion of the settlement and a better organization of production marked by a certain degree of specialization. The ceramics of this phase are identical to the ceramics of the second phase at Jalilpur and the early levels at Kot Diji. Among the other artefacts are grey fired bangles, stone blades made from a dark greyish black chert, a stone celt, various types of stone beads, and human figurines of a type that is not found in the mature Harappan culture. Apart from massive mudbrick revetments, there were five or six different phases of building. The large-scale of construction suggests some form of social organization capable of mobilizing labour and controlling the manufacture of large quantities of brick. The long term production of ceramics in one small area suggests specialization. Among the artefacts which would continue into the mature phase are triangular terracotta cakes, terracotta toys and red fired bangles. In one area, there was no major break between the transitional and the mature phase. Tools of tan brown chert of the Rohri hills near the site of Kot Diji were found in the upper levels of this transitional phase, suggesting an expanded network of exchange and trade. This impression is reinforced by the bangles of marine shell found in these levels. Equally significant are some graffiti on potsherds, indicating the use of symbols for communication.

RISE OF THE HARAPPAN CIVILIZATION

A distinct culture began to appear at Harappa from about 2600 BC. It is called 'Mature Harappan' to distinguish it from the earlier formative phase called 'Early Indus' or 'Early Harappan'. The 'Mature Harappan' culture was marked by walled settlements, bipartite cities and towns, storage structures and other buildings, and extensive construction of houses in baked brick. Not so spectacular as the Egyptian, Mesopotamian or the Chinese in terms of funerary structures, temples or treasures, the 'Mature Harappan' culture was unique in terms of its system of standardized weights, water harnessing, and overseas trade as well as its baked-brick buildings and architectural skills. Common to all these cultures was their reliance on copper and its alloys with tin, lead or arsenic for the tools of production. That is why they are referred to as cultures of the 'Bronze Age'.

The development of bronze metallurgy involved knowledge of mining copper, tin, lead, and arsenic, smelting, alloying, and casting which, in turn, required techniques of pyrotechnology: knowledge of fuels, temperatures, reduction and oxidation, fluxes, and the varying quality of charcoals of different woods. In other words, the Bronze Age marked an advance in science and technology. Metal tools could be made in sizes and shapes different from what was possible in stone, which made skilled carpentry and fine carving of ivory and stones possible. Copper, tin, lead and arsenic had to be procured from distant places. For this, regular interaction between towns, or elite groups, was a necessity. The locus of technological and economic transformation in the Bronze Age, therefore, was the city, and the economy itself had to be sustained by external trade.

The Harappan sites reveal many features of 'civilization' as a stage of advancement of society: sophisticated architecture in a range of building materials, the use of several kinds of stones, shells and metals, a writing system, formal styles of sculpture, and city life made possible by a ruling elite, using coercive power and organizing cults and rituals as well as inter-regional flow of trade, and setting linguistic and aesthetic norms. New formal institutions too were needed, involving laws and hierarchies of command. The Harappan civilization spread over a vast area: from Haryana in the east to Makran in the west, and Badakhshan in the north to Kathiawad in the south.

About thirty sites in the Punjab have been identified as 'Mature Harappan'. The most important of these was of course Harappa. At its largest, the city had a circuit of about 5.5 kilometres. It consisted of two main parts: the 'citadel' and the 'lower town'. The 'citadel' built by the Harappans, with tapering walls which were 13.5 metres wide at the base, covered about 45,000 square metres. Beneath it were the Kot Dijian and earlier levels. To its north, close to the river, was a 'granary' of two rows of rectangular halls which covered a space of about 980 square metres. About 90 metres south of the 'granary', there were a series of round brick platforms, each with a diameter of 3.5 metres and a hole at the centre. Wheeler's view that these central holes served as 'mortars' has been questioned. Two rows of double-roomed self-contained houses, divided by a narrow lane, were located to the north of the walled platform. There were also three mud huts. To the south of the 'citadel' was the excavated part of the cemetery called R 37, which belongs to the 'Mature Harappan' phase.

To the south-east of the 'citadel' was the 'lower town'. The latest excavation at Harappa has revealed several stages of platform building, a major north-south street, mudbrick and baked brick houses, baked brick drains, distinctive ceramics, seals, inscribed pottery, chert tools, stone weights, terracotta cones, figurines, toys and painted pottery. There were at least three levels of the mature Harappa period, indicating significant changes. The first sub-period ended with a phase of decay and disrepair. Then there was a dramatic clean up operation in which new houses, new drains, a new wall and a gateway were constructed. Some older artefacts disappear during this sub period and a few new objects appear in the settlement, including some objects with writing. In the third sub-period, pointed base goblets came to be commonly used as disposable drinking vessels.

The growth from rural to urban culture at Harappa was due partly to its location for trade. Connected with western highlands and the northern plains, Harappa had links also with the Ghaggar-Hakra valley and the southern plains. A steady growth of population and agglomeration of peripheral communities increased its size and socio-ritual activities. Its massive mudbrick walls, revetments and platforms are suggestive of a major socio-political integration. The expansion of the city of the first sub-period of the mature stage appears to have synchronized with integration of the Greater Indus Valley through trade and socio-ritual beliefs. Many different communities, pursuing many different occupations, had come to settle in the city. Some degree of tension appears to be reflected in the narrow gateway but there is no indication of armed conflict or military coercion. The renewal of a part of the city during the second sub-period probably synchronized with decay and disrepair in another part. In the third sub-period there was congestion and lack of civic control, probably due to over-population.

The Harappan site at Kalibangan, covering 12 hectares, has the counterparts of the 'citadel' and the 'lower town' at Harappa. Beneath the 'citadel' was the earlier settlement. The citadel, measuring 240 × 120 metres, was divided into two parts by a wall. The northern part contained residential buildings which do not appear to have been used as the residence of a chief. The southern part had ritual facilities: platforms, brick drains, fire altars, and a clay column in the centre. The whole walled complex was linked with the rest of the town by a paved passage. This part of the town was 360 metres long and 240 metres wide and it was fortified by a wall which was 3 to 4 metres wide. Most of it was divided into rectangular blocks. The streets were 3 to 4.5 metres wide, and the lanes were about 2 metres wide. The houses, opening on the streets, had a courtyard with rooms on three sides. Some of the houses had even a dozen rooms. Terracotta tiles with geometric patterns were used for flooring in some of the houses. There was also a well in some houses. There were no street drains. Beyond the two-walled sectors was a cemetery and a solitary ritual structure. There was an unfortified area with poorer houses, possibly of potters or some other workmen.

During the Harappan phase at Banawali, covering 16 hectares, there were two distinct parts of the town, adjoining each other. The counterpart of the 'citadel' was a rectangular area within a wall of mudbrick. It was divided into two halves by another wall. The counterpart of the 'lower town' was divided into residential blocks by streets running in the north-south and east-west direction. The residential units were rather large, having stores, a kitchen and a bath, besides a number of rooms. One street was over 9 metres wide. The whole town was encircled by a perimeter wall along which there was a deep and wide moat. Among other 'Mature Harappan' sites in Haryana were Rakhigarhi, Siswal, and Mitathal. 'Mature Harappan' pottery and a cemetery have come to light at Chandigarh. In the present Punjab, the partially excavated site at Ropar has revealed a Harappan cemetery and a number of artefacts characteristic of the mature Harappan phase. Some of the other sites which were affiliated to the Harappa culture at least partially were Kotla Nihang and Dher Majra, close to Ropar, and Sanghol on the road from Chandigarh to Ludhiana. Another such place was Manda, on the right bank of the river Chenab, about 30 kilometres west of Jammu. The mature Harappan sites, thus, were scattered over a wide area in the Punjab.

As we may expect *a priori*, the number and variety of artefacts was larger in cities than in towns, and the number and variety of artefacts in towns was larger than in villages. Harappa could certainly be regarded as a city in the context of those times. Kalibangan, Rakhigarhi, Banawali, and Ropar could be counted among the towns. But a small place like Dher Majra would certainly be a village. Stone tools, pottery and ornaments were found in all settlements, large or small. But seals and weights were confined to urban centres. There was, thus, a qualitative as well as a quantitative difference between the town and the village.

Besides Kalibangan, Rakhigarhi, Banawali, Siswal, Mitathal, and other Harappan settlements in Haryana there was a large number of settlements representing what is called the 'Sothi-Siswal' culture. Some of these sites have yielded a few Harappan artefacts. The Sothi-Siswal 'province' thus appears to have been ultimately incorporated into the Harappan world which subsumed local traditions. Since the Harappan urban culture was situated amongst various tribal cultures of hunters and food-gatherers as well as farmers, some skilfully crafted items could travel from the urban centres towards the tribal peoples in return for their produce. It must be pointed out that all Kot Dijian sites were not integrated with the Harappan world. Not only Mehrgarh on the frontier of Sind and Baluchistan but also Rehman Dheri in the Dera Ismail Khan district remained outside the sphere of Harappan influence. Kot Dijian sites in the Bannu basin and near Taxila do not reveal Harappan influence. A political frontier between the two cultural areas appears to have blocked Harappan expansion. The 'Kulli culture' of Baluchistan also remained distinct.

There are hints of contacts between the Indus valley and Central Asia. A seal at Harappa, depicting a heraldic eagle, is strongly suggestive of the link. Similarly, bronze pins with superbly-fashioned animals at their heads, and small bronze flagons with long necks, are indicative of links with Central Asia. Even more important were contacts with Mesopotamia through the Persian Gulf. Mesopotamian kings recorded with pride the arrival of boats from Meluhha, the name used for the country of the Harappans. The weights and seals of the Harappan culture have been found in Mesopotamia. Before 3100 BC the initiative for trade in the Persian Gulf was probably with the Mesopotamians. Later on it passed on to the Harappans. With its rich agriculture, large urban centres, and dense population, Mesopotamia was the greatest consumer of shell, lapis, gold, silver, and carnelian. Harappan shells and etched carnelian beads have been found in Mesopotamia and Mesopotamian inscriptions refer to Meluhha's gold, ivory, lapis lazuli, and certain varieties of woods. Indian monkey and peacock were highly prized in Mesopotamia. That contacts were not confined to trade may be evident from a Mesopotamian type of burial at Harappa.

POLITICAL ECONOMY AND SOCIO-RELIGIOUS LIFE

The wide-reaching economic system of the Harappan civilization was marked by agriculture, trade and manufactures. Standardized weights were in use, and there were storage facilities in cities. A network of communications made artefacts and materials available from distant places, and bronze came to be used for everyday purposes.

Agriculture was the mainstay of the economy of the Indus people. In the region under study, wheat, barley and variety of legumes formed the major crops. Possibly, there were some other crops but their status is uncertain yet. In any case, there is evidence of cotton, millets, mustard, sesame, linseed or flax, and dates. There is no evidence of canals but flood irrigation was practised. The plough was known but more important for cultivation was perhaps the harrow. Among the domesticated animals were buffaloes, sheep and goats, dogs and cats, fowls and possibly elephants and camels. There were more sheep than goats in Harappa. The former could be used not only for meat and milk but also for wool. Probably pigs but certainly the deer were hunted. Peacocks and apes were caught for export. At Harappa, a variety of woods was used in construction, crafts and fuel. Considerable quantities of charcoal as well as dung were used for fuel. Reeds were used for building materials and matting. There was an active and sophisticated fishing industry in Harappa. The diet of the Harappans was quite diversified and it continued to include a significant amount of non-domesticated animal and plant foods. This, it is suggested, may account for good overall dental health of the population.

Trade was of crucial importance for the Harappan economy. Pack animals, wheeled carts, and boats were used for transportation, making it possible to organize overland caravans and overseas commerce. As we noticed earlier, the Harappans had trade relations with Mesopotamia. Among the items of trade in general were foodstuffs, metals, shells, wood, lapis lazuli, jade, amonozonite and turquoise. The major items of import were silver and gold. The exports consisted of ivory and ivory articles, pearls, copper, timber and cotton textiles. The long blade of chert stone from the Rohri limestone hills in northern Sind was used not only in Mohenjodaro and Harappa but also at more distant places like Ropar. The weights and measures used by the Harappans are an index of trade, reflecting accuracy and fineness. A bronze rod from Harappa is marked with four graduated lines, each at an interval of 93.4 mms. Multiples of two and ten were used for weights: as 1, 2, 4, 8, 64, 160, 320. Neither without weights and measures, nor without regulation of exchange and the use of writing, trade on a large-scale was possible.

Among Harappan industries, ceramics held an important place. The pottery at Harappa shows a smooth transition from the earliest to the mature phase. With its gorgeously decorated fine wares, it held an honourable place among the manufactures of the Harappan people. The decorations consisted mainly of intersecting circles, triangles, wavy lines, the scale, the cross, T figures and hearts. There is a strong suggestion of an 'efficient mass production'. At the same time, Harappan pottery was thick walled and heavy, baked red to its core to make it very strong.

Terracotta figurines were found in large numbers at Harappa, Kalibangan, and Banawali. The animals represented in these figurines were probably familiar to the people: rhinoceros, monkey, bull, buffalo, dog, deer and birds. There are females wearing a girdle and loin cloth. Some of them are rather terrifying in appearance. It is generally believed that the female figurines in terracotta represent mother-goddesses and suggest the prevalence of fertility cults among the people. It has been pointed out, however, that no figurines were found in the contexts of ritual practice at Harappa. Nevertheless, some sort of ritual is suggested by the manner in which some of the figurines were manufactured. Their parts were made separately and then joined together, symbolizing perhaps ritualistic 'creation' or 'birth'. The terracotta figurines, both human and animal, were generally used as toys, like toy carts with solid wheels and solid or perforated frames.

Ornaments appear to have been extremely popular among the Indus people. Bangles made of metal, shell, faience, and polished, burnt clay in red and dark grey colours were rather common. Fillets of gold ribbon were used by women for binding their hair. They wore necklaces of several strands. Their fondness for ornaments is suggested also by the gold disc beads and pendants with gold caps which have been unearthed at various sites. Carnelian beads etched with white patterns are suggestive of fine work. The bangles of mature Harappa were of exceptionally high quality, probably, serving a unique social purpose. Even more impressive were faience ceramics which consisted of small vessels as well as bangles, beads, rings, amulets, inscribed tokens, tiny figurines of animals, and stamp seals. The Harappan faience was different from that of Egypt and Mesopotamia in terms of strength and overall uniformity of colour as much as in its dense microstructure. Harappan pyrotechnology and craftsmanship reveal a high level of sophistication.

The building activity at Harappa would not have been possible without a well developed industry of brick-making. A kiln unearthed at Harappa reveals how standardization resulting from specialization. It was a fixed installation dating approximately to 2300 BC, rather substantial and efficient. Depending upon their size, it could bake about 200 vessels at a time. The potters had a highly sophisticated knowledge of the workability of clays, with a variety of forming techniques and methods of combining them. Several potters worked together, and the entire process was performed within the vicinity of the kiln. It can therefore be described as a separate workshop with a relatively high output of standardized manufactures by specialist producers.

Work in metal and stone was another important industry of the Harappan people. They used soft steatite, carnelian, lapis lazuli, faience, shells, gold and silver to make beads, bangles, ladles, cups, figurines of squirrels and rams, pendants, miniature pots, goldwire, silver vases, bars, lamps, and seals. The use of stones, especially of chert blades, was not abandoned, but there was a standard range of tools of copper and bronze: flat chisels, flat axes, single-edged knives, razors, pruning hooks, ox-goads and sickles. Many artefacts were cold hammered but others were cast in moulds. The full range of artefacts was found only in Harappa (and Mohenjodaro) but even the medium size towns like Kalibangan had a large number of artefacts. Fish hooks of metal were in use and so was the thin and sharp share of the plough. A great variety of spindle whorls in terms of materials, size, and design indicates that spinning and weaving were done mostly at home.

Weapons consisted of bronze daggers, spearheads and arrowheads; slings and pellets; mace heads of sandstone, limestone and alabaster were in use.

The tools, more than the weapons, suggest an adequate functional efficiency. The knowledge of metallurgy and chemistry among the people of Harappa is reflected in the mixing of tin with copper, the casting of human and animal figures in intricate moulds, and the manufacture of fine needles. An interest in astronomical observations suggests that experts were familiar with the reckoning of time in days, months and years. On the whole, the material objects which have been unearthed at various places indicate the existence of a fairly advanced technology based on empirical observation.

Sculpture in stone and metal has been found at Harappa and Kalibangan. Two stone torsos from Harappa, though small in size, are regarded as impressive specimens of the art. One of these is of a young woman in a dancing posture. It is headless, and parts of the legs have been broken off. It is in grey stone. The other statuette is in red stone, of a headless male whose arms and legs are also missing. It is sensitively executed. A bronze figure of a bull from Kalibangan is also very impressive. Animal-headed pins and a covered cart of bronze from Harappa show that metal work was used not only for productive purposes, but also for decoration and toys.

In some ways the most important industry of Harappa was seal-cutting. The seals were generally cut out of steatite, a soft stone that was easy to saw and carve smoothly. The operative face was carved in inverse relief. New tools were now available for seal-cutting: bronze knives, small saws, burins, and possibly drills. Though seals have been found at Kalibangan, Banawali and Ropar, they were far more abundant at Harappa which was one of the two most important industrial and commercial centres of the Harappan civilization. The importance of these seals was linked with their role in trade. They were used to stamp clay sealings on bales and other goods. The absence of these seals from a site may be regarded as a fair indication of its small importance as a centre of trade.

The seals from Harappa are generally square or rectangular in shape, though a number of round and a few cylindrical seals have also been found. An animal is characteristically depicted before an object of some ritual significance, called 'sacred brazier' or 'sacred manger', with the pictographic writing above the animal's back. The animal depicted most often is a bull-like creature with its horn thrust forward, known as the 'unicorn'. The other animals are the water buffalo, a short-horned buffalo, a fine humped bull, the rhinoceros, the elephant, the tiger and the allegator (*gharial*). In an interesting sealing, the tiger appears to be drummed up or serenaded by a man carrying a cylindrical drum in a horizontal fashion. There are also seals with single symbols, like the swastika, the endless knot, the multiple cross and the grid.

Apart from being masterpieces of art, these seals carry representations of religious character and provide clues to culture and social life. Their pictographic inscriptions hold the key also to the language of the Indus people. The Harappan script is logographic, with 175 to 400 signs. It occurs on seals, pots, bullae, terracotta, shell bangles, copper tablets and tools, and on ivory rods. It has not yet been deciphered.

The economy of Harappa and its uniformities seem to be unthinkable without some kind of political authority. At one time, Harappa and Mohenjodaro were seen as the 'twin-capitals' of a single empire, while the small towns appeared to serve as provincial capitals and frontier posts or factories. The 'citadels' at Harappa and Mohenjodaro appeared to be the residence of the 'priest king' who controlled the economy of the empire with his 'granaries'. Rigorous enforcement of trade and municipal regulations were seen as indices of a 'highly effective and centralized administration'. Gradually, however, an alternative explanation of these phenomena also emerged. A priestly class, rather than 'a priest king', appeared to have administered the public affairs at various places. Indeed, religion or rather *dharma*, was seen as the 'intensifying factor' of the Harappan civilization; it accounted for the degree of uniformity observable in the culture. This hypothesis does not exclude a certain degree of political control. More recently, however, it has been suggested that the state structure of the Harappan civilization was similar to the state structures of other Bronze Age civilizations. Therefore we can think of 'a ruling elite' exercising political power.

The language that was current is unknown to us. Notwithstanding the claims of some scholars that it belonged to the Indo-European or even the Indo-Iranian family, it is more likely that it belongs to the Dravidian family. But the script appears to have been written from right to left. The absence of any bilingual inscription, the shortness of the majority of the available inscriptions, and their small number have made decipherment extremely difficult. It is clear, however, that the script remained stable over a number of centuries. Accents are added to a large number of letters, suggesting phonetic maturity. It is also clear that the script bears no ascertainable relationship with any contemporary or near-contemporary script. Rightly regarded as 'the most momentous' invention of human beings, writing represented an enormous intellectual advance. Apart from storage of information, and recording for future reference, distant communication was made possible by writing.

In the absence of any literary evidence at present, the religious beliefs and practices of the people are not easy to reconstruct; they can only be inferred from the evidence of buildings, sculptures, terracottas and seals. There has been a tendency to draw comparisons with later historical developments. Objects like stone phalli and rings appear to represent *lingas* and *yonis*. The prototype of Shiva is believed to have been depicted at Harappa as 'a Lord of Beasts' whose cult was associated with fertility. Seated male figures of stone are seen as the prototype of Shiva as 'a Yogi'. The worship of (totem) animals appears to have been common. Composite man-faced animals and 'minotaurs' appear to indicate the coalescence of initially separate animal-cults, and their progress towards anthropomorphism. The worship of trees or tree spirits is indicated, particularly by the *pipal* leaf which appears to carry some religious significance.

It has been pointed out recently that, unlike Shiva as Pashupati, the Harappan 'prototype' was not lord of the domestic cattle, protecting them as they grazed, but a holy person communicating with wild animals. This person could even be a female. Similarly, no votive function is indicated for the 'mother goddess'. The ritual at Kalibangan may have involved the lighting of fire, ablutions, and animal sacrifice. The mythical unicorn and other animals on the Harappan seals underscore the importance of animals in the thinking of the people. There are deity-like entities wearing animal horns, or a particular iconography of human body and animal head, tail, and hoofs, or a combination of human and animal torsos. It appears that wild and powerful creatures had a role to play in the symbolism of the Harappans. In shamanistic religions, wild animals play an important role. Central to shamanism is animism, belief in the souls or spirits who were believed to communicate with living people. The shamans in trance got into touch with these spirits to come up with answers to the serious problems of human life, like disease and drought. The shamans often retreated into forests. There are indications, thus, that a kind of shamanism was prevalent among the Harappans, accounting for their pronounced interest in mythical creatures, wild animals, birds and plants.

Modes of the disposal of the dead provide clues about ideas of death and afterlife. Burials in graves or pottery jars, some post-cremation burials, and a few 'symbolic burials' either in large pots or graves (where corporeal remains are absent), have been found in cemeteries. Apart from burial and cremation there could be exposure of dead bodies to birds and animals, and immersion in rivers. The burials at Harappa contained generally fifteen to twenty pots, and the personal ornaments consisted of shell bangles, copper rings for ears and fingers, anklets and beads of steatite. In a few cases there were copper mirrors and antimony rods. At Kalibangan, the bodies were placed north-south in a pit. Another type was 'a pot-burial without skeletons'. A third type of burial contained pots and other funerary furnishing but no skeletons. There was possibly a separate ground for the working class. At Ropar, each of the thirteen graves exposed contained a skeleton. Except in one, the body was placed with head to the north-west. The grave goods consisted of earthen jars and dishes-on-stand, the number varying from two to twenty-six. There were copper rings and beads and bangles of faience and shell. The provision of food and drink for the nether world indicates that the artefacts buried with the dead were believed to be of use in the afterlife. Both at Harappa and Kalibangan, the evidence of burials suggests social differentiation among the people.

Differences of wealth, amounting almost to class divisions, are reflected in the architectural remains in cities and towns. The great granary on the 'citadel' mound, as much as the 'citadel' itself, suggest the presence of a ruling elite in control of the economy, civil government and religious life. The 'citadel' had a social and symbolic significance, besides being a node of defence. It separated the elite from the ruled. The height, enclosure, buildings, and functions of the 'citadel' indicate social barriers as well as a socio-political hierarchy. The merchants lived in spacious two-storeyed houses with many apartments, bathrooms, courtyards and frequently a private well. There were labourers or slaves in the cities and towns as there were cultivators in the villages. There were 'priests', traders, agriculturists, artisans and other working men at Kalibangan. Thus the society as a whole was well stratified. It was probably a patriarchal society. In any case, the gender difference in the prevalence of hypoplastic suggests that females had less access to essential resources like food, health care and parental investment.

On the basis of an attempt at deciphering the Harappan script it has been suggested that a number of individuals traced their lineage to the Sun and Moon, the Stars and also perhaps the Monsoon Rain. The chiefs' houses, presumably, served both residential and administrative functions. Among other kinds of leaders could be heads of associations of coppersmiths, storehouse overseers, irrigation supervisors, and landowners. Lesser figures would include drummers, perhaps to summon assemblies, and singers perhaps to entertain or perform at ceremonies. Then there were scribes, people in charge of weights and measures, supervisors of the distributors of stores, and grinding of floor and the hunting operations. There were also captains of boats, guardians of crops, and preservers of herds and flocks.

DECLINE AND DIFFUSION

The cultural sequence revealed by recent excavations at Harappa, supported by radiocarbon dating, provides an almost certain chronology, The earliest occupation, called 'Ravi' culture, flourished from 3300 to 2800 BC. It was followed by 'Early Harappan' or Kot Dijian culture from 2800 to 2600 BC. The three phases of 'Mature Harappan' spanned the period from 2600 to 1900 BC. Then there was a transition from 'Mature Harappan' to 'Late Harappan' for a century between 1900 and 1800 BC, followed by the 'Late Harappan' after 1800 BC. The Harappan phase at Kalibangan is generally placed between 2,500 and 2,000 BC, stretched sometimes to 1750 BC. Even so, the Harappan phase at Kalibangan ended without leaving any evidence of a culture that can be called late Harappan. The cause postulated for the sudden disappearance of Kalibangan is the capture of the river Jamuna by the Ganges, resulting in the drying up of the Ghaggar which had been the source of life for Kalibangan and several other settlements.

At Harappa, pottery of a kind dissimilar from that of the mature Harappan occupation has been found at Cemetery H. The structures had fallen into decay, but there were remnants of these structures in fragments of poorly constructed buildings with walls sometimes only one brick in thickness. The Cemetery H culture is looked upon as 'Late Harappan'. On the pottery of the upper stratum of the Cemetery H, peacocks with long streaming features on their heads formed a common motif. Another motif was provided by bulls or cows. There is a dog in one pattern. Other painted designs consist of stars, leaves, trees and other natural objects. The symbolic significance of all these motifs is seen to be religious. The Cemetery H pottery suggests a continuum with mature Harappan on the one hand and the presence of new features on the other.

A recent survey of Bahawalpur has revealed 72 sites containing Cemetery H-related materials which are similar to the mature Harappan elements of Harappa. There is a fair degree of continuity, including the Harappan script. In Cholistan the Cemetery H-related sites consist of high and large settlement mounds near the bed of the dry Ghaggar-Hakra, concentrated near Derawar and to its west where mature Harappan sites were located earlier. The available evidence suggests that people did not entirely abandon the upper Indus region. They adjusted themselves to the changed conditions and remained settled in Cholistan for a certain length of time.

Evidence of the abandonment of cities, towns, garrisons, and villages is, however, equally clear. While few Harappan places remained settled, new villages were founded in adjacent areas. Material culture began to resume local distinctions and regional differences after 1800 BC. In this context, the cultural developments in the eastern Punjab were significant. Archaeological evidence shows the emergence of an indigenous culture in which the Mature Harappan elements are absent, but the pottery shows a continuous development, marked by a fusion of the Mature Harappan and local features. Among the distinctive vessel forms of this culture are carinated bowls, squat dishes-on-stand, and jars with high collared rims. Decoration consists of black painted geometric motifs on the red surface of the vessel or on a thin red slip. There are some similarities between this pottery and the Cemetery H pottery at Harappa. Despite the presence of 'Late Harappan' elements, a sure degree of 'regionalization' is visible. The remains of this culture have been discovered at Mitathal, Banawali, Sanghol, Dher Majra, Bhagwanpura, Dadheri, Daulatpur, Mirzapur, Dhanas and Bhudan. Most of these places had earlier come under the influence of Mature Harappa. The time span of these cultures is estimated to range from about 2000 to about 1000 BC.

In the light of this evidence, we can see that there was no dramatic or catastrophic change leading to a sudden disappearance. There is a strong possibility indeed that some of the villages of the Harappan culture never disappeared. It is quite certain that Mature Harappan vessel forms became rare at Mitathal before they were replaced by new forms without any disruption. What disappeared was the cohesion of the Harappan civilization as an overarching system, involving the disappearance of the modes of elite control, the system of long distance procurement of materials and exchange of goods, and the role of regional crafts. The standardized weights, writing, and the range of bronze tools for crafts were no longer important. Links with Central Asia and Mesopotamia were broken. Therefore, human action, including factors like internal political strife, appears to account for the decline of the Harappan culture much more than natural calamities, environment degradation, or foreign invasions.

READING

Aggarwal 1971; Allchins 1983; Childe 1958, 1967; Dani 1963; Fairservis Jr. 1971; Malik 1971; Pigott 1961; Ratnagar 2001; Sankalia 1974; Srivastava 1979; Wheeler 1960, 1966, 1968.

2

The Rigvedic Culture

THE INDO-ARYANS

In the Swat valley two complete horse skeletons have been found, besides wheel-made burnished or polished pottery, both red and grey: pedestal goblets, some shaped like an hourglass, a floral-like vessel, and a jar cover with a handle shaped like a horse. Metal objects of bronze and copper have also been found: knives, blades and a harpoon. A new element appears to have entered the Swat valley, bringing a marked increase in the use of copper and bronze, horses and horse furniture, distinctive burial rites and perhaps also a cult of fire between 2000 and 1750 BC. The people of this culture, known as 'Gandhara Grave Culture', advanced from the hills towards the plains in the south. One of the mounds at Hathial near Taxila indicates that the site was occupied some time after 1500 BC. A bronze dirk from Fort Munro (Rajanpur) in the Dera Ghazi Khan area is far superior as a weapon to anything known to the Harappans. It is dated 1200–1100 BC. From the cairn graves of Moghul Ghundai in the Zhob valley have come bronze objects like a tripod jar, horse bells and a bangle, assigned to 1000–800 BC.

The people of the Gandhara Grave Culture are identified as Indo-Aryans who entered the Indian subcontinent through Afghanistan in a series of migrations. It is now generally agreed that the original home of these peoples was in the Eurasian steppes, extending from the borders of China to the east of Europe. There, however, they were a part of the people now called the Indo-Europeans. Diversification among them resulted in the emergence of a people called the Indo-Iranians, and a further diversification resulted in the emergence of the Indo-Aryans who migrated to Afghanistan through Iran. The languages spoken by these three sets of people are now called the Indo-European, the Indo-Iranian and the Indo-Aryan families.

The Indo-Aryans produced the oldest and a most voluminous

literature, known to the world as the Vedic corpus. This corpus consists of four collections of hymns (*samhitas*): the *Rigveda*, the *Yajurveda*, the *Samaveda*, and the *Atharvaveda*. To each of these *samhitas* is attached a prose manual containing explanatory matter, known as Brahmanas. The concluding portion of the Brahmana is known as Aranyaka, which is followed by a commentary known as Upanishad. This entire corpus was the work of nearly a thousand years, composed and collected largely between 1500 and 600 BC. It was transmitted orally from generation to generation before it was recorded in writing about two thousand years later.

The *Rigveda*, composed largely between 1500 and 1000 BC, is divided into ten 'books' (*mandalas*). Six of these, from the second to the seventh, are more or less homogeneous, the work of a specific seer and his descendants. These 'family books', arranged on a uniform plan, appear to form the nucleus of the *Rigveda*. The unity of the ninth book lies in the fact that all its hymns are addressed to a single deity, Soma. Among the authors of the eighth book, the family of the Kanvas has left its distinct imprint, and the early part of the first book has an affinity with the eighth. The tenth book of the *Rigveda* was composed probably towards the end of the period: it appears to stand apart because of its subject matter, its form, and its language.

The language of the *Rigveda*, called 'Vedic' by some scholars to mark its distinction from the classical Sanskrit which developed later, is not homogeneous. Apart from a definite change in the tenth book of the *Rigveda*, dialectic differences are reflected in the other books. In fact, some elements in the language of the *Rigveda* are found neither in the Indo-Iranian nor in the Indo-European family of languages. Recent linguistic analyses have confirmed the presence of proto-Dravidian elements in the vocabulary and phonetics of the *Rigveda*. Some of the proto-Dravidian words relate significantly to agricultural activities, pointing to the local agricultural communities as their source.

THE PEOPLE IN THE *RIGVEDA*

The sages of the *Rigveda* do not set out to describe the geography of their habitat but they do refer to its rivers. The western tributaries of the river Indus, now known as Gomal, Kurrum and Kabul, are mentioned as Gomati, Krumu and Kubha. To the north of the river Kabul was the modern Swat, called Suvastu, signifying 'fair dwellings'. In a hymn to 'the rivers', the Indus (Sindhu) surpasses all others in might. It rushes on 'bellowing like a bull'. Most active of the active, the unrestrained Sindhu is like 'a dappled mare, beautiful, fair to see'. Several roaring rivers run to it 'like mothers to their calves'. The eastern tributaries of the Indus, the Jhelam, Chenab, Ravi, Beas and Satlej, are frequently mentioned. With the Indo-Aryans moving eastwards, the rivers between the Satlej and the Jamuna are mentioned: the Saraswati, Drishadvati, and Apaya. In fact the Saraswati became in due course the most important river for the Indo-Aryans. There are some references to the Jamuna, and the Ganga is mentioned once or twice in the *Rigveda.*

Although there is a reference to twenty-one rivers, the sages of the *Rigveda* looked upon seven of them as the most important. There are frequent references to 'seven rivers' and to the peoples of the seven rivers. There is hardly any doubt about six of these seven rivers: the Indus, the Jhelam, the Chenab, the Ravi, the Beas and the Satlej. However, at an early stage, the seventh river was probably the Kabul. At a later stage, it was certainly the Saraswati. The peoples of the seven rivers may therefore have been the inhabitants of the valleys of the Indus and the Saraswati, and their tributaries. The *Rigveda* provides evidence on this land of 'seven rivers' (*saptasindhu*).

The sages of the *Rigveda* frequently refer to 'the five people', the Anus, the Druhyus, the Purus, the Turvashas, and the Yadus. At one place they are all mentioned together. Elsewhere, they are bracketed in twos, threes or fours. Occasionally, one or another of them is mentioned separately, but nowhere are they shown in a situation of conflict among themselves. They appear to have been closely allied. Among their sages were Kanva, Indra Vaikuntha, and the Bhrgus. Among their gods were Indra, Agni, Soma, Ashvins, and Maruts. There are references to their wealth and their power, and their armed conflict with others. There is a reference, for instance, to the riches of the Yadus in cattle, the 'vigorous strength' of the Purus and Druhyus, and the 'undeniable strength' of the Turvashas and Yadus. In one hymn, the Purus are 'winning lands'. In another, they are settled on both the banks of the river Saraswati in 'the fullness of their strength'.

However, all five peoples begin to be overshadowed by the people referred to as Bharatas and Trtsus, whose sages are Bharadvaja, Vishvamitra, and Vasishtha, and their gods, Indra, Agni, and Indra-Varuna. Two of their chiefs are mentioned more often in the *Rigveda* than any other, Divodasa, and his son Sudas. The Bharatas and their chiefs are mentioned in association with the rivers Ravi, Beas, Satlej, and Jamuna.

In a hymn addressed to the rivers Beas and Satlej, Vishvamitra prays to them to let the Bharatas ford safely with 'their wagons and chariots'. In another hymn, the Bharata chief Divodasa defeats a chief called Shambara. In yet another, Vishvamitra is the escort of Sudas and assures him of a successful *ashvamedha*. Sudas defeats a chief called Bheda, but the greatest success of his career is his victory over a confederacy of 'ten kings', including the Anus, Druhyus, and Turvashas. Many of the Druhyus were drowned in the Ravi and, together with the Anus, they lost thousands of men. The Trtsus destroyed 'seven castles' of the enemy. That the confederacy was supposed to be far stronger than the Bharata-Trtsus is admitted by their sage Vasishtha who composed the hymn: Indra 'did to death a lion' even 'with a goat'. 'He pared the pillar's angles with a needle.'

Some of the other people who participated in 'the battle of ten kings', presumably as a part of the confederacy, were the Alinas, Bhalanas, Pakthas, Shivas, and Vishanins. They are not mentioned anywhere else in the *Rigveda*. It is evident that the sages of the *Rigveda* refer to people in the context of conflict, involving success or failure. The people who side with Bheda against Sudas are also mentioned only once. They are the Ajas, Shigrus, and Yakshus. A few others are mentioned in similar situations: the Gungus, Kikatas, and Arjikas. The existence of some more people is suggested by scholars: the Krvis, Srnjayas, Arjuneyas, Ushinaras, and Matsyas. To figure much more frequently in the *Rigveda* are yet some other categories of people, referred to as Dasa, Dasyu and Pani. Thus, over a score of groups of unequal importance are mentioned in the *Rigveda*. Knowing the perspective of its sages, it may not be wrong to assume that they do not mention all the people who lived and moved in the land of the 'seven rivers' in that age.

It is more important to note that all the peoples mentioned in the *Rigveda* were not Indo-Aryan. The contexts in which the Gungus, the Kikatas, and the Arjikas are mentioned suggest that they were non-Aryan. Bheda is explicitly mentioned as a Dasa chief. His supporters, that is, Ajas, Shigrus, and Yakshus, also appear to be non-Aryan. The Dasas, Dasyus, and Panis had their own 'tribes' or 'clans' (*vish*). But in the eyes of the Indo-Aryans they all formed one 'race' or a single category. At several places the Dasas are equated with the Dasyus. Together with the Panis, they represent the mythical opponents of Indra. They represent the forces of darkness, whereas Indra and the other gods of the Indo-Aryans represent the forces of light. On the empirical plane, the Dasas, Dasyus, and Panis are the dark-complexioned, indigenous people. The Indo-Aryans, by contrast, are 'fair-complexioned' or 'honey-hued' (*madhuvarna*). This difference is taken for granted by the sages of the *Rigveda*. For them groups stand divided primarily into the Arya-*varna* and the Dasa-*varna*.

The indigenous people were different from the Indo-Aryans not only in their complexion but also in their physical features and their culture. The Dasyus are called 'noseless' (*a-nasah*), that is, snub-nosed. Alternatively, they are 'mouthless' (*a-asha*), that is, dumb, or the people whose language is not intelligible to the Indo-Aryans. That the religious beliefs and practices of the indigenous people were different from those of the Indo-Aryans is hammered by the sages of the *Rigveda* in various ways. They hold an 'alien creed'; they offer no food to the Aryan gods and give no gifts to priests; they are 'godless bands of men'; they are Indra's 'slanderers'. They are 'the sorcerers, the prayerless'; they bring 'no sacrifice'. Indeed, they are 'foolish, faithless, rude-speaking niggards, without belief or sacrifice or worship'. One sage regrets that all around him are 'the Dasyu, riteless, void of sense, inhuman, keeping alien laws'. The Panis are greedy 'wolves'; they steal the cows of other people and eat them.

The Rigvedic sages pray to Indra to strike 'fear into the Dasa', to strike them, and to make earth 'a covering' for them. Indra is expected to overcome 'the Dasa race', and to subdue their tribes for 'the Arya'. It is gratifying for a sage to know that Indra has 'tamed' the Dasyu and subdued the people 'for the Arya'. Ashvins baffle the guiles of Dasyus and blast them away with their trumpets. Indra casts down their 'abject tribes'. The aid of Mitra-Varuna is invoked so that 'we ourselves' may subdue them. Indra, who is known for piercing the Panis, is invoked by all the Arya tribes. Making a clear distinction between the Arya and the Dasyu, Indra punishes 'the lawless' and gives them up to those who worship Aryan gods. The idea that the gods help those who worship them through hymns and sacrifice is frequently expressed in the *Rigveda*.

The differences in religious belief and practice between the Indo-Aryan and the indigenous peoples were not the only, or even the main, cause of their protracted conflict. Even in the mythical conflict between Indra and his opponents, the point at issue is not merely 'the light' but also 'the land' and 'the waters'. The sages of the *Rigveda* ask for 'glory' but more often they ask for 'might' through material resources. They look forward to getting a share of the 'booty'. They are keen to see the wealth of the enemy passing into the hands of their patrons. 'Slay everyone who pours no gift' is followed by 'bestow on us what wealth he hath'. That is how a part of Shambara's wealth reaches the sage: 'We have received in turn from Divodasa, Shambara's wealth, the gift of Alithigva'. Even in 'the battle of ten kings' the expectation on both sides is to 'win the wealth'. In one hymn there is an indication that the Panis' hoarded wealth included the wealth in horses and cattle. Other domestic animals can be added to the list. Then there are references to food and grain, and to gold and ornaments. More significant are the references to slaves, both men and women, who formed a part of the spoils. There is also the question of land and water. The Indo-Aryans needed ample pasturage. They feel happy when Soma is 'winning us land and waters'. There is at least one reference to contention for grain-lands. The whole context inspires the sage to induce his patron to 'bring these existing worlds into subjection'.

The Indo-Aryans felt a sense of solidarity against others. The sages of the *Rigveda* fondly refer to 'the pious Aryan tribes', the 'Aryan folk', the 'fair-complexioned friends' of Indra, the 'Arya worshipper', and 'the Aryas might and glory'. Ashvins spread the light 'unto the Arya'. Agni brings forth 'broad light to the Arya'. Agni was born to give strength to the 'Arya'. Indra is 'the Arya's Comrade'. He 'disclosed the light to light the Arya'. He declares: 'I have bestowed the earth upon the Arya'. Indeed, the gods granted their prayer for cows, horses, plants, forest trees, the earth, the waters and the hills; they made the Sun mount to the Heavens; and they 'spread the righteous laws of Aryas over the land'.

Nevertheless, both Divodasa and Sudas fought against Aryas as well as Dasas. In one hymn, Turvashas and Yadus go down before Divodasa. In another situation, Indra gives Turvasha up to Sranjaya. Sudas' *ashvamedha* was meant to mark his superiority over all possible opponents, both Arya and Dasa. The hostile parties on both sides in the battle of ten kings were in fact Arya. In this battle both sides invoked Indra and Varuna, but the gods helped Sudas. In any case, the victorious heroes boasted that the gods were on their side. Indra-Varuna came to their aid on the field of battle when 'the white-robed Trtsus with their braided hair, skilled in songs' worshipped them 'with homage and with hymn'.

It is tempting to visualize that in due course the Indo-Aryan and the indigenous peoples came to terms with one another. In a number of verses, they stand bracketed. In one context, the opposing foes, 'both the Arya and the Dasa', are struck down by Indra. With the help of Indra and Varuna, Sudas slays 'his Dasa and his Aryan enemies'. In another hymn, the sage prays to Indra and Agni to slay 'our Arya foes' and 'our Dasa foes', and drive away 'our enemies'. More significant is the statement that Agni has 'quelled' the hatred of both the Aryas and the Dasas. In another hymn, all Aryas and Dasas belong to the 'good lord of wealth', Indra. Now the god subdues the godless man, 'whether he be a Dasa or be an Arya'. Indra views all, the Dasa and the Arya, and goes by one's essential merit: 'I look upon the wise and drink the simple votary's Soma juice.'

It is highly significant in this context that the Rigvedic sages accept gifts from Dasa chiefs and praise their liberality. 'A hundred has the sage received, Dasa Balbutha's and Taruksha's gifts. These are thy people, Vayu.' Among the recipients of their gifts is a respectable sage, Vasha Ashvaya, who gets oxen 'like a herd', a hundred camels, and a stately woman adorned with ornaments of gold. Well known for giving 'a thousand liberal gifts' is Brbu, the Pani chief who set himself far above the others, 'like the wide bush on Ganga's bank'. He is praised by all the singers. There are strong indications, thus, that some of the indigenous chiefs and their people had come to be associated with the Rigvedic culture.

Pastoral people are more mobile than agricultural communities. It is not surprising that one and the same people in the *Rigveda* can be seen associated with different places in different contexts. It is significant, therefore, that some people came to be associated with certain areas. Indeed, a broad picture appears to emerge from scattered references to the various peoples of the *Rigveda*. In the trans-Indus territories, the Pakthas and Bhalanas are associated with the river Kurrum, the Vishanins with the river Gomal, the Alinas with the river Swat and the Gandharas with the river Kabul. The Shivas and Srnjayas are associated with the area between the rivers Indus and Jhelam. Dominant between the Jhelam and the Saraswati are the Anus, Druhyus, Purus, Turvashas and Yadus. The Bharatas are well settled between the Saraswati and the Jamuna, performing their sacrifices on the Drishadvati and the Apaya as well as the Saraswati.

The Aryas had an advantage over their non-Arya opponents in the weapons of war which, indeed, were far superior to the weapons of the Harappan times. The vital parts of the Arya warrior's body were covered with armour. There are references to armlets and breast-plates, helmets of metal, and to coats of mail. The warriors were armed with bows and arrows (in quivers), lances and spears, axes and daggers. The arrows could be tipped with dear-horn or metal, and sometimes with poison. There is a reference to 'an archer's arrow tipped with flame'. In their battles, the Aryans used chariots with spoked wheels, which were light enough to carry two warriors. Drawn by two horses yoked abreast, the chariot was the fastest vehicle known at that time.

The *Rigveda* bears testimony to the heroic tradition created and cherished by the Aryas. They refer to the battle as 'war-dance'. They praise their warriors and honour their past heroes. They prize skilled charioteers, and 'champing, neighing, loudly-snorting horses'. The terrible charge of their horses is irresistible, and they swoop down like hungry falcons. Their deep neigh is 'like the thunder of heaven'; it strikes terror in the hearts of the enemy. The horse was also the most beautiful animal for the Aryas and they loved to see it 'meet the mare'. Its crucial importance was reflected in its sacrifice (*ashvamedha*) to the gods who themselves loved the horse and the chariot.

RELIGIOUS IDEAS AND PRACTICES

In the Rigvedic hymns, there are references to 'thirty-three' gods, related to the earth (*vasus*), the air (*rudras*), and the sky (*adityas*)–covering all the three realms of the universe. However, the actual number of deities to whom hymns are addressed is more than thirty-three. The number of hymns addressed to more than one god is nearly 150. More than sixty of these are addressed explicitly to 'all gods' (*vishvedeva*). Many are addressed to two or three gods, jointly with Indra, Agni, Vayu, Ashvins, Varuna, Mitra, Soma, and Vishnu. Then there are hymns which, strictly speaking, are not addressed to deities. Their number is not more than fifty but they have a significance of their own.

Indra, Agni, and Soma are the three gods to whom the majority of the hymns of the *Rigveda* are addressed. Nearly 240 are addressed to Indra alone, in addition to about 40 in which another god is joined with him. Over 200 hymns are addressed to Agni, in addition to a dozen joint hymns. About 120 hymns are addressed to Soma. The number of hymns addressed to Ashvins, Maruts, Mitra-Varuna and Dawn ranges from about sixty to twenty. The number addressed to Savitar, Surya, Pushan, Brhaspati, Adityas, Vishnu and Rudra ranges from about ten to five. There are at least fifteen other deities who receive only one, two or three hymns. Included among these are Heaven and Earth, Bhaga, Saraswati, Yama, Prithvi, Ushas, Rtu, Aditi, Ratri, and Aryani. The number of female deities is very small, and none of them is of much importance.

Scholars of religion find it difficult to characterize or define the Rigvedic religion. There are monotheistic ideas but no monotheism. There are henotheistic ideas but no henotheism. The simultaneous belief in several gods makes for polytheism in actual operation. The powers and functions of different gods often overlap, and strictly speaking there is no pantheon. Besides the conception of divinity reflected in the attributes of the major deities, it is important to know what is offered to them and what is expected from them.

Indra is the king of all the gods, the thunder-armed soma-drinker god of the blue sky and rain, the bounteous lord (*maghavan*), all-sustainer, the mighty (*shakra*), lord of hundred powers (*shatakratu*), lord of the brave and god of battles. He gives victory over enemies and rivals. However, he is invoked jointly with gods like Agni, Pushan, Soma, Varuna, Vayu and Brhaspati. Indrani figures in several hymns as his consort. Prayers, sacrifices and refreshments please Indra: 'Thou hast made prayer the means of thy exalting, therefore we wait on thee with hymns, O Indra. May we, by the pressed soma, soma-drinker, bring thee, with sacrifice, blissful sweet refreshment.' In another hymn Indra rejoices in the sacrificial cake offered to him, and in the songs sung in his praise, as a lover rejoices in his bride. Praise and reward go together. Indra gives waters, herbs that have no poison, forests, kine, steeds, men, treasures, safety of the body, charm of sweet speech, days of pleasant weather, and riches. Indeed, in Indra 'unite all paths that lead to riches, like rivers that commingle with ocean'. One sage is frank enough to ask: 'Tell thou this, if at thy hand aforetime the earlier singers have obtained good fortune, what is thy share and portion?' It sounds almost like a contract. However, Indra cannot be taken for granted: 'he loves no more the men he loved aforetime; he turns and moves away allied with others'.

Agni, the god of fire and light, lord of heaven and earth, is identified with the Sun, and Moon, Varuna, and Varuna-Mitra. He is the son of Dyaus; he is the son of Dawn; he is the son of Earth, of Heaven-and-Earth, Water and Tvastar. He is man's father and brother; he is born from the mouth of Purusha. He is the slayer of foes and he is invoked in battle. He clears the forests. He is the ripener of plants, the punisher of sins, the priest of gods and their messenger; he is the oblation-bearer, and sacrifices reach other gods through him. No sacrifice is possible without him. He is the universal king who is identified with all gods. He is the regulator of the Sun and the seasons. Praises and gifts are offered to him. What is expected from him is 'goodly fields' and 'pleasant homes', the highest wealth which is 'the object of man's desire', removal of sins, safety, prosperity, and happiness. He is the spiritual husband of maidens, consecrator of marriage, and giver of children. He is invoked for 'hero-sons'.

Soma is the 'father and begetter of gods'; he is the 'father' of Heaven-and-Earth; he is identified with the Sun and the Moon; he is the father of Indra and Vishnu; he is the Brahman of the gods, leader of the poets, and *rishi* of the sages; he is omniscient, the giver of rain, the slayer of heroes, lord of valour, and the saviour in battles. Never does he guide and aid the wicked, or him 'who falsely claims the warrior's title'. Mighty and glorious, he is the guide of mortals. Pre-eminent for wisdom, he is wealth-finder, a good friend, and the healer of disease. Praise, oblations, and sacrifice are offered to him and he bestows milch-cows, swift steeds, healing herbs, running waters and the ability to speak effectively in councils.

The chief attribute of Indra, Agni, and Soma is power, each being independent of the others. They share much, but not every trait. Indra is the giver of victory *par excellence*, and he is rather distant from men. Agni is closer; he clears forests, ripens plants, and punishes sin. Soma is distinguished by wisdom and omniscience. The offerings to all the three gods consist of prayers, praises, 'refreshment', and the best articles of food from pastoral and agricultural produce. What they can bestow on men is what matters the most: running waters, green pastures, timely rain, goodly fields, cattle, horses, victory in battle, slaves, domestic happiness, hero-sons, good health, long life, security, and eloquence. The beneficiaries of these gifts in theory are all men, but actually much more so the princes and the priests. Remarkably, there is little concern with personal piety, and virtually none with the life hereafter.

The number of hymns addressed to a deity is not necessarily an index of its significance. Varuna, for example, is the great upholder of physical and moral law. The wrath of this moral governor is roused by sin, and he is severe in its punishment. The hymns addressed to him are devout and ethical in tone. Prayers are offered to him for forgiveness of guilt. Vishnu, referred to as the god of three strides, takes three steps to cover the universe to save mankind. Rudra is fierce and destructive but he is also 'auspicious' (Shiva). He is the greatest of physicians. The god who was to lose his status and to survive only as a vague notion of 'fortune' is Bhaga. He is invoked at dawn like Indra,

Varuna, Mitra, Ashvins, Pushan, Soma, Rudra and Brahmanaspati. He is son of Aditi, 'strong', 'early conquering', thinking of whom even the mighty chiefs say 'give me Bhaga'. He bestows wealth and bliss and he discovers treasures. He augments cows and horses, and men and heroes. He is the god of good fortune through whose protection one can attain 'the height of affluence'. Both the mighty and the weak call on him to give them riches. 'Now, now must Bhaga be invoked by mortals, lord of great riches who distributes treasures.'

Hymns of great beauty are addressed to goddesses, but without adding much to their importance. To the Indo-Aryans, the river Saraswati was what Ganga became later, the most sacred stream. Many a sacrifice was performed on the banks of the Saraswati. She is referred to as the 'mighty flood', but she is also the inciter of all pleasant songs and the inspirer of gracious thoughts; her light is illuminating. Dawn (Ushas) bestows brave sons, horses, and troops of slaves. Then there is the deified Speech (Vak) who has her own gifts to bestow. She announces and utters the word that gods and men alike welcome: 'I make the man I love exceedingly mighty, make him a sage, a Rshi, and a Brahman.' However, the goddesses of the forest (Aryani) and of night (Ratri) inspired the poets to write more beautiful poetry.

At the centre of the Indo-Aryan worship was the sacrifice. It lifted 'mortal man to highest immortality'. Since it was believed to ensure existence and preservation, the sacrifice was equated with Manu, the father of the Aryan peoples. It was performed in an assembly (*vidatha*) which was regarded as an inviolable asylum. The sacrificial fires were lit from the 'house-fire' perpetually maintained by the householder. *Soma* juice was invariably offered to the god and it was taken by the priests. A hymn describes the process by which *soma* was prepared. Logs of wood were used as fuel and holy oil (clarified butter, or *ghrita*) was poured on the burning fire when hymns were chanted in praise of a god or gods. Sacred grass was strewn for the gods to sit and rest. The sacrificial animal was anointed and taken round the sacrificial post three times before it was slaughtered.

There are two hymns in which there are references to the horse's beauty, the goat which was slaughtered first, the hewers of the post and those who carried it, the carver of the knob on the horse's stake, the ministers employed at the solemn rite (the invoker, the ministering priest, the atoner, the fire-kindler, the *soma*-presser, the sage, and the reciter), the courser's trappings, halter, heel-ropes, head stall, girths and cords, the grass in his mouth, the flesh eaten by the flies or left sticking to the post or the hatchet or to the slayer's hands and nails, the perfect cooking of meat on the spit and in the cauldron, the trial fork and the vessels and dishes used, hooks and carving boards, and the distribution of meat. The horse consecrated to the gods and accepted by them did not die: it went to them with every article associated with it on the earth. The sacrifice was expected to bring 'all-sustaining riches', good cows and horses, many offspring, 'freedom from sin', and 'lordship'. The horse-sacrifice (*ashvamedha*) was meant to ensure regeneration and to sanctify power.

The growing importance of the sacrificial ritual raised the importance of the priests. They came to claim that they knew how to please the gods and to secure their aid. In a very real sense, therefore, they attributed the success of their patrons to their own songs and prayers. For example, it is the prayer of Vishvamitra which 'keeps secure the race of Bharatas'. When Vishvamitra was the 'escort' of Sudas, Indra grew friendly towards him. The sons of Vishvamitra can ensure Sudas' success in an *ashvamedha*: 'let loose Sudas' horse to win him riches. East, west and north, let the king slay the foremen, then at earth's choicest place perform his worship'.

They who performed services for the sacrifice looked for reward in the form of generous *dakshina*. The amount of *dakshina* received by Kakshivan from the chief named Bhavya, who dwelt on the bank of the Indus, is exceptionally large: one hundred necklets, one hundred steeds, one thousand cows, and chariots with mares to draw them, besides many horses of dusky colour. Another composer boasts of the *dakshina* he received from three chiefs: ten coffers and ten mettled horses from one; ten horses, ten treasure chests, ten garments and ten lumps of gold from another; and three chariots, with an extra steed for each, and a hundred cows from the third.

The composers express their views on *dakshina* without reserve. For both the singers and their princely patrons who give *dakshina*, Agni provides 'higher bliss'. Many men give *dakshina* with their hands outstretched because 'they dread dishonour'. They who are liberal are never ruined; they suffer no harm, and they face no trouble. In fact, they get fragrant dwellings and brides with fair apparel, they obtain their draughts of liquor, and they conquer their enemies. But accursed are they who enjoy riches through the hymns addressed to gods and do not give ample *dakshina* to the composers. May their riches flee from them. Through sacrifices, the priests gained wealth and prestige; their patrons (*jajamanas*) gained legitimacy and power.

If the words of the sages could please the gods, they could not fail to scare demons and evil spirits, of whom there were plenty. There was a charm to drive maladies from all parts of the body: nostrils, eyes, ears, chin, head, brain, tongue, neck and neck tendon, breast bone, spine, shoulders, arms, viscera, rectum, heart, kidneys, liver, spleen, thighs, knee-caps, heels, forepart of the feet, hips, stomach, groin, hair, and nails. This is an impressive description of human anatomy. There is a charm against miscarriage, 'the malady of evil name' that has beset 'the labouring womb'. The charm is meant to drive away that 'which destroys the sinking germ, the settled, moving embryo', and that 'which will kill the babe at birth'. There is a charm also for safe delivery: 'Like as the wind, like as the wood, like as the sea is set astir, so ten-month babe, descend together with the afterbirth.' The Rigvedic composers appear to have entertained a strong belief in the power of words (*mantras*).

The need of words was not obviated by the use of herbs as medicine. The 'spirit of disease' is asked in one hymn to fly away with the bluejay and the kingfisher. 'Fly with the wind's impetuous speed, vanish together with the storm.' Another charm or spell was believed to be efficacious against all venom in reptiles, scorpions, insects, poisonous roots and artificial poisons: 'So have the pea hens three times seven, so have the maiden Sisters Seven carried thy venom far away, as girls bear water in their jars.' There were charms against misfortune, evil dreams and rivals, including the rival wife. There was also a herb which was believed to quell 'the rival wife', or subdue a fellow-wife, to gain the husband for oneself. The pigeon and the dove were birds of bad omen. The *kapinjala*, especially coming from the south, was of good omen: it sang like the Brahman's son at libation to proclaim happy luck in all directions.

It is interesting to note that 'prajapati' is an attribute of the gods like Soma and Savitr. Towards the end of the Rigvedic period, Prajapati becomes the 'lord of creatures'. Vishvakarma is 'the sole god' who produces earth and heaven and welds them together. He is mighty in mind and power. He is the maker and the disposer, who knows all existing things, and who gives names to all other deities. Both Prajapati and Vishvakarma are spoken of as the creators of the universe.

In another account, the material for creation was provided by Purusha. When he was sacrificed, his head became the sky, his navel the air, and his feet the earth; from his mind sprang the moon, from his eyes the sun and from his breath the wind. And now Purusha is 'all this world, what has been and what shall be'. There are other accounts of creation associated with the sun, the waters, and *hiranyagarbha* (germ of gold). In one hymn, the existent (*sat*) evolves from the non-existent (*asat*): 'from what was not arose what is'. The most daring and sustained speculation on creation is found in the Song of Creation. The ideas related to creation point towards the unity of god on the one hand and towards pantheism on the other.

There is a hymn on *mayabheda*, 'the discernment of *maya*'. It is a kind of spirit that runs through everything in the universe: 'I saw the Herdsman who never rests, approaching and departing on his pathways. Clothed and gathered in diffusive splendour, he continually travels within the worlds.' Was this spirit in the universe and yet apart, like the soul in the body? In a late hymn of the *Rigveda*, there in a kind of spirit in the body. Whereas the body is perishable, the personality or the soul does not perish. The soul is spoken of as departing to waters or plants. The concepts of *maya* and *atman* are not there in the *Rigveda*, but these vague notions could become the basis of these concepts later.

ECONOMIC AND SOCIAL LIFE

The Indo-Aryans loved meadows rich in grass where animals grazed before the day was hot. They felt unhappy about even a spacious country if it was void of pastures. They cherished cows of various hues. In a hymn on the 'cows', Rudra is asked to be gracious to 'food that moves on feet'. In another hymn, the god is invoked to grant health to cows, mares, rams, and ewes, as much as to men. Many similes and metaphors in the *Rigveda* are drawn from the cow. The gods are implored to come quickly to the sacrifice 'as milch-kine hasten to their stall'. Indra drives the people with his might 'as the bull drives on the herds'. Indra is triumphant like 'a bull among the herd of cows'. The cow lows and licks the forehead of its calf, fondly calling its mouth to the warm udder. Oxen and cows are looked after by the herdsman. Outside the realm of poetry, the cow served as a kind of currency.

Agriculture did not remain unknown to the pastoral Indo-Aryans. They begin to pray for a 'lasting home'. Agni is praised as 'the king of lands where men are settled'. Ashvins become the ploughers of 'the first harvest in the sky'. The plougher goes to the field singing. The oxen are yoked to the plough with straps and binding thongs; the ploughman plies the goad, and the plough furrows happily. The ploughman unyokes the pair of oxen at the end of his work and takes them to the place where they drink water. There is hardly any doubt that the Rigvedic peoples took to plough agriculture. The field (*kshetra*) full of barley is reaped in an orderly fashion. A poet grasps the sickle metaphorically and hopes to fill his hand with barley, 'cut or gathered up'. They who do not worship Indra are thrashed like 'sheaves upon the floor'. The grain comes down from the winnowing basket. Indra begins to crave the gift of corn as much as animals and gold. There are references to wells which, presumably, could be used for irrigation. However, agriculture depended almost entirely on natural precipitation. The cultivators pray for rain. The hymn on 'frogs', which is interpreted generally as a satire on Brahmans, can be seen as a panegyric for frogs which were believed to have the magical power of bringing rain. In any case, the cultivators feel happy when 'the murmuring moisture' falls to the ground. There are references also to measurement of fields and their allocation, presumably in the assembly (*sabha*).

Adjacent to cultivated fields and pastures there were considerable tracts with natural growth and forests. The existence of wild animals is an index of the prevalence of wilderness. The hunting of wild bulls, boars and the deer is referred to in the *Rigveda*. The wild elephant, called *mrighastin* or the beast with a hand, 'eats the forests up' and the mighty lion (*simha*) roars. A rudy wolf can waylay a man to scare him out of his wits. Equally unwelcome is a 'wild beast in pasture land'. There were wild buffaloes (*mahisha*), thirsty stags, and antelopes in their beauteous form. There were other animals like the spotted deer, ape, jackal and bear. A common sight was that of a pigeon turning to its mate. A number of other birds are referred to in the *Rigveda*: eagles, falcons, hawks, vultures, peacocks, quails, parrots, cuckoos, owls, doves, swans, kingfishers, bluejays, emmets, *chakvas*, and *kapinjalas*. There were serpents and mongooses and there were scorpions. Then there were a number of tamed animals: horses, cows, rams, ewes, goats, camels, buffaloes, dogs, asses, and perhaps monkeys.

The professions and occupations mentioned in the *Rigveda* go beyond the orbit of warriors, priests, bronzesmiths, chariot-makers, herdsmen, fowlers, and the ploughmen. Carpentry and smithy were not confined to chariot-making and forging armours and weapons. The carpenter remained long at his work, so long indeed that his back began to ache. There are references to boat-building and the tanning of leather. Songs are woven for the Ashvins 'as skilful men weave garments'. There is a reference to 'female weavers', and to 'the weaver's thread' being devoured by rats. Medicinal herbs and leeches were used for healing. Some of the daily tasks are mentioned in a hymn to Rbhus: one drives the crippled cow to the water, another trims the flesh on the carving board, and yet another carries off the refuse at sunset, while all day long the aged parents find it hard to help their children. In a hymn to Dawn, who awakens all moving creatures to their 'different vocations', one wakes up 'to high sway, one to exalted glory, one to pursue his gain, and one to his labour'.

The metals used by the Rigvedic peoples were gold and bronze. They used necklets (*nishkas*), bracelets, anklets and earrings as ornaments. Kettles and other domestic utensils of metal were manufactured in smithies. Sheep wool was used for making clothes, sometimes adorned with gold. The major items of food were milk, butter, *ghee* and grain which was ground between mill-stones to make cakes with milk or butter. Fruit and vegetables were eaten more frequently than flesh which, on ceremonial occasions, was either roasted on spits or cooked in pots. Apart from *soma*, which was reserved for ceremonial purposes, *sura* was drunk for its intoxicating effect. It made men so arrogant that they began to revile the gods.

Rigvedic society was by no means egalitarian. In a pastoral setting, the *gomat* was the man of wealth. One way of increasing wealth was to breed cattle. Another was to capture cows, among other things, as booty. Some of this booty was retained by the chief and a substantial portion was distributed among the priestly families. The articles thus distributed consisted of cows, horses, chariots, gold and female slaves. Not all the families of a clan (*vish*) received equal shares in this distribution. Indeed, the clan consisted of the *rajanya*, who constituted the ruling families, and the *vish* who represented the rest of the clan. The chariot-riding warriors of the *Rigveda* were now the guardians and protectors of the *vish* who were the producers. In this process, the *vish* became increasingly involved in producing items to be used by the *rajanyas* as oblations and gifts to Brahmans. To meet the increasing demand, more land could be brought under cultivation with the services of those who were available, whether from within or from outside the *vish* lineages.

In this context, the *Purushasukta* hymn in the tenth book of the

Rigveda appears to invoke divine sanction for a social situation that had begun to emerge, and to claim the superior most status for the Brahman:

> When they divided Man (Purusha), into how many parts did they divide him? What was his mouth, what were his arms? What were his thighs and his feet called? The *brahman* was his mouth, of his arms was made the *rajanya*. His thighs became the *vaishya*, from his feet the *shudra* was born.

This appears to imply a kind of social status in the descending order, from the Brahman at the top to the Shudra at the bottom of the scale. Since the hymn was composed by a sage who presumably identified himself with the Brahman, the claim of the highest position for the Brahman is understandable. It is also clear that with the increasing importance of hymnology and ritual sacrifice the priestly class emerged as an important section of the society.

The *rajanya* were concerned with war and rulership and they enjoyed greater economic advantages than the Brahmans. But they needed their support to legitimize their political power. Neither the *rajanya* nor the Brahman formed a part of the *vish* anymore. Therefore, the Vaishya now consisted of the holders of land and cattle, together with the artisans who were still respectable and important. The Shudras were certainly at the bottom of the social scale, consisting of slaves and the subjugated segments of the indigenous peoples. But all the indigenous peoples were never reduced to the status of Shudras.

The social order projected in the *Purushasukta* hymn is no longer confined to tribal units. The social categories cut across the tribes (*janas*) to postulate a social collectivity divided into horizontal strata. Equally important is the assumption that this stratified social order constituted an organic whole like the body of the Purusha. It may be added in this connection that the phrase *pancha-jana*, taken generally to refer to 'the five people', could also symbolize the totality of the people as an image derived from the five fingers of the hand which occurs in the *Rigveda*. Just as some Dasa chiefs were accepted as *aryas*, some indigenous sages were accepted as *brahmans*. Among them were Agastya and Vasishtha. The eminent Brahmans like Kavasha, Ailusa and Dirghatamas were *dasiputras*. A hymn of the ninth book speaks of a poet whose father was a leech and whose mother used to work at a millstone. It is difficult to say how long freedom continued to be exercised in the choice of an occupation. But even in theory, the *varnas* do not appear to have become hereditary in the Rigvedic society.

By far the most important social institution of the Rigvedic peoples was the family. It consisted of three or four generations living together as a single unit. The sons and their wives and children, and the grandsons and their wives, formed a part of the family. Sometimes a worthless son-in-law, or wife's brother, also lived with the family. The seniormost male member of the family acted as the head. There are verses in the *Rigveda* which suggest monogamy. The husband and wife (*mithuna*) worship together as 'the pair' and serve the gods 'with uplifted ladles'; in one mind they kneel before the gods. In another hymn 'close to her husband clings the wife' and, in embraces intertwined 'both give and take the bliss of love'. References to wooing and courting also suggest a degree of freedom and equality. The young men freely follow the maidens, and the idea of love dies hard. The wife of Agastya invites his caresses in old age, and complains of his coldness. She is sad that old age impairs the beauty of our bodies, but a wife in old age could come near unto her husband. A widow could remarry.

At the same time, there are verses in the *Rigveda* which indicate the existence of polygamy. Indra dwells like 'a king among his wives'. One poet is oppressed by enclosing ribs on every side like 'rival wives'. There is a reference to the 'yearning wives' of a husband. The Rigvedic family was patriarchal. Women remain active in their household chores. The only woman outside the home is the dancer who 'puts her broidered garments on' and bares her bosom, presumably to entertain men. A young woman without brothers is feared to go astray. The bride is embellished by her mother, and she gets a dowry. She is expected to give birth to ten sons. The importance of the male child is underlined by the custom of adoption: the sonless father can adopt his daughter's son. The sons were expected to obey the father's behest unquestioningly. The few comments on the female gender are far from complimentary. Indra says that the mind of women is hard to instruct, and 'her intelligence is small'. There can be no friendship with women: 'their hearts are those of hyenas'.

The Indo-Aryans had a great zest for life. 'We have gone forth for dancing and for laughter, to further times prolong our existence.' They wished for a long life and looked forward to old age. 'Tearless and free from sorrow', their wives adorn themselves with fragrant balms and unguents and deck themselves with jewels. Death is implored not to touch 'our offspring' and not to injure 'our heroes'. The widow in mourning is asked to come back to 'the world of life' and to marry another man. The Indo-Aryans were fond of the good things of life and enjoyed all the pleasures it offered. 'Liberality' on the part of an individual was a great virtue. Riches, like the chariot wheel, are ever rolling, coming now to one and then to another. Therefore, there is no point in being 'a niggard'. Indeed, he who eats 'with no partakers' is all guilt. A liberal friend outvalues him 'who gives not', just as a Brahman who is eloquent outvalues the one who is not.

It is possible to look upon the Indo-Aryan amusements as reflecting this zest for life. Indra is invoked as much in war as in 'the steed's race course'. The prize-winning horse is better looked after than the others. Indra is invoked for success in the race: 'O Indra help our chariot on, yea, Thunderer, though it lag behind: Give this my car the foremost place.' The honour of winning the race became all the more important because of the high stakes. Gambling was common. Indra seizes the riches of his foes 'like a gambler gathering his winnings'. The aid of the gods is invoked in this 'luckless game' as much as on the field of battle. 'The gamester seeks the gambling-house, and wonders, his body all afire, shall I be lucky?' There is no turning back: 'Dice verily are armed with goads and driving hooks, deceiving and tormenting, causing grievous woe.' The gambler who wins a little is lured more and more, to be destroyed eventually as a loser. His wife is left forlorn and wretched. His mother mourns the son who wanders homeless. Therefore, the poet advises: play not with dice: no, cultivate the land. Enjoy the gain, and deem that wealth sufficient. Significantly, the dice were initially used in the *sabha* for the allocation of land for cultivation.

The chariot race provided amusement for men but singing and dancing provided pleasure for both men and women. The 'maidens' are explicitly mentioned in connection with dance. Associated with dance was laughter. The ploughman sang on his own but singing was a cultivated art, performed with musical instruments: the drum (*dundubhi*), the flute (*vana*), and the lute (*vina*), representing percussion, wind and stringed instruments.

POLITY

In early studies Rigvedic polity was seen as monarchical. Occasionally the king was elected by an assembly (*sabha*) from amongst the royal race, or the noble families, but the office of the king appeared to be hereditary. His main duty was to protect the people who, in turn, rendered obedience to him and supplied him with voluntary gifts. There were no fixed taxes. He held the chief command in war. It was his duty to perform sacrifice on behalf of the tribe, either directly or through a priest known as the *purohita*. The king patronized a family of singers too. The political unit was constituted by the tribe (*jana*) which consisted of a number of clans (*vish*). Each *vish* was an aggregate of villages (*gramas*). Each family in the *grama* was headed by a patriarch. The fighting organization was based on the three divisions of the *jana*, the *vish* and the *grama*. The power of the king was limited by the will of the tribal assembly (*samiti*).

In partial modification of this early understanding of Rigvedic polity it was suggested that two tribal councils shared the responsibility for government. The *samiti* was a general gathering; the *sabha* was a meeting of the great men of the tribe. The chief of the tribe, the *raja*, had a rudimentary court, attended by courtiers (*sabhasad*) and chiefs of septs (*gramanis*). He had an army commander (*senani*) in addition to the chief priest (*purohit*). Apart from booty, the Raja collected tribute from his subjects for meeting the financial requirements of administration. Judicial administration was confined to payment of compensation as a punishment for murder. Some tribes were governed directly by the tribal council of kings (*rajas*), making the polity oligarchic.

More recently, a case has been made for the existence of 'republics' among the Rigvedic peoples. It is argued that there are several references in the *Rigveda* to the *sabha* without any ruler. The words *rajan* and *sabha* do not occur together in such contexts. The tribes which had *sabhas* had no *samitis* either. To be a member of the *sabha* one had perhaps to be distinguished either in warfare or property in cattle and grain, or in eloquence and learning, or by a large family of adult males. A few hymns of the *Rigveda* clearly refer to people 'who choose their ruler'. It may be presumed that the people in this context were the heads of patriarchal families. The person selected or elected as the ruler (*rajanam*) was probably expected to possess the qualities most appreciated by the tribes concerned: skill in fighting, chariot-racing and oratory.

Much more frequently, however, the *Rigveda* refers to the assembly of chiefs or princes. The *raja* is chosen not by the *vish*, but by *rajas*-in-assembly. Indeed in one hymn Indra is surrounded by his friends, like a wandering tribal chief surrounded by the lords of clans. In another hymn, Agni is invoked to establish concord and harmony in an assembly of equals. It was at these assemblies that one among the *rajas* was chosen to preside and protect. The office was not hereditary to begin with. There is no mention of any heir-apparent. Thus, the chief of the tribe was the first among equals.

Rigvedic polity can be appreciated in terms of a structure that was based on lineages as corporate groups of unilineal kin with a formalized system of authority. The extended family based on three or four generation lineage formed the basic unit of the system, and several unilineal descent groups made up a clan, tracing its origin to a single ancestor. Significantly there are more references to lineages than to chiefs in the *Rigveda*. The Rigvedic *jana* (tribes) incorporated a number of *vish*. These clans may have been egalitarian earlier but by now they were bifurcated into the *vish* and the *rajanyas*, the latter constituting the ruling families. It was from amongst these families that the Raja was chosen. The chariot-riding lineages of the *Rigveda* were pre-eminently the guardians and protectors of the *vish* and the junior lineages of the *vish* were the producers of both pastoral and agricultural items. The latter provided presentations to the former, informally on special occasions for redistribution, in the form of *bali* to a *raja* chosen by other *rajas*. In this situation, the *vish* stood in a subordinate relationship to the *raja*. What sustained the *rajanya* and the Brahmans was the tribute of the *vish*, in addition to the booty. When booty could not meet the expanding demand, the *vish* were obliged to increase agricultural output.

The evidence of the *Rigveda* can be appreciated further in the light of this evolutionary polity. *Bali* was a 'tribute' or a prestation, and not a tax, offered by the *vish*. *Bhaga* was a share in the distribution of prestation or in the spoils after a raid. The term *shulka* in the *Rigveda* was used in the sense of a measure of value and not for tax. The meaning of these terms changed in the *Dharamasutra* literature from 'tribute', 'distribution' and 'value' to forms of tax.

The specific functions of the Rigvedic assemblies are not clear. The *samiti* and *sabha* were the gathering points of the *rajanya*, the former being more open than the latter. These terms occur more frequently in the tenth book of the *Rigveda*. The term *vidatha* appears to refer to a ritual occasion on which, among other things, the distribution and sharing of wealth took place. The *gana*, in its origin, could have been a cattle-raiding peer group.

The concentration of power in the families of chiefs, in combination with other changes, encouraged the emergence of hereditary chiefship. The struggle for power among the chiefs is reflected in the aspirations of an ambitious chief in a hymn of the *Rigveda*: 'Make me a bull among my peers', he prays; 'make me my rivals' conqueror'. 'I have mastered all your thoughts', he goes on to add, 'your synod and your holy work'. Having raised himself above the rest he expects them to look up to him with awe and respect: 'Speak to me from beneath my feet, as frogs from out the water croak, as frogs from out the water croak.' In due course, election and selection were suppressed by attempts at hereditary succession. However, the establishment of a 'monarchical' system did not imply a political authority functioning within a territorial limit by delegating its powers to functionaries, financed by taxes collected on an impersonal basis, and acting as an instrument for integrating social segments identified by economic functions in addition to their ritual roles. In other words, there was no full-fledged state in the Rigvedic period.

READING

Basham 1959; Gonda 1975; Griffith 1976; Griswold 1973; Keith 1925; Kuiper 1991; Sharma 1968; Thapar 1966.

3

State Formation and Social Stratification (*c.* 1000 BC–200 BC)

According to D.D. Kosambi, the Rigvedic culture in the Punjab was finally 'wrecked' by the invasions of Alexander and the extension of the Maruyan empire to the Punjab. It is true that Rigvedic culture changed less in the *saptasindhua* during the early centuries of the second millennium BC than in the upper Ganga plains where it was influenced by a new environment. The new developments occurred more in the area between the Jamuna and the Satlej than in the area west of the Satlej. Around the middle of the first millennium BC, the north-western parts of the Punjab came into closer contact with Persia, and in the second half of the fourth century BC the western Punjab experienced the invasions of Alexander. Soon afterwards, the establishment of the Mauryan empire brought the entire region into close contact with the Ganga valley.

The post-Rigvedic period, to the fall of the Mauryan empire, was marked by important socio-cultural changes. Evidence for this change comes from the later Vedic literature, early Sanskrit and Buddhist works, the accounts of the Greek writers, Ashokan inscriptions, and archaeological evidence. Much of this evidence relates directly to either the north-west or the south-east of the region but nearly all of it has an indirect bearing on the Punjab as a whole. This reveals something of the political developments, polity and administration, economy, social order, religious developments, and literature and art of this period.

POLITY AND ADMINISTRATION

In the later Vedic literature, there are references to the Kurus in association with the Panchalas in the south-east and to Gandharas in association with the Kambojas in the north-west of the region. In between, there were peoples known as Ambasthas, Kekayas, Madras, Salvas, and Shibis. These incidental references to the people of the region by no means cover all groups. The nature of the later Vedic literature precluded the possibility of any exhaustive listing. Panini's *Ashtadhyayi*, composed in the sixth century BC in the north-west, refers to a score of people, including the Andhekas, Arjunayas, Audambaras, Kunindas, Kshudrakas, Malavas, Sauviras, Trigartas, Vasaiyatas, Vrshinis and Yaudheyas in addition to the Ambasthas, Gandharas, and Salvas. The *Mahabharata* appears to be even more comprehensive. It is significant that seven peoples mentioned in the later Vedic literature and by Panini figure in the Epic: Ambastha, Gandhara, Kamboja, Kekaya, Kuru, Madra, and Shibi. There are eight others who are common to the *Ashtadhyayi* and the *Mahabharata*: Arjunayas, Kshudrakas, Kunindas, Malavas, Sauviras, Trigartas, Vasaiyatas and Yaudheyas. Just as Panini mentions several people who do not find mention in the later Vedic literature, so the *Mahabharata* refers to peoples who do not figure in Panini's work. Notable among them are Abhiras, Abhisaras, Dasharmas, Jartikas, Shudras, Sindhus, and Vatadharas. On the basis of this evidence, it may be safe to suggest that a number of groups survived for several centuries in one or another part of the region, and a few of them possibly became subordinate to others. The Bharata-Trstus and the Purus coalesced to constitute the Kurus. Similarly, the Panchalas included probably the Turvashas and the Yadus.

Before the end of the sixth century BC the region came into political contact with Persia. The first great ruler of the Achaemenian empire, Cyrus, annexed the trans-Indus territories before his death in 530 BC. The capital of Gandhara at this time was at Pushkalavati, near Charsadda. The third Achaemenid, Darius, crossed the Indus during his long reign of over thirty-five years, beginning in 522. Archaeological evidence reveals Persian presence at least in the upper Sindh Sagar Doab. According to Herodotus, the Indian possessions of the Achaemenian rulers formed the twentieth province of their empire. As the most prosperous province, it yielded the largest tribute. Under Xerxes (486–65 BC), Indian contingents appear to have fought as a part of the Persian army. They were dressed in cotton clothes and armed with spears, reed bows, and arrows of cane tipped with iron. Persian rule lasted in these parts till about the middle of the fourth century BC.

In the third quarter of that century, the trans-Indus territories were independent of Achaemenian rule. Pushkalavati, the old capital of Gandhara, was under the Ashtakas. In the upper Sindh Sagar Doab, there was the kingdom of the Ambhis with their capital at the old city of Taxila. In the Hazara area, there were the Urashas, and to their north-east in the Punchh and Naushehra region were the Abhisaras. The kingdom of the Paurava (Porus) was in the upper Chaj Doab, Another Puru was ruling in the upper Rachna Doab. In the upper Bari Doab, there were at least three peoples: the Saubhas, the Kathas, and the Bagalas. In the lower part of the Doabs were Shibis, Arjunayas, Kshudrakas, Malavas, and Ambasthas, with the Kshtras and Vishtis still farther away towards the Panjnad. Beyond the Panjnad, in the direction of Sind, were the Shudras.

In 330 BC, Alexander defeated Darius III, and burnt his capital, Persepolis. Continuing his march eastward he reached the borders of India. The Ashtaka king of Pushkalavati offered resistance and, when his capital fell after a siege of one month, it was thoroughly sacked. Alexander crossed the Indus in 326 BC. Ambhi, the king of Taxila, readily submitted to him, presumably because of his standing rivalry with the neighbouring rulers. In any case, he supported Alexander in his attack on Porus across the river Jhelam, crossed by a feint. The interceptors sent by Porus were wiped out in a sharp cavalry action. The main battle with Porus lasted an entire day and ended with great slaughter. Hopelessly overmatched and severely wounded, Porus surrendered to Alexander with dignity. In the words of Plutarch, 'this fight took the edge off the Macedonians' courage, and stayed their further progress in India'. Alexander thought it politic to reinstate the Paurava king in his dominions. When the younger Puru in the Rachna Doab submitted without fight, his territory too was added to the dominions of Porus. In the upper Bari Doab, the Kathas offered stiff resistance to Alexander and suffered the consequences with great courage. When Alexander reached the right bank of the Beas, his Greeks refused to cross the river. Feeling helpless against their collective will, he decided to return.

Alexander re-crossed the rivers Ravi and Chenab and reached the Jhelam. Boats had been prepared for his journey by water to the mouth of the Indus. His zest for 'exploration' nearly cost him his life. He was severely wounded in one of the battles against the Malavas and Kshudrakas and he had to fight against the Arjunayas too. He was out of the Punjab by 325 BC. The immediate effect of his invasion was the extermination of some republics and kingdoms, the enlargement of a few states, notably the kingdoms of Porus, Ambhi and the Abhisaras, and the presence of garrisons under Greek commanders in the Punjab.

The last of Alaxander's generals, Eudamus, left the north-west in

317 BC. By this time Chandragupta Maurya appears to have established his power up to the Indus. Some historians hold the view that he occupied the Punjab first and the territories of Magadha only afterwards. It is highly probable that he was associated with the north-west much before he succeeded to the throne of Magadha, and not unlikely that he met Alaxander personally in 326-25 BC. In any case, two decades later he was more than a match for Seleucus Nikator who had succeeded Alexander in this region. When Seleucus tried to extend his power towards the Punjab in 305 BC, he was worsted. The treaty that followed in 303 BC, indicates that the Mauryan king had the upper hand. Seleucus ceded Kabul and Kandhar, and probably Baluchistan and Herat, to Chandragupta and received five hundred elephants in return. The empire founded by Chandragupta was extended by his son Bindusara and his grandson Ashoka. It became the first subcontinental empire in India, with the Punjab as its integral part for over a century. Mauryan rule in the Punjab appears to have exercised greater influence on the life of its people than the Achaemenian.

Turning to the polity of this period, we notice first that the Rigvedic tribal identity gave place to territorial identity in the early centuries of the first millennium BC. The later Vedic literature refers to some *janapadas* in the Punjab. For example, the Kurus at the one end and the Gandharas at the other, with the Madras and the Kakeyas in between were associated with *janapadas*. The term *janapada* literally means an area where a people (*jana*) set their foot, that is, where they settle. A *janapada* was named after its ruling lineage. Since the economy included pastoralism and even hunting as well as agriculture, large forested areas adjoined the settlements, such as the Kuruvana of the Kuru Janapada. In the early Buddhist literature, *janapadas* contain market towns as well as villages, and involve administration and the collection of taxes. An important aspect of this development was that all the people of the *janapada* were not linked by the ties of kinship.

Panini refers to two categories of polity in the Punjab: the *gana-sangha* and the *ekaraja*. The former can be looked upon as oligarchies and the latter as monarchies. The *janapadas* of the Madras, Malavas, Kshudrakas, Andhekas and Vrshnis were among the *gana-sanghas*. The last two, according to Panini, were ruled by Kshatriyas who, exercised greater control over their territory and its people than the *rajanya* of earlier times. They encouraged agriculture to minimize the need of cattle-raids. They were consecrated as *rajas* and they were all equal, except that some distinction was made between the older and the younger generations. The term *arya* was now restricted to them and the Brahmans; it was not extended to the Vaishyas. Prestation could have been replaced by regular taxes but there is no evidence that taxes in the *gana-sangha* were collected by its ruling chiefs through a common agency. Every chief appears to have managed the internal affairs of the pocket of territory under his control. According to Panini, the country between the Indus and the Satlej, referred to as Vahika, was dominated by *gana-sanghas*.

Panini mentions the monarchies of the Ambasthas, Gandharas and Sauviras. Whereas the number of 'rulers' in the oligarchies could be pretty large, in the *ekaraja* polity there was room only for one. With the establishment of monarchies, the connotation of *raja* changed radically. The acceptance of monarchy introduced some new features in the polity of the *janapada*. The need for authoritarianism was emphasized, the collection of revenues on a regular and systematic basis was sought to be justified, and great concern was shown for the problem of social harmony.

Panini was probably more familiar with the kingdom of Gandhara than the others. In any case Gandhara appears to have been the most important kingdom of the north-west in the sixth century BC. It is not without significance, therefore, that Panini treats *bali* as a tax, thinks of *bhaga* as a share in the produce, and refers to *shulka* as a kind of customs duty. There is no direct evidence on the arrangements made for the collection of taxes, or any other aspect of administration. The evidence of the later Vedic literature may have some relevance for the monarchies of the Punjab. This literature underlines the divinity of the king through his consecration by the *rajasuya* ceremony. The performers of the horse-sacrifice (*ashvamedha*) are extolled as the more powerful kings. The *sabha* is mentioned in connection with judicial rather than political matters, and the *samiti* as a large body concerned with matters related to legislation. The king begins to wield the rod of punishment (*danda*) which symbolized authority backed by force. The acts regarded as criminal were related to social and individual conduct as well as to life and property: murder, robbery, theft, treachery, abduction, adultery, incest, and drinking intoxicating liquors.

Panini refers to the *parishad* as a source of strength for the king. In the later Vedic literature, the *parishad* appears to be an advisory council for deliberating religious, political and judicial matters. The king himself administered civil and criminal justice. A number of *ratnins* are mentioned in connection with the consecration of the king:

purohita, *senani*, *suta*, *gramani*, *kshttra*, *samagrahitar*, *bhagadugha*, and *akshavapa*, among others. They supported the king not only symbolically but also at the functional level. However, it is difficult to equate them with 'ministers' or 'officers'. There was no administrative machinery and no system of delegating power. The smallest unit of population was the village (*grama*). It was linked with the local market (*nigama*), and through that with the town (*pura* or *nagar*). Panini talks of *grama-dharma* and divides the land of the village into three categories: wasteland (*ushara*), pasture land (*gochara*), and cultivated land (*karasha*). The last is also described as furrowed (*sitya*) and ploughed (*halya*). Panini's *kassaka* was either a professional ploughman or a peasant. The cultivation of land in the village was managed by a number of households (*grhyas*), each with its head who commanded the labour of *dasas* and Shudras as well as the family labour. The public matters of the village were handled by the *gramini* who served as a link between the village and the king.

The establishment of the Achaemenian empire and then of the Mauryan brought about important changes in administrative matters. The Indian province of the Achaemenian empire was far larger than the kingdom of Gandhara. The governor was appointed by the emperor from amongst the members of his family or an old ruling family. His chief duties were to preserve law and order, to collect taxes and to remit tribute to the imperial treasury, to execute imperial decrees, and to maintain high roads in a state of security. He had an army to enforce authority but the commanders of fortresses in the province were responsible directly to the emperor. A secretary in the provincial capital kept the emperor posted with the important happenings in the province. Tribute and tax were collected through local agencies as well as the agents of the governor. There is no reason to believe that the Indian province with its capital at Taxila was any different. It may be safe to assume, then, that some members of the conquered peoples were employed in civil and military positions, and received rewards. Some of the old ruling interests were associated with the new administration at subordinate levels. It is almost certain that the units of administration which earlier were primary and secondary now became secondary and tertiary. The older structure of power was partly accommodated at the lower and local levels of the imperial administrative framework.

The province that covered the Punjab under the Mauryas was larger than the Indian province of the Achaemenian empire. The capital remained at Taxila, but the Mauryan province extended probably up to the Jamuna. Like the other provinces of the empire, this north-western province was placed under a viceroy. Ashoka is believed to have served as its viceroy for some time under Bindusara. The viceroys were generally close relatives of the emperor. The *kumaras* and *aryaputras* of the Ashokan edicts are probably such princes and relatives. The viceroy was assisted by a council of ministers appointed by the emperor, and they had more powers in relation to the viceroy than the ministers at the imperial court in relation to the emperor. Most of the other important officials of the province were also appointed by the emperor but the viceroy had the power to appoint some lower officials.

The province was divided into several large units and the highest officials, the *mahamattas*, were generally represented in the province by the administrators of these primary units as well as the viceroy and his ministers. They controlled various aspects of administration. As the highest cadre of officials, the *mahamattas* provided the backbone of the imperial administration. Each unit was divided into districts, with three sets of officials: the *pradeshikas*, the *rajukas*, and the *yuktas*. The *pradeshikas* were in charge of the overall administration; they supervised the collection of revenue and the maintenance of law and order in towns and the countryside. The *rajukas* worked as judicial officers. An edict lays down that there should be uniformity in judicial procedure and punishment. The disputes brought before them were concerned largely with agricultural problems, assessment, remission of taxes, land and water disputes among the cultivators, among herdsmen about grazing, and disputes among village artisans. Possibly, the *rajukas* were responsible also for surveying and assessing land. Thus the *rajukas* formed the backbone of rural administration. For a group of villages within the district, *gopas* and *sthanikas* served as the link between the district authorities and the village headmen. The *yuktas* were subordinate to both the *pradeshikas* and the *rajukas*, serving them as accountants and clerks.

The Mauryan administration in the Punjab was more centralized than the Achaemenian. However, the degree of centralization has been overemphasized. Local interests had to be reconciled, and it is probable that the oligarchies were dealt with leniency by the Mauryan administrators. The administration of the city of Taxila was conducted through a number of sub-committees in which the heads of guilds and prominent individuals were involved. Apart from the maintenance of law and order, which was a political necessity, the administrative machinery of the province as a whole was aimed primarily at collecting the revenues from land and taxes on trade and manufactures. Ashoka's schemes of promoting public welfare tended to reinforce the general pattern of administration and perhaps made it more efficient. Just as the Punjab came into closer contact with the rest of India, the sub-regions of the Punjab came into closer contact with one another. Regional and sub-regional variations were somewhat reduced but certainly not obliterated.

TRADE AND URBANIZATION

The process of urbanization had started in the Punjab before the establishment of the Mauryan empire. Panini refers to *puras* and *nagaras* which were not simply fortified villages. The capitals of oligarchies were centres of political activity. This activity, however, was not the only factor in the rise of towns. Panini refers to *apanas*, as places of exchange or shops, which indicates the origin of urban places. Panini's reference to *vaniya* and *adya*, who were the counterpart of the *sreshthins* of the Ganges plain, indicates the presence of traders and money-lenders in the Punjab. This finds further support in Panini's reference to coins which came into currency in addition to exchange through barter. The coin of the highest value in circulation mentioned by Panini is the silver *shatmana*. The standard coins were the silver *karshapana* and the copper *masa* and *kakani*. There were probably coins of smaller denominations in both silver and copper. No less significant are Panini's references to skilled and unskilled workers employed on daily or monthly wages. Among the daily wage earners were domestic workers. The close connection of the rise of towns with trade, and of trade with coins, is well acknowledged by now. What is even more important, surplus produce was an essential ingredient of urbanization, carrying the implication of development in agriculture. The increasing importance of the *grihyapati* and the *kassaka* acquires great significance in this context.

The Achaemenian empire which stretched from the north-west of India to the Mediterranean Sea had brought the Punjab into contact with several countries, with important implications for commerce. The high roads maintained by the Achaemenian administration were indispensable for the movement of troops, but they could be used for trade as well. The posting stations and *sarais* at intervals of about 22 kilometres were helpful to the traders. The silver coins found in the north-west provide another indicator of trade. These coins were equivalent to double, half, and quarter of the Persian *sigloi.* Coins of gold were also in use. The seals in Aramaic and Kharoshthi scripts also indicate the existence of trade between the north-west of India and the Persian empire. There is absolutely no doubt that Taxila became an important urban centre under Achaemenian rule.

Three distinct townships have been identified at the Bhir Mound in Taxila. The lowest two are placed by John Marshall in the pre-Mauryan period from the late sixth century BC. The main street running straight from north to south belongs to the first phase; it was maintained subsequently on increasingly higher level. The streets and lanes divided shops and dwelling houses into blocks. The masonry was less massive and rough in the second than in the first phase, indicating further development.

Objects of metal, stone, terracotta, bone, ivory, shell and glass have been unearthed from the Achaemenian period. Iron was used for swords, daggers, and tools. Copper and bronze were used for pendants, finger-rings and kohl-rods. Gold and silver were used as much for necklaces, ear-rings and amulets as for coins. Stone was used for pestles and mortars, mullers, moulds, pivots, amulets and sacred objects. Terracotta objects consist of 'nude mothers', male and female figures standing side by side, toy animals, decorative pieces, and ornaments. Some other objects in terracotta are an oil vessel, a wine vessel, a cooking pot with a round bottom and an open-mouth vessel resembling a modern *handi*, a flat-bottomed jar of medium size, a spouted pot, a small pot resembling the modern *lota*, a drinking cup, bowls and saucers, a basin, a vase and a couple of lids and stoppers. Bone, ivory, shell and glass were used for beads, bangles, combs, hair-pins, kohl-rods, ear-cleaners, toothpicks, pendants, amulets, handles of mirrors, fans, draughtsmen, counters, and arrow heads. All these objects reflect the material aspect of the life of the people of Taxila. It may be added that archaeological evidence by its very nature remains an understatement: the material objects actually used by the people are likely to have been more impressive than what is left at the sites.

Under Mauryan rule, the Punjab was well integrated with the empire in the sphere of trade. The Royal Highway from Pataliputra to Taxila was considered the most important route. Through Kabul and Balkh, one route went up to the Black Sea; another went up to Ecbatana, below the Caspian, through Kandhar and Herat. A third route went up to Seleucia on the Tigris, passing through Persepolis and Susa. The people of the Punjab were familiar with boat building and river voyages in the time of Alexander. There is no reason to believe that they did not participate in the river traffic down the Indus during the Mauryan period. In Buddhist literature, there are frequent references to long journeys undertaken by merchants on the trade route to Taxila and beyond. Situated on the meeting point of three major routes, Taxila became a pre-eminent city.

Numismatic evidence suggests the prevalence of flourishing trade during the Mauryan period. Nearly 1,600 coins have been found from the Bhir Mound. More than 1,300 of these came from two hoards, one buried around 300 BC and the other around 200 BC. About 250 other coins were issued in the fourth, the third, and the second century BC. These coins were 'long bars', or 'round and concave', or rectangular, or oval. Copper coins struck locally were also current at Taxila during the third century BC. Another category of coins current in Taxila, referred to as *nigama* coins, are believed to have been issued by the guilds of Taxila. Their significance for trade is quite obvious. The punch-marked coins appear to have become current during Mauryan rule. In any case, coins were much more widely used now than earlier.

The Greek writers refer to a large number of towns in the Doabs of the Punjab. There would be towns on the route for trade from the Jamuna to the Satlej. The sites at Topra and Kalsi have not yet been excavated. The lack of information need not be interpreted as the absence of towns. The northern Black Polished Ware and punch-marked coins, both of which are associated with the Mauryas, have been discovered at Ropar. A number of sites with Painted Gray Ware have been discovered in the Saraswati-Drishadvati region. Both the NBP and the PG ware have been discovered at Sanghol on the Chandigarh-Ludhiana road. In fact it has been suggested that the PGW appeared a little earlier in the Ravi and the Satlej valleys than in the Ganga-Jamuna Doab. Its predominance implies a larger area of distribution and a larger size settlement, with an increasing use of iron technology, marking a shift from pastoral and agrarian economy towards an economy that was partially urban.

We turn to Taxila again because it is the best excavated site. It was also the most important city of the period. The main street of the Mauryan city had an average width of about seven metres. There were at least three other streets, running from north to south but not in a straight line. Their average width varied from three to six metres. The lanes running from east to west were much narrower, and quite a few of them formed blind alleys. Evidence of vehicular traffic, whether carts or chariots, is provided by wheel-guards to protect the corners of houses. There were small open spaces in the lanes to allow packed animals to pass. There were soak-wells in squares for public convenience, but there was no other public sewage system. Soak-wells of various types were used in residential and other buildings from the very beginning. Public bins were in use, cleared regularly by sweepers. The lanes, being higher than the main streets, served as water courses during the rain. There were no wells in the city because the water table was very low. It may be presumed that water for use in the city was brought from the neighbouring stream.

The walls of residential houses become compact and neat during the Mauryan period. They were built mostly with limestone and *kanjur*, and plastered with mud mixed with chopped straw. In some cases they were whitewashed. An interesting feature of the buildings was their alignment: walls were generally raised on old foundations. This made for continuity in the pattern of settlement through different phases. The houses of the affluent residents of the city were rather large. One such house covered about 335 square metres. It had an open court of about 65 square metres, with twenty rooms on three sides, covering about 270 square metres. The ground floor was meant probably for slaves and dependents. In any case, there was a second storey for the members of the family. A few of the houses were even larger, having two open courts. The houses had flat roofs covered with mud. Rooms on the streets could be used as shops. They had narrow slits to serve as windows. The courts, bathrooms and kitchens were paved with cobblestones. As a rule, the court, the bathroom, the kitchen and the privy had a soak-well each. The largest building exposed so far is a pillared hall, covering an area of nearly 2,800 square metres.

The use of metals appears to have increased during the Mauryan period. Iron was now used for household utensils, agricultural implements, tools, and weapons. There was, thus, a much larger variety of iron objects: bowls, spoons, ladles, sieves, scale pans, spears, javelins, arrowheads, swords, daggers, elephant goads, axes, adzes, chisels, tongs, pliers, tweezers, anvils, nails, hooks, spades and hoes. Objects of copper, bronze and brass include an ear-cleaner, a round bowl, a vase, a kohl-rod, bangles, bracelets, armlets, brooches, hair pins, kohl-phials, cups, ink-pots and pens, bells, tools, and surgical instruments. Beads made of copper and iron have also been found. Gold and silver were used for earrings, pendants, and finger rings. The material culture appears to have become richer.

Stone began to be used now for inlay, encrustations, sculpting, dishes, saucers, cups, bowls, trays, burnishers and polishers. The stone cutters of Taxila were probably employed in making Ashokan pillars with their beautiful capitals. The terracotta objects added during the Mauryan period include several female and male figures of some religious significance, pot-bellied dwarfs, toy carts, toy animals running on wheels, playing dice, and votive and ritual tags. Some of the pottery items are painted or glazed, and embossed or stamped. But most of them are plain. Among the new items are store-jars, a narrow-necked flask; large water pots with rounded bottoms, a pear-shaped vessel resembling the pots used on Persian wheel, open-mouthed pots, water bottles for transport, handled jugs, a pan, a lamp, and drain pipes. The pottery of Taxila was largely local. However, the black polished ware came as a luxury item from the Ganges plain.

Bone, ivory, shell and glass were used for making several kinds of objects for practical use and ornamentation. Shell bangles and beads of various kinds were popular. Among the semi-precious stones used for beads were agate, amethyst, beryl, carnelian, chalcedony, lapis lazuli, malachite, onyx and quartz crystal. Among the common stones were abri, granite, limestone and steatite. Then there were amber, coral, shell bone and faience from which beads were made. There were beads of metal and terracotta too. Above all, there were beads of glass, clourless and in blue, green, yellow, orange and red. If two colours of the rainbow were missing, others like amber, black, grey, turquoise and opal added to the riot of colours.

Metals, stone, glass and agate were used for seals and sealings found at Taxila. These are of two categories: one, either Persian or bearing Persian influence, and the other Indian. The scaraboid seals appear to be characteristically Persian. On one such seal of clay, there is a winged stag. On a seal of black agate there is a *nandipad* symbol and a lion. The designs were executed with a drill. Regarded as characteristically Mauryan are pyramidal seals of stone, glass and copper. The design on these was executed with a graving tool. These designs appear to carry some religious significance. Terracotta sealings have also been found in Taxila of the Mauryan times.

Taxila was a centre of exchange not only of goods but also of ideas. In Buddhist literature, the city is depicted as a great centre of learning. Even if stereotyped, the image invoked by the *Jatakas* is not without interest or significance. There are over a hundred references to Takkashila (Taxila) as a city, a capital city and a centre of learning. There were teachers of world fame who taught there, often taking up to

500 pupils, each of whom was expected to pay 1,000 pieces of money. A few could be accepted on a promise of payment after the completion of their education. The chief pupil could help the teacher in his tasks, and the teacher was entitled according to the norms of the times to make use of the stick, when it became necessary, even on princes.

The world-famous teachers at Takkashila imparted what may be called higher education. The pupils went there to 'complete' or to 'perfect' their education after having been educated elsewhere till the age of sixteen. The teachers of Takkashila generally admitted to their academies young princes and sons of Brahmans, the youths of warrior and Brahman castes. The *Jatakas* refer specifically to the princes of Banaras, Mithila, Indraprastha, and a Prince of the Shivis. The Brahmans of Kashi, Panchala, a lad of Mithila, a son of the family priest of the Kuru King of Indraprastha, and Brahmans of the north country in general flocked to Takkashila for higher studies. The princes who went there for higher education became viceroys and kings; the Brahmans who went there became ministers, family priests of kings or teachers of world fame at places like Banaras. Occasionally, the sons of merchants could be admitted to higher studies at Takkashila, but not Chandalas. Two of the latter who got admission posing as Brahmans were discovered on account of their speech and were thrown out. The higher studies at Takkashila consisted of the learning of the 'three Vedas by rote', the 'sacred texts', 'all the branches of knowledge', 'elephant lore', 'the science of archery', 'magic charms', 'all the liberal arts', 'all the arts and sciences', consisting probably of Vedic ritual, grammar, astronomy, astrology, mathematics, medicine, military science, and political economy.

THE SOCIAL ORDER

The later Samhitas and the Brahmanas contain statements on the ordering of society into four *varnas*: the Brahman, the Kshatriya, the Vaishya and the Shudra. These statements indicate that the ideal of a four-fold social order was crystallizing. The functions and duties, and the privileges and status, of the four *varnas* are also set out. The Shudras are at the bottom of the scale, without any right to property, fit only to serve others. The Vaishya, pursuing agriculture, industry, trade and pastoralism, are meant to provide the means of subsistence for the *varnas* superior to them. The Kshatriya fight for the protection of the country, and maintain peace; they receive revenues and income from land. The Brahmans are close to the Kshatriyas, in some texts slightly below them and in others slightly above. They stand clearly contrasted with all the other *varnas* as the privileged eaters of oblations. They also enjoy certain privileges and exemptions denied to others.

The Grihyasutras clearly differentiate the status, occupations, obligations, duties and privileges of the four *varnas* in matters religious and secular. The idea of impurity makes its appearance; the gulf between the Shudras and the other three widens; the sacraments and the right to renunciation are denied to the Shudras; and the outcastes emerge in the form of Chandalas who live on the outskirts of villages and towns. Furthermore, differences are made for each of the three higher *varnas* in almost all sacraments. The Brahmans alone can sacrifice for themselves and others, and they alone can receive gifts; their special duty is to study and teach the Vedas. The Kshatriyas are close to the Brahmans in power and prestige. The Vaishyas stand at a distance from both of them. However, fire can still be borrowed from a Vaishya rich in cattle, or from one who has performed many sacrifices. The Dharmasutras uphold differences between the four *varnas* in the matter of punishments and financial and social concessions. Significantly, the offspring of a Shudra male and a Brahman female did not become a Shudra but a Chandala.

Like the position of the Shudras, the position of women deteriorates further in the later Samhitas, Brahmanas and Sutras. The age recommended for the marriage of a girl becomes lower, before puberty in fact. A good wife does not talk back; she eats after her husband. Remarriage of the widow is prohibited in some texts. The 'marriage' of a girl who has been carried off or abducted is recognized as legitimate. The birth of a daughter is not welcome; she is a source of misery. Matrimony is a holy bond but only for women. Polygamy is favoured, especially for begetting a male child. The son alone is the saviour of the family. Some of the later Dharmasutras condemn even *niyoga*. The well known principle that the males are the masters of women makes its appearance. Their fathers protect them in childhood, their husbands protect them in youth, and their sons protect them in old age; a woman is never fit for independence.

The statements in the later Samhitas, Brahmanas and Sutras on the social order cannot be taken as empirical realities. Being mostly normative, their thrust is on what should be and not on what is. The *varna* framework, it is suggested, was not a reflection of the socio-economic hierarchy so much as a structure for the integration of varying sub-systems. Furthermore, in post-Rigvedic literature differences are perceived between the Kuru-Panchala region and the *janapadas* of the Punjab. Whereas in the former there is relative purity of the ritual, in the latter the rituals have been discarded. These *janapadas* fall in status because they have ceased to perform the *yajnas*. Indeed, it is probable that the *gana-sanghas* of the Punjab did not attach much importance to the rituals. Panini makes a few observations here and there which have a bearing on the social order. First of all, he talks of social categories more in terms of *jati* than of *varna*. The *aryas* are distinguished from the rest as possessers of wealth. Birth into the *arya-varna* bestows social status. A Brahman could sometimes be the king. A *dasa* restored to his former position acquired the status of *arya-krita*. These observations are suggestive of stratification but not of rigidity. Nevertheless, Panini observes that the lower category of Shudras were treated as outcaste and forced to live outside the villages and towns.

In Buddhist literature, Chandalas are described as *bahinagare*, literally living outside the town as excluded groups. They are associated with pollution: the daughter of a *setthi* washes her eyes on seeing a Chandala, and a Brahman is worried that the breeze blowing past a Chandala will blow on him as well. The word 'untouchable' is not used but the sentiment is present. However, the Chandala of these stories is the Buddha or a *bodhisattva* in his earlier birth, which carries the implication that such stigmas are not desirable. Indeed, a king marries a Chandala woman and makes her son his successor. Buddhist sources underline the importance of the *khatris*, *gahapatis* and *kassaks*, and refer much more frequently to *jati* than to *varna*, which suggests that *jati* was the most evident category of social perception. However, *jatis* were ranked into high and low categories, postulating a dual division. In the late first millennium BC there was no exact correlation between *varna* status and economic status. As ritual status, *varna* gained primacy only where *yajna* and *grihya* rituals were of central importance. This does not appear to be the case in Vahika, the land between the Satlej and the Indus.

Magasthenes, as quoted by Diodorus, Strabo and Arrian, refers to seven divisions of the Indian people in the early third century BC. One of these seven were 'philosophers'. They actually consisted of Brahmanas and Shramanas. The former performed priestly functions, presiding over animal sacrifices and other rituals performed by kings, or members of the ruling elite, or the wealthy landowners. Some of them specialized in learning and adopted teaching as their profession. The

Shramanas were monks and nuns of various religious orders. The Buddhist monks too specialized in new kinds of learning and imparted teaching in monasteries. The Shramanas appear to have included other ascetics as well. They were known for their austerities and wisdom. We do not know about the relative importance of the Brahmanas and the Shramanas in terms of numbers and social prestige, but there is no doubt about their conspicuous presence in the Punjab.

The second category of people mentioned by Magasthenes was that of the cultivators. A large number of people had settled on land since the days of the *Rigveda*, making cultivation of land an important profession. As a single category, the cultivators were probably the most numerous. Among them were owners of land who needed tenants to cultivate it. Then there were the average landholders, cultivating the land with the help of their family members. Perhaps some state farms were cultivated by tenants who received a certain share of the produce. The other cultivators generally paid one-sixth of their produce, or some other share, to the state. There were pastoral tribes not only on the peripheries of the region but also between the cultivated tracts. Magasthenes appears to refer to them as herdsmen as the third category of Indian people. In towns and cities there were artisans, shopkeepers and merchants who formed the fourth category. Most of them, if not all, were associated with guilds. With increase in the number of urban centres, their number had increased since the sixth century BC. Magasthenes refers to them as a single category.

There were three other categories of people, all connected with the state: soldiers, overseers and councillors. As a part of the standing army of the state, the soldiers would form a substantial number. Some people in the Punjab specialized in the profession of arms and were possibly available for recruitment. The overseers were the officials referred to in the *Arthashastra* as the *adhyakshas*, or the superintendents of various departments of the state. The councillors were the highest officers known as *mahamattas*. The last two categories were represented in the Punjab, though it is quite likely that most of the *mahamattas* did not belong to the region. The other officials were probably inducted mostly from the Punjab. Ashoka refers to his subordinates at three rungs: high, middle and low. It may be reasonable to imagine that the first came largely from outside the region, and the bulk of the third came from the region itself; the middle category could come from both the sources. This is how we can account for the *pradeshikas*, *rajukas*, *yuktas*, *gopas* and *sthanikas*. Lastly, the Greek writers tend to assume that all categories of people in India had specific rules for marriage and occupation. This would make sense if we treat their statements as applicable to *jatis* and not to *varnas*. The Greek writers were not talking of seven 'castes' but of seven 'branches' among the people.

The categories of people mentioned by Magasthenes appear to account for a very large part of the population in the Punjab, but not for all. The inscriptions of Ashoka refer to slaves and servants. The people in the countryside appear to have consisted of landowners, cultivators and tenants. There is no mention of the categories of people who provided many services required in agriculture, and in social life. We may be sure that there was a good occupational diversity and social stratification in the Punjab. But we do not know how important was the *varna* ideal in the eyes of its people, or how rigid were the rules of marriage and commensality. The fact that the writers of the Ganges plain looked upon the Vahika as 'unorthodox' suggests a relative lack of rigidity.

Indeed, the taunts hurled by Karna at the Madra prince Shalya in the *Mahabharata* indicate that the 'eastern' people looked upon the Vahikas as different from themselves. The Madras, Gandharas, Sindhus, Sauviras, Trigartas, Arattas, Vasatis and Khashas stand excommunicated by the Ganga, Jamuna, Saraswati and the Himalayas. Thus, the Vahikas appear to be living mostly beyond the Satlej. The observations made by Karna are both specific and general. The total picture that emerges is that of a people who eat wheat flour cakes, parched or fried barley, garlic, fish, and meat of cows, camels, donkeys, pigs, sheep and fowls. They do not properly clean the wooden and earthen platters in which they eat. They drink liquor distilled from molasses. Then they indulge in loud laughter and merriment, singing songs with no rhythm or music. Generally unrestrained in their loose talk, they become more so when intoxicated. In their houses, all men and women mix freely with one another: parents, sons, daughters, parents-in-law, sons-in-law, daughters-in-law, sisters and brothers, friends and guests, maids and attendants. Their women were fair, tall and healthy, and they ate large quantities of food; they put on woollen shawls over their shoulders and lacked in modesty. They prefer *suviraka*, the famous liquor of the Sauvira *janapada*, to their sons and husbands, and they sing songs in praise of strong drink. A Vahika takes birth as a Brahman and becomes a Kshatriya, and then a Vaishya, a Shudra and a barber; he again becomes a Brahman and then a slave. The Madra Kshatriyas acted as priests and they were worse than the eunuchs of the vintners among the *mlechhas*.

Nevertheless, a Vahika exile in the Kurujangala yearns for the land where he could ride a camel, a donkey, or a mule in the groves of *shami*, *pilu* and *kaira*, and join his gang to plunder the lonely wayfarer. He yearns for his wheat cake, barley meal and buttermilk. He yearns for his tall and fair wife in the woollen shawl. And he dreams of his native land where charming ladies wear shawls and big bracelets, and anoint their eyes with collyrium, besmear their eye-corners with red arsenic paste, and dance to the tune of sweet music. In short, he is nostalgic about his region.

In this 'epic' description of the Punjab, the affinity of the people of the Satlej-Jamuna Divide with the people of the middle Ganges plain is assumed, and the people of Vahika present a contrast to them both. This contrast relates to food, drinks, dress, economy, social behaviour, ritual, and women. There is thus a difference in the socio-cultural articulation in the plain between the Indus and the Satlej on the one hand and the plain between the Satlej and the Jamuna on the other.

RELIGIOUS IDEAS AND PRACTICES

For the religious ideas and practices in the Punjab we may first turn to the later Samhitas. The *Samaveda* was so closely connected with the *Rigveda* that there is hardly anything in it that is both new and significant. Indra, Agni and Soma remain its principal deities and sacrifices are offered to them. The *Atharvaveda* was recognized as canonical much later and that too not by all those who accepted the three earlier Samhitas. In any case, the *Atharvaveda* was not compiled in the Kuru-Panchala region and it was not known to Panini in the Punjab. The *Yajurveda* was composed and compiled in the Kuru-Panchala region, and it was known to Panini.

The pantheon of the *Rigveda* is retained in the *Yajurveda* but with some modifications. Prajapati, who was foreshadowed in the later hymns of the *Rigveda*, comes more and more to the fore in the *Yajurveda* as the chief of gods. Rudra begins to appear on the scene more frequently as Shiva, and his other epithets are also mentioned: Shankara and Mahadeva. Vishnu begins to occupy a more prominent position. His constant identification with the sacrifice is a new feature. The demons, now regularly called Asuras, appear perpetually as a group of evil beings opposed to the gods who are good, giving rise to a number of myths. The Apsaras begin to be more prominent, and many of them are referred to by individual names. Snake worship makes its appearance as an element in the Yajurvedic religion. Furthermore, the sacrifice itself becomes the centre of thought and desire: its correct performance in every detail becomes all important. It compels the gods to do the will of the officiating priest who, is a sense, holds the gods in his hands. The ritual began to be more and more a mystery to all except the Brahmans.

The sacrificial ceremonial, with practical directions (*vidhi*) and explanations (*arthaveda*), is the primary concern of the Brahmanas. The Rigvedic Brahmanas, known as the *Aitareya* and the *Kaushitaki*, were probably composed in the Kuru-Panchala region. The Somavedic Brahmanas come from two schools: the Jaiminiya and the Panchavimsha. The latter contains a minute description of sacrifices on the Saraswati and the Drishadvati. The Yajurvedic Brahmanas are known as the *Taittiriya* (for the *Black Yajurveda*) and the *Shatapatha* (for the *White Yajurveda*). The latter refers to the Gandharas, Shalvas, and Kekayas. Its geographical data indicate that Kuru-Panchala was the centre of Brahmanical culture. The famous Yajnavalkya is associated with this Brahmana, and Janamejaya, the celebrated king of the Kurus in the *Mahabharata*, is mentioned for the first time. However, the Pandavas figure in none of these Brahmanas. Arjuna is an appellation of Indra. The story of the love and separation of Pururavas and Urvashi, shadowed forth in a hymn of the *Rigveda*, is narrated much more elaborately in the *Shatapatha Brahmana*, which also contains the legend of the Deluge.

The Brahmanas speak not only of *vidhi* and *arthaveda* but also of theologico-philosophical speculation in their last part, called the Upanishad, literally 'sitting down beside' or confidential sessions, carrying the implication of 'secret or esoteric doctrine'. These portions were known also as *vedanta*, not the essence or the culmination but simply the end of Vedic literature. The Upanishads of the *Rigveda* are now known as the *Aitareya* and *Kaushitaki*, those of *Samaveda* are known as the *Chandogya* and the *Kena*, and those of the *Yajurveda* as the *Brhadaranyaka* and the *Taittiriya*. The transition from the Samhitas to the Upanishads is provided by the Aranyakas or 'forest books'. The Upanishads virtually represent a new kind of religion. Elaborating the speculative side of the Brahmanas, they uphold *jnana-kanda* or esoteric knowledge against *karma-kanda* or ritual. The basic theme of the Upanishad is the nature of the world-soul, Brahman or *atman*. The former represents the cosmic principle which pervades the universe, and the latter represents the psychic principle manifested in man. The great fundamental doctrine of the Upanishads is the identity of the individual soul (*atma*) with the world-soul (*parmatma*) or Brahman. This realization leads to bliss through the absorption of the former in the latter.

In one of the later Upanishads, the world is explained explicitly as an illusion produced by Brahman as a conjurer (*mayin*). This notion is inherent in the oldest Upanishads. The theory of transmigration (*samsara*) went hand in hand with the doctrine that true knowledge led to supreme bliss by the absorption of the individual soul in Brahman. In the *Shatpatha Brahmana* the notion of being born again after death, and dying repeatedly, is associated with the idea of retribution. The theory is elaborated in the *Chandogya Upanishad*. What regulates new birth is man's deeds. In the *Brhadaranyaka Upanishad* we come upon the beginning of the doctrine of *karma* or 'action' which alone survives death as 'good' or 'bad' (and determines new birth). They who practise sacrifice and good works pass through the world of the fathers to the moon and then they return to earth to be born as men; others become birds, beasts and reptiles. In the *Chandogya*, the wicked are born as Chandalas, dogs or swine. Panini was familiar with the three Samhitas, suggesting that they exercised some influence in Vahika too. He also refers to the worship of the Bharata heroes in the Punjab, which was something new.

The Greek writers refer to Dionysus as an Indian God who was worshipped in the hills. He is identified with Indra, showing the survival of this deity into the fourth century BC. The Greek writers also refer to Herakles, who is identified with Vasudeva. He was popular in the plains. D.D. Kosambi suggests that Indra was yielding place to Krishna because pastoral life was yielding place to an agrarian economy for which the Vedic sacrifice and constant fighting were a costly nuisance. Krishna was preferable to Indra because he was a protector of cows and not a god demanding their sacrifice.

According to the Greek writers, Alexander showed interest in sages who were practising austerities at Taxila. One of them had a shaven head but another had long hair. Each had a group of disciples, and both of them were accustomed to addressing all and sundry in the market-place. There is no record of their philosophic ideas but they enjoyed enough prestige to take anything they wanted without payment. Alexander conversed with ten 'sophists' among the Mallavas and persuaded another sage to accompany him.

This information begins to acquire great significance when we see it in conjunction with the evidence of the *Rigveda*. A hymn in the tenth book of the *Rigveda* refers to *munis* who wear long loose hair; they are girdled with the wind; and their bodies are besmeared with ochre-coloured dust. They can fly through the air and assume any form. Distinct from the Brahman, the ascetic rose far above the heights achieved by the sacrificial priest. He could see the past, present and the future; he could mount the heavens, and was graciously received at the courts of gods; the divinities could descend to earth and visit him in his hermitage; and he could work miracles by the powers attained through asceticism. Above all, he came into possession of esoteric knowledge. It was through such ascetics or renouncers that the conception of Brahman and *atman* came into currency, together with the associated ideas of transmigration (*samsar*) and the law of deeds (*karma*).

Archaeological evidence too is suggestive of some religious beliefs and practices at the popular level. Terracotta and clay objects like the 'nude mother' and other female deities have been found at Taxila. Votive or ritual tanks and amulets also appear to carry religious significance. The Pillared Hall at Bhir Mound could have served as 'a shrine of some sort'. The house attached to it could have been occupied by priests and their attendants. In the debris of this building were found terracotta reliefs representing a male and female deity standing side by side and holding hands. Such plaques could be sold to or distributed among the worshippers.

Ashoka is said to have sent missionaries to various parts of the Indian subcontinent, including Gandhara and Kashmir. There are some minor inscriptions in which Ashoka's concern specifically for Buddhism finds expression. He professes his respect for and faith in the Buddha, the Dhamma and the Samgha. He underlines the importance of certain sermons in particular, as on the excellence of the discipline, the lineage of the noble one, the future fears, the verses of the sage, the *sutra* of silence, and on the admonition to Rahula on the subject of false speech. These are the sermons on which the laity and the monks should frequently meditate. At the place of the Buddha's birth the emperor got a stone pillar erected, with a stone enclosure around it, and exempted the village of Lumbini from tax, fixing its contribution of grain at one-eighth of the produce. Ashoka was seriously concerned with the unity of the Samgha. Any monk or nun who created a schism was to be dressed in white garments and sent away. This order must be endorsed by laymen on the days of confession and penance, and also by special officers. There is no doubt about the emperor's deep interest in

Buddhism. Though Buddhism was probably not unknown in the Punjab before Ashoka, his reign marked the first important phase in the history of Buddhism in this region.

No discussion of Buddhism under Ashoka can be complete without his Dhamma. When we turn to the pillar inscription of Topra in the east of the Punjab and the rock inscriptions at Mansehra and Shahbazgarhi in its north-west, we find that Ashoka does not equate Dhamma with Buddhism. His conception of Dhamma is primarily ethical: to do good to others; to discard violence in favour of non-injury to living beings; to control 'passions' which lead to violence, cruelty, anger, vanity and jealousy; to cultivate self-control, compassion, liberality, truthfulness, purity of conduct and thought, restraint, moderation, impartiality, gratitude, devotion, courtesy, and consideration. The Dhamma is addressed to all provinces, people of all religions, and people of all classes in both towns and villages. Dhamma was to be propagated and implemented through the *mahamattas* and *rajukas*, proclamation through edicts for both restriction and exhortation, and public welfare. The objectives of the Dhamma were ethical improvement of the individual, social harmony and social reform–all these leading to the grand objective of happiness in this life and, much more so, in the next. Ashoka feels gratified after an increasingly systematic effort of a score of years that the love of Dhamma was on the increase, not through the exercise of power so much as through persuasion.

After this summary statement about the Dhamma, we may turn to what is actually said in the inscriptions found in the Punjab. In the pillar edict of Topra it is stated that 'happiness in this world and in the next is difficult to secure without intense love of Dhamma' which consists of 'the least amount of sin, many virtuous deeds, compassion, liberality, truthfulness and purity'. The passions that lead to sin are 'such as violence, cruelty, anger, vanity and jealousy'. The *rajukas*, placed over many hundred thousands of souls, are entrusted with the control of 'the award of rewards or the imposition of punishment'. Impartiality in their proceedings and judgements is expected to promote 'the welfare and happiness of the country people'. Having the propagation of Dhamma in view, Ashoka 'set up pillars bearing records relating to Dhamma, appointed Mahamatras to deal with the affairs connected with Dhamma, and issued proclamations on Dhamma'. For the same purpose, banyan trees and mango groves were planted along the roads to provide shade for beasts and men, wells were excavated at intervals of 8 *krohs*, and rest houses were constructed. The 'Dhamma-Mahamatras' were occupied with the affairs of the Buddhist Samgha, with the Brahmanas, the Ajivikas, the Nirgranthas and with all the other religious groups 'not specifically mentioned'. Among the good deeds are 'obedience to mother and father, obedience to elders, courtesy to the aged, courtesy to the Brahmanas and Shramanas, to the poor and the distressed, and even to slaves and servants'.

In the rock inscriptions at Mansehra and Shahbazgarhi, we are told that the 'Dhamma-Mahamatras' are occupied with 'all the religious sects' for establishment and promotion of Dhamma 'even among the Yavanas, Kambojas and Gandharas, the Rashtrikas and Paitryanikas and the other people dwelling about the western borders of my dominions'. They are occupied with the welfare and happiness of 'the servile class and the community of traders and agriculturalists as well as the Brahmanas and the ruling class and likewise of the destitute and the aged'. Their concern extends to prisoners in all cities and towns. 'King Priyadarshi, Beloved of the gods, wishes that all religious sects should live harmoniously in all parts of his dominions.' The common objective of all religious groups is 'self-control and purity of thought'. If a person does not possess these, his liberality is worthless. People perform various ceremonies on the occasions of illness, weddings, births, setting out on journeys and on similar other occasions. The womenfolk in particular perform many ceremonies which are 'trivial and meaningless'. The ceremonies associated with Dhamma, on the other hand, produce great results: 'proper courtesy to slaves and servants, reverence to elders, restraint in one's dealings with living beings and liberality to the Shramanas and Brahmanas'. Significantly, the Shramanas are mentioned here before the Brahmanas. Whereas the other ceremonies may at best 'produce results in this world only', the ceremonies connected with the Dhamma earn 'endless merit' for the next world even if they do not produce results for this world. 'Only the happiness of the people in the next world is what is regarded by the Beloved of the Gods as a great thing': this is ensured not by armed conquest but by 'conquest through Dhamma'.

The evidence of the inscriptions clearly indicates that the Dhamma of Ashoka was essentially an ethical pattern devised on the basis of a variety of religious and moral teachings of contemporary thinkers. Since he himself was a Buddhist, the Buddhist strand in the pattern is more evident than the rest. But to equate his Dhamma with Buddhism is wrong, and it would be unjust to maintain that the Dhamma was an attempt to make Buddhism the state religion. Ashoka's equal regard for the Shramanas and the Brahmanas comes out clearly. Among the Shramanas were not only the Buddhists but also the Ajivikas and the Jains. Furthermore, religious groups 'not specifically mentioned' are also bracketed with them. The Brahmanas were surely represented in the Punjab, and so were the Buddhists and some other ascetics. It is not clear, however, whether or not Jains or Ajivikas were present among some other groups.

LANGUAGES, LITERATURE AND ARTS

The *Kaushitaki Brahmana* of the *Rigveda* contains the statement that the study of language was specially cultivated in the north of India, and that students who returned from there were regarded as authorities on linguistics. We do not know the places where this study was cultivated but we do know that Panini had a number of predecessors. The study of language was intimately linked with religion in the sense that correct recitation and understanding of the sacred text were regarded as essential requirements of worship. Therefore, interest in phonetics, etymology, grammar and metre developed quite early. The *Taittiriya Aranyaka* mentions phonetics (*shiksa*) as a subject which dealt with letters, accent, quantity, pronunciation and euphonic rules. The basis for such studies was provided by 'word-text' (*pada-patha*) of the Vedas. Connected with *pada-pathas* were the *Pratishakhyas* which furnished a systematic account of Vedic euphonic combinations. Panini used them for his *Ashtadhyayi*.

In the study of etymology, collections of rare or obscure Vedic words, arranged for the use of teachers, were prepared as *Nighantus*. These could be used for exegesis. Yaska had before him five such collections when he wrote his Vedic commentary, the famous *Nirukta*. Besides being important from the point of view of exegesis and grammar, the *Nirukta* is significant as the earliest extant Sanskrit prose tract of the classical type, considerably earlier than Panini. He must have lived long before Panini for a considerable number of names of important grammarians are mentioned between them. Yaska's *Nirukta* also shows that the *Rigveda* had a fixed form in his time, and its text was essentially identical with the text now available.

Grammatical studies were cultivated to a considerable extent before Yaska. He talks of two schools: the 'eastern' and the 'northern'. He mentions nearly a score of predecessors among whom were Shakatayana, Gargya and Shakalya. Yaska has an interesting discussion on the theory of Shakatayana that nouns were derived from verbs. Gargya is rejected by him because of his view that all nouns are not derived from verbs. The whole system of Panini's grammar is founded on Shakatayana's theory of the verbal origin of nouns. Coming to be regarded as an infallible authority, Panini superseded all his predecessors. Their works, consequently, have perished. Yaska alone survives because he was not directly a grammarian. His work represents Vedanga 'etymology'. Panini's own work can be regarded as the starting point for the post-Vedic classical Sanskrit.

Panini's work in itself has a great cultural significance. His interest in grammar and linguistics underlines the importance of Vedic language and literature in the Punjab, particularly when we know that he had a number of predecessors. He moulded the future of the language precisely because his work came as the culmination of interest in systematic analysis of language. His work is significant also for revealing his familiarity with the later Vedic tradition. He was a master not only of the *Rigveda* but also of the *Sama* and the *Yajura*. He describes the language spoken by a group of priests who were familiar with the language of the northern schools of the Vedic tradition, which was close to the later Vedic prose in structure. Thus, Panini's work reveals a certain degree of close contact between Vahika and the Kuru-Panchala region.

Another great name associated with the Punjab is that of Kautilya. On the basis of thorough analyses of the *Arthashastra* in recent decades it can now be stated with some confidence that it was originally composed by him around 300 BC. It was commented upon and edited by later writers till the text now available was prepared by Vishnugupta in the third or the fourth century AD, including whatever interpolations had been incorporated by then. The second book of the *Arthashastra* appears to be the original core, with a few other books closely allied to it. This treatise on political economy gives a clear and methodical analysis of economic and political thought in its application to the existing conditions. Kautilya can legitimately be looked upon as the theorist of the Mauryan system of administration and taxation. Panini and Kautilya are perhaps the best examples of profound thought coupled with a strong element of empirical observation. Their works appear to be closely related to the life around.

The official language and script of the Achaemenian empire was Aramaic. The Aramaic script was inadequate to express all the sounds of the language spoken by the people in the north-west of the subcontinent. Gradually a new script was evolved for the local Prakrit. This new script was Kharoshthi. Its popularity is indicative of the prevalence of Prakrit in the Punjab. It may be added that the use of writing was helpful not only to the administrator but also to the trader.

The inscriptions of Ashoka throw some light on matters related to languages and scripts. When Ashoka decided to give wide publicity to his ideas and programmes he decided to use Prakrit as the medium. The inscriptions from Topra and Kalsi in the Satlej-Jamuna Divide are in Prakrit written in Mauryan Brahmi. The language of the inscription at Mansehra in the upper Sindh Sagar Doab is also Prakrit, though the script used is Kharoshthi. This is also true of the inscription at Shahbazgarhi across the river Indus. The language of the fragment of an inscription discovered at Taxila is Aramaic, which would indicate that there were some Persian residents of Taxila. The inscription at Lampaka (Lamghan) is in Aramaic. In the inscription at Kandhar, Greek as well as Aramaic is used, indicating the presence of Greek and Aramaic speaking people in Kandhar. It need not be ruled out, however, that inscriptions in Greek and Aramaic languages were meant for the traders coming from the west as well as for the local people. The evidence of Ashokan inscriptions is suggestive of the popularity of Prakrit throughout the Punjab.

No public monuments of the period have yet come to light. A.H. Dani feels that Mauryan monuments have yet to be excavated. There must have been *sarais* on the Mauryan highways. But they have left no evidence behind. Marshall suggests that the Dharamarajika stupa at Taxila was founded in the time of Ashoka and that beside it was an Ashokan pillar which was broken into pieces later. Two pillars have actually survived: one is now in the Ferozeshah Kotla complex at Delhi and the other at Hissar. These are the only examples of Mauryan sculpture from the Punjab. Originally these two columns were almost certainly similar to the other known Ashokan columns.

All Mauryan columns were chiselled out of grey Chunar sandstone and had a lustrous polish. Each column consisted of two parts: the shaft and the capital. Circular in shape and slightly tapering, the shaft was made from a single block of stone and had graceful and elegant proportion. The capital was monolithic like the shaft, but consisted of three parts: an inverted lotus, abacus, and a crowning figure. The beautifully arched and elegantly rubbed floral bell of the capital contrasts with the chaste, plain and smooth, tall and tapering shaft. The abacus, either circular or rectangular, is often carved on its side with elegant floral designs or figures of birds and animals. It supports the crowning figure or figures of animals which are sometimes of the highest workmanship 'ever known in animal sculpture anywhere in the world'. The impetus originally came from Achaemenian Persia. But the Mauryan columns possess an undeniable originality of their own in both form and character. The total aesthetic effect of the columns was never to be surpassed in later Indian art. In fact, the Mauryan art made no permanent contribution to the growth of Indian art. One of its functions was to impress and overawe the populace. Like the columns and the animal figures themselves, Mauryan art stands aloof and apart, symbolizing imperial power at its height.

READING

Agarwal 1963; Bogard 1985; Burrow 1965; Cowell 1893; Dani 1968; Ghosh 1990; Joshi 1977; Keith 1920; Marshal 1975; Mcrindle 1877, 1896; Nikam and Mekeon 1949; Rhys Davids 1903; Roy 1994; Sharma 1989; Sircar 1957; Thapar 1973, 1987; Trautmann 1971; Wagle 1966.

4

Socio-cultural Diversification (*c.* 200 BC–AD 400)

The politics of the Punjab after the decline and fall of the Mauryas was marked by foreign invasions in succession, resulting in the formation of new states which continued to have more or less close contacts with the countries on the West. Consequently, the trends of trade established during the Mauryan period were reinforced, and urbanization received a new impetus. The growth of urbanism carried important implications for the socio-economic and cultural life of the people, including religion and the arts. We shall concentrate on a period of six centuries from about 200 BC to about AD 400 to view these important developments. This period was remarkable also for the resurgence of a number of indigenous powers.

POLITICAL DEVELOPMENTS

The immediate successors of the Mauryas had to contend with the Greek successors of Alexander for power in the Punjab. The latter established their rule in the region during the first quarter of the second century BC. They were followed by the Shakas, the Parthians and the Kushanas. The Guptas appeared on the scene in the fourth century AD but did not directly rule the north-west of India. Instead, some of the peoples of the region established sub-regional or local polities. The involvement of a large number of peoples in the politics of the Punjab during this period makes the situation complex but none the less fascinating.

Exactly a hundred years after Chandragupta Maurya's war with Seleucus we find an Indian prince, Subhagasena, entering into a treaty with Antiochus III. The Indian prince was, however, the losing party, required to pay tribute to the Greek ruler. We do not know if Subhagasena had any connection with the Mauryas, but his submission to Antiochus III made Gandhara subordinate to the Greek power. The Greek governor of Bactria, named Euthydemus, whom Antiochus III had recognized as an independent king in 206 BC, started on conquests in the direction of India before his death around 190 BC. His successor, Demetrius, crossed the Indus; his coins have been found all over the Punjab. He was busy in his Indian campaigns, probably in Sind, around 170 BC when his throne was usurped by Eucratides. About twenty-five years later, Eucratides' successor, Heliocles, was ousted from Bactria by the Shakas. He crossed the Hindu Kush and dislodged a successor of Demetrius from Gandhara.

Meanwhile, Pushyamitra Shunga, the commander-in-chief of the Mauryan armies under a successor of Ashoka, had taken over the government at Pataliputra, presumably in an attempt to resist Greek advance into the Mauryan dominions. The successors of Demetrius in the Punjab were sandwiched between the Shungas in the east and the successors of Eucratides in the west. Significantly, Antialcides, the ruler of Taxila who belonged to the house of Eucratides, sent Heliodorus as his ambassador to the court of the Shunga Bhagabhadra. At that time, Strato I, who belonged to the house of Demetrius, was ruling over the eastern Punjab. Two Greek houses were thus rivals for power in the region. Numismatic evidence reveals the existence of more than 30 rulers in about 170 years. Apparently, 'joint' or 'subordinate' kings were entitled to issue coins. Menander, a king of the house of Demetrius with his capital near the present day Sialkot, proved to be the most eminent of all the Indo-Greek kings of the Punjab. Known to the Buddhist tradition as Milinda, he was immortalized in the Pali work entitled *Milindapanha*. He is now thought to have ruled in the first (rather than the second) century BC.

The Shakas who were ruling in Bactria were hard-pressed by the Yueh-chi people of China before the end of the first century BC. Moving towards India, they occupied Gandhara. The first Shaka ruler at Taxila was Maues, who was succeeded by Azes I, Azilises, and Azes II. The earliest date assigned to Maues is 20 BC and the last date assigned to Azes II is AD 79. If these dates are accepted, the Shakas would appear to have ruled for about a century. However, there are some difficulties. The dates assigned to the Shaka rulers overlap: 20 BC to AD 22 for Maues; 5 BC to AD 30 for Azes I; AD 28 to 40 for Azilises and AD 35 to 79 for Azes II. This problem is resolved if there was 'joint rule'. Information on the Satraps appointed by them to administer the provinces gives an indication of the territories over which they ruled: Kabul, Gandhara, the Swat valley, Taxila and some other parts of the Punjab. A Satrap named Rajula administered the east Punjab at one time, and later became the *mahakshatrapa* of the Mathura region. For some time thus, the Shakas ruled over the entire Punjab.

Yet another difficulty arises due to the fact that one Phraotes is mentioned by a contemporary observer as ruling in Taxila in AD 43–4, whereas Gondophernes was ruling there in AD 45. Both these names suggest connection with the ruling house of Parthia. The governor of Parthia under the Greeks had become independent at about the same time as Euthydemus, and founded a new dynasty. If Phraotes conquered Gandhara and Taxila, Gondophernes extended his power to the Punjab as well. Possibly, the Shaka Azes II became subordinate to Gondophernes. This would be in consonance with the idea that the Parthian empire was a loose federation, with territories administered by 'vassal' kings. Gondophernes was succeeded by Pakores. In AD 64, however, the Peshawar region was under the Kushana ruler Kadphises I. The latter was succeeded by Vima Kadphises and then the famous Kanishka in AD 78. Thus, the third quarter of the first century saw the rulers of three dynasties exercising power in the north-west of India: the Shakas, the Parthians, and the Kushanas.

In the last quarter of the first century the whole of the Punjab was part of an empire that extended from Balkh to Banaras under Kanishka. The Kushanas were a branch of the Yueh-chi who had started moving towards the west under political pressure and ousted the Shakas from Bactria. Like the Shakas, they imbibed much Greco-Roman culture before they made their conquests in India. In fact, the Kushanas looked upon themselves primarily as Bactrians. The location of their empire gave them access to both the east and the west. Four of Kanishka's second-century successors are known: Vasishka, Kanishka II, Huvishka, and Vasudeva. With a short obscure phase around AD 140, they exercised power in the Kushana empire till Vasudeva's death in AD 176. Thereafter, a number of Kushana kings continued to rule in the Punjab but their exact connection with Vasudeva is not known. Among them were Kanishka III and Vasudeva II who ruled till about 230.

The Kushana governors of the Punjab appear to have become independent. But they had to face the Sassanian successors of Ardashir, who had founded an empire by defeating the Parthians around AD 225. The Kushanas were obliged to accept Sassanid supremacy. In the third quarter of the fourth century, the Kushana chief Kidara became independent of the Sassanid emperor, probably with the support of Samudra Gupta. Kidara consolidated his power in Gandhara, Kashmir and the eastern Punjab. If Kidara accepted Gupta suzerainty, the Gupta empire can be said to have extended to Gandhara and Kashmir. But even the eastern Punjab was not directly administered by the Guptas during the fourth century.

During foreign invasions some of the peoples of the Punjab such as the Mallavas, the Shibis and the Arjunayas, migrated to other parts of the subcontinent. But there were others who bided their time: the Audambaras, Rajanyas, Trigartas and Kunindas along the hills from the Ravi to the Jamuna, and the Agreyas, Vrishnis and Yaudheyas in the lower portions of the Satlej-Jamuna Divide. Their struggle for political survival entitles them to resurrection from oblivion.

The Audambaras held power between the Ravi and the Beas, with occasional extensions beyond. Their coins resemble those of Demetrius, indicating that they had become independent of Shunga rule in the latter half of the second century BC. One of their four known kings was Mahadeva who took the title of 'king of kings'. It may be safe to infer that the polity of the Audambaras was monarchical. The other three kings of the first century BC were Shivadasa, Rudradasa and Dharaghosha. At the turn of the first century BC the Audambaras witnessed a dynastic change. One of the coins of this time bears the legend 'of the victorious king Rudravarman, the Vimaki'. Rudravarman appears to have been the founder of the Vimaki dynasty. He was succeeded by Aryamitra, Mahimitra and Bhanumitra. The coins attributed to the Audambara kings have been found in the areas of Pathankot, Jwalamukhi and Hoshiarpur. The neighbours of the Audambaras on the east were the Rajanyas whose coins have been found in Hoshiarpur district. The Brahmi legend *rajana-janapadas* on their coins indicates that their polity was oligarchical. The Trigartas continued to be associated with the Jalandhar Doab. Their coins of the second century BC bear the Brahmi legend *trakata-janapadas*, indicating that their polity too was oligarchical. Whether or not they still formed a confederation is not clear.

The eastern neighbours of the Trigaratas were the Kunindas, inhabiting the lower hill ranges between the Satlej and the Jamuna. They appear to have risen to power in the first century BC under Amoghabhuti, presumably after Menander and before Maues. The silver coins of the Kunindas compare well with the Indo-Greek silver coins. The legend in Brahmi reads *rajnah kunindas amoghabhutisa*. There is a legend in

Kharoshthi also. Symbols on these coins include the deer, tree-in-railing, crescented *chaitya*, *svastika,* and a female deity holding a flower in her right hand. The Kunindas issued copper coins too, generally bearing Brahmi legends and sometimes Kharoshthi legends. The Kunindas appear to have issued the largest number of silver coins among all the 'republican' states known in Indian history. Recovered from about thirty places, not only in the hills between the Satlej and the Jamuna, Mandi, Garhwal, Kumaon, Almora and Nainital, they have been found in the plains between the Jamuna and the Satlej and at Taxila. This information suggests the importance of trade for the Kunindas. A Kuninda coin of about AD 200 bears the name Chatreshvara, with the titles *mahtamana* and *bhagavata.* On the obverse appears the name of Karttikeya as the lord of war. This was probably the second phase of Kuninda power, established by force of arms against the successors of the Kushana Vasudeva.

The pattern which appears to emerge from this evidence suggests that indigenous peoples tried to reassert themselves whenever the power of the Greeks, the Shakas, or the Kushanas declined. This impression is reinforced when we turn to the Yaudheyas. A large number of coin moulds have been found near Rohtak, with the legend *yaudheyanam bahudhanyaka.* The latter term is generally taken to mean the Haryana region, including Rohtak. In the *Mahabharata*, the Yaudheyas are referred to as Rohitakas, that is belonging to Rohitaka or Rohtak. The coin moulds suggest that the Yaudheyas had extended their territory beyond Rohtak. The coins of the Yaudheyas suggest three distinct phases of their history. The late second and the early first century BC form the first phase of independence after the decline of the Mauryas and Shungas. A legend on the coins of this phase reads '*maharaja*'. If this represented a personal name, the polity could still be 'republican'. If not, the legend indicates a monarchical system. No coins are available for the first century after Christ, indicating that the Yaudheyas were suppressed by the Shakas. The coins of the second century AD are poor in quality. Possibly the Kushanas did not fully release the Yaudheyas from political yoke. The coins of the third and fourth century are fine in quality, and reveal Kushana influence. The legend clearly shows that after about AD 175 they were flushed with success: it reads 'victory of the Yaudheyas' (*yaudheyyaganasya jayah*). The Yaudheyas worshipped Karttikeya as the lord of war. The commander-in-chief of the republic was called *maharaja-mahasenapati.* During the fourth century, they extended their influence up to Sunet, near

Ludhiana, where a number of their coins and coin-moulds have been found. Their copper coins bear the legend '*yaudheya-ganasya jaya*', and a sealing bears the legend '*yaudheyanam jaya-mantradharanam*'. Both of these were meant to celebrate their victorious career.

At Sunet, the Yaudheyas had replaced another people, the Vrishnis, as rulers. The latter are mentioned by Panini, and Kautilya refers to their polity as 'republican'. According to the *Bhagavata* and *Vishnu Purana* as well as the *Mahabharata*, Arjuna had brought the Vrishnis to the Panchanada from Dvaraka. Their presence in Sunet during the second or first century AD is indicated by a seal with a Kharoshthi legend. Seals and sealings with Brahmi legends confirm the Vrishnis presence at Sunet in the second and third centuries AD. A silver coin with Brahmi and Kharoshthi legends, and a twelve-spoked wheel, was issued in the name of Krishna as the protector of the Vrishnis. This is evident from a comparison of the legend on this coin with the legend on later sealings found at Sunet. The legend reads '*vrishni-rajanya-ganasys tratuh*'. The Mahasenapati of the Vrishnis also issued coins with the Sudarshana Chakra of Krishna. The copper coins of the Vrishnis found at Sunet, Sanghol and other places in the same region bear Brahmi legends, and an eight-spoked or twelve-spoked wheel. They also indicate that the Vrishnis ruled in this area for a century or so after the death of Vasudeva II from the middle of the third century AD. The names of some of their rulers are known, but not the chronological order: Vyaghra Sattra, Vyaghra Sena, Jaya Sasya, Yajna Soma and Sattragupta. We may add that the people known as Agreya ruled at Agroha in the Hissar area in the second century BC. There could be other cases still unknown.

TRADE, URBANIZATION AND URBAN LIFE

Through all the political changes in the time of the Indo-Greeks, Shakas and Kushanas, mercantile life continued to grow. The occupation of north-western India by these non-Indian peoples led to trade with regions which had remained untapped earlier. The Indo-Greek kings encouraged contact with western Asia and the Mediterranean world. The Shakas, Parthians and Kushanas brought Central Asia into the orbit of trade, which in turn led to trade with China. Overland commerce with western Asia and the Hellenic world went through the cities of the north-west, notably Taxila. The most widely used highway westwards was from Taxila to Kabul, from where roads branched off in various directions. The northern route through Bactria reached the Black Sea, and a southerly route from Kandhar went to the eastern Mediterranean. Kandhar was also connected with Persepolis and Susa. Taxila became a collection point for goods from different parts of the world.

With the rise of trade, the number and size of towns began to increase in the Punjab. Craftsmen of different types began to emerge. Monetary exchange and luxury goods began to increase. The physical appearance of cities and towns began to reflect new levels of wealth. A new city known as Sirkap, was founded by the Bactrian Greeks to the north of the Bhir Mound in the second century BC. It was planned on chess-board pattern, and its wall was 5.5 kilometres long. A third Taxila was founded by the Kushana rulers to the north of Sirkap. Known as Sirsukh, it had a perimeter of about 5 kilometres. We know that Taxila enjoyed a life of at least one thousand years from the fifth century BC to the fifth century AD, touching the peak between the second century BC and the third century AD. The excavated portion of the main street of Sirkap measures over 600 metres from north to south. It was flanked by shops on both sides. The residences of the rich, on the average, cover nearly 1,360 square metres. The excavated portion of a palace-like building covers an area about 100 metres from north to south and about 80 metres from east to west.

Greek and Western Asian antiquities no less than the Indian give an impressive view of urban life in Sirkap. The tools, moulds and stamps (for stamping textiles and pottery), and the dies for fashioning coins and ornaments, testify to artisanal skills. Glass beads and tiles were manufactured. The presence of an affluent class is indicated by a magnificent collection of gold and silver jewellery. Large cooking pots of copper, and wheeled braziers for moving fire from room to room, have been found. Grinding mills found at Taxila were something new. The list of its antiquities is too long to be reproduced, but there is hardly any doubt that the city was a leading centre of crafts.

As evidence of its trade with distant lands, Roman amphorae have been found at Taxila. Its connection with the east is shown by the presence of red sandstone. Coins and coin moulds are indicative of trade and exchange. Nearly 96 per cent of over 7,500 coins recovered from Sirkap come from the Shaka-Parthian levels, and contain the old punch-marked, local Taxilan, Greek and early Shaka issues as well as the late Shaka, Parthian and Kushana issues. Their variety is astounding. The Shaka coins alone are of more than forty types. Sirsukh, the city of the Kushanas, has been only partially excavated. It does not compare well with Sirkap, but the coins recovered from Sirsukh are very large in number.

Over a score of Kushana sites have been identified in the Jammu region but not excavated. Ten sites of the period have been identified in the Philaur tahsil of the Jalandhar district. Jalandhar itself was an important town. Over a score of Kushana sites have been explored in the Ludhiana district and two of these have been excavated. There are several known settlements of this period elsewhere in the Punjab, at Ropar, Bhagwanpur, Bara, Ghuram, Agroha, Daulatpur, Raja Karan ka Qila and Sugh. Thus the entire region was dotted with urban centres during the early Christian centuries. Sunet, near Ludhiana, became an urban centre around 200 BC and remained a flourishing town till about AD 300. Several structural phases have been revealed by excavations. The town had an elaborate drainage system. Beads and bangles of terracotta, bone dice, ivory bangles, terracotta seals and sealings have been found. Far more impressive are the coins found at Sunet which appears to have served as a mint-town and a commercial centre. In fact nearly 30,000 coin moulds have been found, indicating wide prevalence of money economy. The large number of seals and sealings indicates the importance of administrative activities.

Coins of the Indo-Parthians and the Kushanas as well as those of the indigenous rulers have been found at Sanghol. The presence of a coin mould suggests that it was a mint-town. It has six structural phases till the time of the early Kushanas. A stupa has been discovered at Sanghol, built probably in the Kushana times. Besides monasitc cells, the stupa complex has yielded a copper chisel and more than ninety small barrel shaped gold beads. Like Sunet, Sanghol appears to have been a thriving town for much of this period.

A major literary work of this period may be taken to describe urban life more or less faithfully: the *Milindapanha*, written sometime during the first century AD. A certain degree of idealization cannot be ruled out, but the creative imagination of the writer could not have been divorced from the empirical realities of the times. Seventy-five occupations are mentioned in his ideal city of Shakala (Sialkot). Some of these had no direct hand in production, like the Brahmanas and the Shramanas, or even the traders. Then there were dancers, wrestlers and acrobats, and sixteen specialized categories of fighters in the infantry and the corps of elephants, horses and chariots. And then there were musicians, cooks, washermen, bath-assistants and bawds.

However, the number of craftsmen in the city was not small. There is mention of goldsmiths and other metal-workers; workers in shell, ivory and precious or ordinary stone; makers of arms; dyers and workers in textiles; potters and builders; workers in transport; and those who prepared various kinds of sweets and other edibles. There were craftsmen who worked in gold, silver, tin, copper, brass and lead. The weavers worked in silk and wool as well as cotton. Some of them specialized in making cloth for the army and for the deities and the priests.

There were many other categories of people in the city. There were laundrymen, cleaners and spinners as well as tailors. There were butchers, fishmongers and sellers of grass, wood, leaves, fruits, roots, boiled and cooked rice, and cakes. The needs of urban housing, food and dress were thus adequately met. There were merchants who dealt in scents. The term used for them is *ganddhi.* The cloth merchants of Shakala brought silk and cotton from distant places in India. As a model city, Shakala was full of gold, silver, bronze, precious stones and coins.

Jalandhar is described in the *Padma Purana* as a 'city studded with gems'. There is a reference also to its fortresses, tall mansions and gates. The houses of the city were ablaze with gold so much so that peacocks dreaded them as they dread fire. The faces of the girls of Jalandhar 'resembled the full moon at dusk'. The fragrant breeze of its gardens captivated the minds of women and 'inflamed them with love'. Existing as a town in the first century BC, Jalandhar appears to have become a prosperous city in the time of Kanishka. There is hardly any doubt that cities and towns of the period were centres of technology, production and exchange. The presence of Brahmanas in the urban centres and of Shramanas in the neighbourhood suggests that cities were also the centres of learning and religious institutions. There is enough evidence to suggest that cities and towns were the centres of art.

The major artistic expression of the period is known today as the Gandhara school of art. It relates primarily to sculpture. In the Gandhara region first, and then in Taxila and other places, this art flourished for nearly five centuries under the Shakas and Kushanas who transmitted the cultural traditions of their Hellenistic predecessors and played the role of protectors and interpreters of West-Asian Hellenism. The Gandhara art is Hellenistic and Indian at the same time. Sculptures represent, among other themes, stories and legends from the life of the

Buddha and the Bodhisattvas. The reliefs are faithful to Indian traditions, myths and legends but appear to lack spontaneity and emotional sympathy. The figures of the Buddhist 'pantheon' look like the figures of the Graeco-Roman pantheon, sometimes with a moustache, or a turban, with ornaments. Draperies are arranged in the style of the Roman *toga*. Indian sages appear to be the bearded sages of the classical tradition of Greece and Rome. This is true also of the mythical figures. Nevertheless, the independent and individual statues of the Buddha and the Bodhisattvas appear to have a character and aesthetic value of their own, both in features and treatment.

It is possible to identify three distinct phases of the Gandhara art. The figures and draperies of the Shaka phase strongly recall Hellenistic ideals. Under the Kushanas began a certain degree of schematization. The drapery is more symmetrical and tends to become a decorative display. The figures are short in stature, stumpy in appearance, and rough in treatment, exhibiting a kind of rude strength. Then from the third century AD, the Gandhara art begins to express an intense feeling, a telling realism, and an individuality of character. It is generally agreed that in its third phase, called 'Indo-Afghan' by Marshall, the Gandhara art 'attained a command of form and a vitality of expression' lacking in the earlier period. This was partly due to the fact that clay and stucco were now the materials used in place of stone. The plasticity of the new materials could be much better exploited by a good artist.

The eastern Punjab on the other hand reveals the popularity of school known after Mathura. The spotted red sandstone of Sikri was its identification mark. The Mathura Buddhas and Bodhisattvas are quite distinct from their Gandharan counterparts. However, examples of the refined type of the Gandharan Buddha can be seen in the Mathura region under the Kushanas. Certain reliefs and decorative motifs also reveal Gandharan influence. At the same time, a statue recently discovered at Karhali in the district of Patiala has a clear affinity with the Mathura school. Numerous beautiful pieces of sculpture in spotted red sandstone have been found at Sanghol. On the whole, probably, the eastern Punjab was culturally closer to Mathura.

Much of the Gandhara sculpture was a part of architecture insofar as it was represented on panels depicting the events of the Buddha's life, or the lives of the Bodhisattvas, that adorned stupas and monasteries. The stupa was a sacred structure because it contained a relic of the Buddha, or of one of his chief disciples. It was erected on a spot associated with an event in his life or an important event in the history of Buddhism. Monasteries developed later on spots where the wandering Buddhist monks used to rest during the rainy season. The principal element of the stupa was a dome. It was surmounted by an umbrella (*chhatra*) and surrounded by a passage for circumambulation (*pra-da-kshinapatha*) generally fenced by a railing or a wall. This plan is clearly demonstrated in the Great Stupa at Manikyala in the upper Sindh Sagar Doab. The structure known as Shahji ki Dheri at Peshawar was built by Kanishka as a relic-tower. It consisted of a basement in five stages with a wooden superstructure of thirteen storeys about 120 metres high. An iron column at the top with a number of umbrellas raised the total height of the tower to about 200 metres. It was decorated with every sort of precious substance and it was admired by all for its exquisite beauty and graceful proportions. A monastery was attached to this 'highest tower in Jambudwipa'.

The best known stupas are those of Taxila, where more archaeological work has been done than elsewhere. The height of the Dharmarajika stupa ruins is about 15 metres, and the overall diameter is about 45 metres. The surviving structure is likely to be of the Shaka-Parthian phase. A terrace and four flights of steps at its base were constructed later. The last element to be added was a band of ornamental stonework in probably the fourth or the fifth century AD. There were three successive floors of the *pradakshinapatha*. There was also a lion pillar in imitation of the well known lion pillars of Ashoka. Much later than the foundation of this Great Stupa, a number of small stupas were built in a ring. Such miniature votive stupas have been found in large numbers at different sites and provide a good idea of what the bigger monuments looked like.

Before the beginning of the Christian era, the stupa had become the nucleus of each monastery (*sangharama*) and the visible manifestation of the Buddhist faith in India. The earliest monasteries in the north-west appeared during the first century AD. They consisted of detached structures, each with a specific function. The quadrangular *vihra* as a single enclosed complex, meant to meet all the needs of the monks, developed as the faith gained popularity and became institutionalized. Close to the Dharmarajika there was a range of apartments for the monks. These buildings were the earliest to appear. Regular *vihras* developed later. The mound that covers the ruins of monasteries near the Dharmarajika has an area of about 150 metres from north to south and by about 120 metres from east to west. Not far from the Bhir

Mound is a site known as Kalawan, with a stupa and monastery. There were several other important stupas and *sangharamas* near Taxila, as at Giri, Ghai, Jandial, Mohra Moradu, Pippala, Jaulian, Lalachak and Bhamala.

Architecture and sculpture do not exhaust the art of the period. The Indo-Greek and Shaka coins are aesthetically of a high order. Their execution is chaste and elegant, their workmanship is refined, and their general design is in the best Hellenistic tradition, particularly those which bear Greek legends. The portraits on them express refined realism. At a later stage, square and rectangular shapes begin to appear and the Attic standard begin gradually to fade away. Legends become bilingual, Greek and Kharoshthi or Brahmi. The Indo-Parthian coins are crowded in design, and record the impress of Indian feeling and form. The early Kushana coins are still more Indian in feeling, though they retain the original features of dress and demeanour. In execution and design, the Kushana coins are much more elegant and refined than the Indo-Parthian coins. From the third century onwards Persian and Sasanian influences become visible.

A large number and variety of engraved gems have been collected from several sites in the Punjab. They are generally Hellenistic in design and execution, with motifs largely from Greek mythology. They reveal a developed sense of composition and relief. The source of their motifs is largely Greek mythology. Athena, seated or standing, Aphrodite, gods and goddesses of Greek legends, fighting warriors, spirited lions or elephants are the common motifs. The legends are in Greek, Kharoshthi and Brahmi. The Greek inspiration was replaced by the Roman in the first and second centuries AD. This art did not, however, take roots in Punjabi soil. In the jeweller's art, for instance, the indigenous craftsmen showed great skill. Gold and silver jewellery was popular among the rich and not so rich. Some new types of pottery appeared under the Kushanas. Terracotta objects were made to gratify the aesthetic sensibility of the humbler people.

The information on art and artefacts available for the Satlej-Jamuna Divide is small but not insignificant. Remains of stupas and monasteries have been found at Sanghol, Sugh, Fatehabad and Bhuna. A sealing from Sanghol depicts three stupas and bears a legend that was regarded as sacred: 'The Buddha has told the cause of all things that proceed from cause, and he has told how the cause comes to its end–such is the word of the sage alone.' Gandhara and Kushana Buddhas and Bodhisattvas have been found at Sirsa, Sugh, Jhajjar and in the

Rohtak district. A Bodhisattva figurine has been found at Sugh. The signet ring of an Indo-Greek king at Sunet indicates that Indo-Greek influence had crossed the Satlej. At Sanghol, a sealing has been found bearing the image of Pallas with a shield in her outstretched right hand and a thunderbolt in her left hand. This belongs to the time of Gondophernes. Secular art has not gone unrepresented in the eastern Punjab. A sculpture from Bhuna in the Karnal district represents a scene of love. A sealing from Sanghol represents a woman offering a cup of wine to a man. Another sealing depicts with realistic vigour an elephant trampling a lion. Seated on its hind legs, the lion is often depicted in glyptic, expressing strength and ferocity. The humped bull has been depicted, couchant or trotting. Some of the other animals portrayed realistically are the tiger, bear, stag, horse, scorpion, and the dancing peacock.

BUDDHISM, SHAIVISM AND VAISHNAVISM

The art of the period gives the impression that Buddhism emerged as the most popular faith during this period. The oldest and the most orthodox form of Buddhism, known as Theravada (Sthaviravada in Sanskrit), and its most important branch, Sarvastivada, that became popular in northern India, had spread to Gandhara and Kashmir by the time of Kanishka. This form of Buddhism came to be known as the Little Vehicle (Hinayana). A new form came to be recognized by the time of Kanishka and spread all over north India before the end of the second century AD. It was known as the Great Vehicle (Mahayana). Its hallmark was the doctrine of the *bodhisattva*. It was believed that the Buddha in his previous lives had worked selflessly for the good of all but bided his Buddhahood. The appearance of the Bodhisattva in Gandhara sculpture is clear evidence of the popularity of Mahayana. In fact, three important Bodhisattvas figure prominently in the Gandhara art: Maitreya, Avalokiteshvara and Manjushri. The practice of image worship and the idea of *bhakti* also became an integral part of Mahayana Buddhism.

The account of Fah Hian as much as the art of the period bears witness to the prevalence of Buddhism in the Punjab. The language, the clothes and the food of the ordinary people in the Gandhara region was just the same as in 'the Middle Country' (Madhyadesha). The law of the Buddha was universally honoured. The monks had their fixed abodes in *sangharamas*. In Udyana, 500 monasteries belonged to the Little Vehicle. In Bannu there were about 3,000 monks of the Little Vehicle. About the same number of monks in Rshi belonged to both the Little and the Great Vehicle. It was believed that the Buddha had personally visited Udyana. The Swat valley was associated with a Bodhisattva who had saved a dove from a hawk by giving his own flesh. In Gandhara a Bodhisattva was believed to have sacrificed his eyes, and people had erected a tower on that spot.

Fah Hian believed that the tower raised by Kanishka at Peshawar had been prophesied by the Buddha. His alms bowl was preserved in another monastery and every kind of religious honour was paid to it daily in the forenoon and the evening. The offerings of the poor were believed to be more gratifying to the Buddha. The relic of the skull-bone of the Buddha was in a Vihara near Jalalabad. The king had great reverence for this relic and the Vihara was covered with plates of gold and decorated with 'the seven precious substances'. The king used to offer flowers and incense and repeatedly bend his head to the ground in adoration. Only after this morning worship did he attend to public affairs. 'The chief men and nobles also attend to these acts of worship first, and then to their household duties.' This was their unfailing duty every day. The relic was returned to its shrine after the worship was over. Flowers and incense were sold at the gate of the Vihara every morning. All the neighbouring princes deputed commissioners to present religious offerings to the relic. The Buddha's tooth relic was in Nagrak and it was worshipped in the same way as his skull-bone. The Buddha's staff was in a Vihara not far from Nagrak. The Buddha's robe (*sanghati*), in a distant Vihara, was worshipped with devotion to bring rain in a drought. In a cave not far from Nagrak the Buddha had left his shadow. It could be seen by the devout from a distance of ten paces but vanished on going nearer. Close to this cave was a tower raised in honour of those who had attained Buddhahood for themselves (Pratyeka Buddhas). In Taxila the Buddha had sacrificed his head as a Bodhisattva and that was why the country was called Takshashila or 'the severed head'. At Manikyala, the Buddha was believed to have fed his body to a starving tiger. The stupas raised at these two places were among the four known as 'the Great Stupas' in the north-west. Fah Hian observed that 'kings, ministers, and people of all the surrounding countries vie with each other in making religious offerings at these places, in scattering flowers, and burning incense continually'. In Pi-cha, which may be taken as a reference to Bhera, the Law of the Buddha was 'prosperous and flourishing'. This was true of both the Little and the Great Vehicle. The people of this country were surprised but gratified to see devotees coming from China to seek the Law of the Buddha. Fah Hian does not appear to have passed through the north Punjab on his way to Mathura. He noticed a large number of temples with over 10,000 priests on his way to Mathura, but he gives no details.

Some general observations made by Fah Hian are quite significant. Since the Buddha's *nirvana*, the kings and nobles of 'all these countries' had been erecting Viharas for the monks and endowing them with lands, gardens, houses, and 'also men and oxen to cultivate them'. The records of these endowments were engraved on plates of copper and handed down from one king to another 'so that no one has dared to deprive them of possession, and they continue to this day to enjoy their proper revenues'. All the resident monks had chambers, beds, coverlets, food, drink and clothes provided for them 'without stint or reserve'. For their part, the monks continually engaged in work of benevolence, recitation of scriptures, and meditation. In all monasteries, towers were raised in honour of the Buddha's famous disciples: Sariputra, Mogalana and Ananda. Towers were raised also in honour of the three *Pitakas*, *the Abhidhamma*, *Vinaya* and the *Sutta*. Exhorted by the principal religious families in the neighbourhood after the first month of residence, the monks assembled in a great congregation and repeated the Law. Then 'they present religious offerings to the tower of Sariputra, every kind of incense and flowers, and through the night they burn lamps provided by those men for the purpose'. Women ascetics had 'requested Buddha to permit females to become disciples'. The novices (*samaneras*) were particular about worshipping Rahula, the son of the Buddha by his wife Yashodhara. The professors of the *Abhidhamma* paid religious offerings to that work, and the masters of the *Vinaya* did the same honour to theirs. The men of the Great Vehicle worshipped Prajna Paramitra who symbolized divine wisdom, Manjushri who underscored the idea that all creatures have the nature of the Buddha, and Avalokiteshvara who as the 'saviour of men' symbolized intense love for man.

There is hardly any doubt that some of the rulers of the Punjab patronized Buddhism. The names of Menander and Kanishka are well known but there were others too who patronized Buddhism, though not exclusively. The members of the ruling class followed the example of the rulers. In the inscriptions of the period there are references to donors. In all probability, rich merchants were among these donors.

The spread of Mahayana Buddhism made it possible for the laity to follow the path at least partially, and Fah Hian's evidence suggests that the people in the neighbourhood of monasteries were interested in the Buddhist religious worship.

Vestiges of Vedic religion remained in the Punjab. Fah Hian refers to Indra in a few legends. Indra figures in the sculptures of Gandhara, and so does Brahma, besides a number of other celestial beings of the *Rigveda*. New gods and goddesses were worshipped by the Indo-Greeks. The Indo-Parthians may have brought with them the practice of fire worship. There is some evidence of Sun worship.

Far more important was the emergence of Rudra-Shiva as a major deity. A sealing from Sunet shows a trident axe above the legend *maheshvara*. Another sealing has the legend *rudrasharma* below a trident. There are other sealings or seals which depict a trident axe or a trident and spear or else a trident and *linga;* there is also the trident goad with a vase and an axe, and a trident shown with a snake. A sealing from Sanghol shows a four-armed deity holding a trident in one and an antelope skin in another of its four hands. This is taken to be the earliest known anthropomorphic representation of Shiva in the Punjab.

The influence of Shaivism among the Audambaras, Yaudheyas and Kunindas during the four centuries following the end of Shunga rule has been emphasized by historians. A legend on some of the Audambara coins, read as *bhagavata mahadevasya rajarajnah*, was at one time interpreted as 'of Mahadeva, the worshipper of the *bhagavat* the king of kings'. It was therefore contended that Mahadeva was a royal devotee of *bhagavat* or Vishnu. This legend, now read as *bhagavato mahadevasya rajarajasya*, is interpreted as 'of the god Mahadev, the king of kings'. It is therefore suggested that Shiva was the family deity of the Audambaras. On the coins of Shivadasa, Rudradasa and Dharaghosha the word *mahadevasya* precedes the ruler's name, suggesting that these coins were issued in the name of the divine as well as the temporal head. Furthermore, a Shaiva temple is depicted on some Audambara coins. The figures of Karttikeya and Shiva with a bull appear on the coins of the Yaudheyas. The legend on these coins, and on the coins of the Kunindas during the second and third centuries AD, reinforces the impression that they had pronounced Shaiva leanings.

The development of Vaishnavism during this period was as important as the emergence of Shaivism. The origin and development of Vaishnavism from 200 BC to AD 500 has been studied by Suvira Jaiswal.

There is convincing evidence that Narayana, Vishnu, Sankarshana, Baladeva, Vasudeva, Krishna, Shri and Lakshmi were individual deities at one time and, with the exception of Vishnu, popular non-Vedic deities. At a later stage, Narayana came to be identified with Vishnu, Sankarshana with Baldeva, Vasudeva with Krishna, and Shri with Lakshmi, and they all came to constitute the Vaishnava pantheon. The evidence of the *Mahabharata*, *Bhagavadgita* and *Harivamsha* enables us to see the process through which this transformation was taking place in the early Christian centuries. Before we come upon the term Vaishnava for the devotees of Vishnu, we come upon Bhagavatas, Pancharatras, Ekantins and Sattvtas as the worshippers of Narayana-Vishnu-Vasudeva. The identification of Vasudeva Krishna with Narayana-Vishnu, which had begun in the second century BC, was complete by about the middle of the sixth century AD when Vasudeva-Krishna became 'Vishnu incarnate in all his potency'. Shri-Lakshmi, a pre-Aryan fertility deity, absorbed many ideas associated with Aryan and non-Aryan goddesses. She came to be conceived as Vishnu's *shakti* by the fourth century AD. During these developments, Vaishnavism came to be marked by the doctrine of *bhakti* which implied affection but not yet love, the doctrine of *ahimsa* which primarily meant vegetarianism and non-injury to living beings, and the doctrine of incarnation which did not imply the superiority of the principal deity embodied in the later concept of *avatara*. At an early stage, there were only four incarnations of Vishnu: the boar (*varaha*), the man-lion (*narasimha*), the dwarf (*bavana*), and Vasudeva. Parashurama and Rama were soon added, followed by others like the Fish, the Tortoise, the Kalki and Dattatreya so that the number of the incarnations of Vishnu came to be generally accepted by the eighth century as ten. Eventually, this number rose to twenty-four, or even twenty-nine, including the Buddha.

Among the Vaishnavas the worship of images in temples became prominent. This consisted of a more or less elaborate ritual, called *puja*. What was called the 'Vedic' form of worship was confined to the three upper *varnas*, but the 'tantric' worship was open to all. Women were recognized as devotees. Certain days became particularly sacred, like the *dvadasi* of Kartik. The discus and the conch came to have a special sanctity, and so too some special marks on the forehead. Stress was laid on *japa* or repeated recitation of sacred syllables, formulae or names of the deity. Music and dance formed an important part of temple worship, especially on festival days. However, idols could be worshipped by the family or even by an individual, indicating the existence of household shrines. The most important festival was the *Chaturmasya* (not yet the Janmashtami or the Ramanavami). It was believed that Vishnu went to sleep on the eleventh of the bright fortnight of Har to wake up four months later on the eleventh of Kartik. During these months, his work was done by Indra. The celebration of the Chaturmasya was marked by festivities on the first five days beginning on the eleventh of Har, and on the last five days ending with the eleventh of Kartik. Another popular practice among the Vaishnavas was to observe *vratas* or vows which required total or partial abstinence from food and certain acts of worship. The Vedic ritual of sacrifice was thus replaced by a totally different kind of ritualistic worship which was not confined to the priestly and ruling classes. The social base of Vaishnavism, potentially, became much wider than that of the Vedic religion.

In the context of the development of Vaishnavism during this period, the available evidence begins to make a lot of sense. In a text of a later period, the man-lion incarnation of Vishnu is placed in the Madra country, which suggests that Narasimha, known as Narsingh in the Punjab, was the god of a popular cult before his worship was absorbed into Vaishnavism. The Greek ambassador Heliodorus is described in the Besnagar inscription as a Bhagavata who dedicated a Garuda banner to Vasudeva. Since Heliodorus came from Taxila, Bhagavatism was evidently known in the Punjab. During the rule of Mahakshtrapa Shodasa, son of Mahakshtrapa Ranjuvula, a lady named Tosha (a foreign sounding name) had the images of the five Vrishni heroes (*panchviras*) installed in a temple. An inscription of the time of Shodasa records the construction of a gateway and a railing at a temple of Bhagavat Vasudeva. The Kushana rulers were by no means averse to Vaishnavism and one of them bore the name Vasudeva. A fifth-century rock inscription of Tusham in the Hissar district describes Vishnu as 'a mighty bee on the the waterlily that is the face of Jambavati' (one of the queens of Vasudeva-Krishna). Vishnu is identified with Vasudeva by the devotee of the Bhagavat in this inscription.

The evidence of seals and sealings from Sunet and Sanghol indicates the presence of Vaishnavism in the Satlej-Jamuna Divide. There are a number of sealings from Sunet which bear the legend *jitam bhagavata*. This may be a reference to Vasudeva. The mace, discus and conch on a sealing with the legend *jaya-svami* are suggestive of the same deity. A more detailed legend is *sri jitam bhagavata svami narayanena*. There are several glyptics which carry 'vishnu' as a part of the legend. The use of Vishnu and Hari in proper names, as much as the symbols associated with Vishnu, indicates the prevalence of Vaishnavism in the Divide. No anthropomorphic representation of Vishnu has yet been found. The names of Rama, Krishna and Balabhadra are found on some glyptics, but without any representations of Vishnu's incarnations.

On a gold coin of Huvishka a deity holds discus in one hand and an *urdhvalinga* in another, making him a precursor of the composite god Hari-Hara. It has been suggested that the Kushana practice of erecting shrines for their dead ancestors was derived from the example of Vrishni shrines for the five heroes. There are a few sealings suggestive possibly of Sun worship, the worship of Shakti in connection with both Shaivism and Vaishnavism, particularly the latter, and the worship of Hari-Hara. A Kharoshthi sealing from Sunet bears the legend *Jaya-pachalaya*, with the motif of a half-elephant and half-lion below a discus. This appears to refer to the five Vrishni heroes. Probably a shrine was dedicated to them at Sunet. Their worship was prevalent till the third century AD.

LANGUAGES AND LITERATURE

The period under study was marked by great literary activity. Secular literature began to be produced in several forms, and religious literature was no longer only Brahmanical. The Buddhists and Jains produced voluminous literature of their own. Prakrits were used for literary expression in addition to the 'classical' form of Sanskrit that was evolving. On the whole, thus, the period became remarkable for the volume, range and variety of its literary output.

It is not generally known that the term Sanskrit came into currency much later than the Rigvedic period. In the time of the Brahmanas, Middle Indo-Aryan was in some ways distinct from the language of the north-west (Udichya). The language called 'eastern' (Prachya) was distinct from both. Panini developed the north-western language in the direction of 'classical' Sanskrit, a movement which was reinforced by Katyayana and Patanjali. Their Sanskrit was simpler than the Rigvedic language, but it was used only by the priestly and ruling classes. Poetry and prose in this language got encouragement through royal patronage. The Brahmans used it even more enthusiastically for religious purposes. Paradoxically, with the development of Prakrits in different parts of the country, Sanskrit became its *lingua franca*.

Significantly, therefore, some of the Buddhist and Jain writers began to write in Sanskrit. A development of great social and cultural significance, the rise of classical Sanskrit cannot be seen as a 'revival'.

Equally significant was the emergence of Prakrits as the media of literary expression. In the Prakrits used by the characters of Ashvaghosha's play recovered from Turfan, experts see the prototypes of Magadhi, Ardha-Magadhi and Shauraseni Prakrits. The Buddhist canon was written in the eastern and the north-western Prakrits as well as in Pali. The Prakrits used by the characters of Shudraka's *Mrichchhakatika* are more important than Sanskrit, and reveal a larger variety than what we find in any other Sanskrit play: Shauraseni, Avanti, Prachya, Magadhi, Shakari, Chandali and Takki. The Prakrit known as Takki was more clearly distinct from both Magadhi and Shauraseni than the others. It is not clear if Takki was the term used for the north-western Prakrit. In a popular theory, Paishachi is identified with the Prakrit of the north-west, with the implication that it was the farthest removed from classical Sanskrit. Inscriptions from Gandhara and Kabul, and their environs are found in the north-western Prakrit. An inscription of the time of Kanishka gives a quotation from a treatise in this Prakrit. Furthermore, this quotation refers to canonical works in Prakrit.

That secular literature too was composed in Prakrits is evident from Hala's collection of poetical stanzas known as the *Gathasaptashati* which represents the work of a number of poets. A precious treasure of romantic tales in prose in the Paishachi language was Gunadhya's *Brihatkatha* which was given its Sanskrit garb by Ksemendra and Somadeva in the second millennium. That the Prakrits overshadowed Sanskrit during the period is demonstrated most effectively by the number of inscriptions which have come to light: 1,500 in Prakrits and only about a dozen in Sanskrit. However, not many inscriptions in Prakrits are to be found after AD 400. Prakrits remained current outside India even after the fourth century.

Though the number of languages used in this period was more than half a dozen, the scripts used in inscriptions and coins were only three: Kharoshthi, Greek, and Brahmi, all of them used in the Ashokan inscriptions. Kharoshthi and Greek were used not only by the Indo-Greeks but also by the Shakas and the Kushanas in their coins and inscriptions. Kharoshthi was used for literary works in the north-western Prakrit. Though the use of Brahmi as well as Kharoshthi and Greek was known all over the Punjab, Brahmi was more frequently used in the eastern parts, and Kharoshthi and Greek in the western parts. The use of Kharoshthi was not confined to the Punjab or the north-west. It was carried to Central Asia. In the Punjab, however, it went out of use after the fourth century and its place was taken by Brahmi. In fact, with the increasing use of Sanskrit, Brahmi became the most popular script in the Punjab.

The Buddhist literature was written largely in Prakrits during this period. The Jain canon is of little relevance for our purpose, first because the earliest available literature is not older than the fifth century, and second because Jainism remained far less important than Buddhism in the Punjab. Much of the Buddhist literature was composed in the second half of the first millennium BC, and much of it was known in the Punjab. To the Buddhist canonical literature were added non-canonical works in the early centuries of the Christian era. There is a possibility that the *Milindapanha* was originally composed in the north-western Prakrit and, therefore, in the Punjab or in one of its neighbouring areas.

The entire Buddhist canon has survived only in Pali. Of works in other Prakrits, only fragments have come to light. In terms of form and content, the Pali canon consists of nine *angas*: sermons in prose and verse, explanations, stanzas, epigrams, short sayings of the Buddha, stories of previous incarnations, miracles, and teachings in the form of questions-and-answers. They have been collected in 'three baskets' (*Tipitaka*, *Tripitaka* in Sanskrit): the *Vinaya*, the *Sutta* and the *Abhidhamma*. The first deals with the rules of the monastic orders; the second, with the ethical principles of Buddhism; and the third relates to the metaphysical principles of the Buddhist doctrines. A fair idea of the volume of this literature may be formed from the fact that the *Vinaya Pitaka* consists of four texts; the *Sutta Pitaka* consists of five *Nikayas*, the last of which consists of fifteen texts (including the *Jatakas*); and the *Abhidhamma Pitaka* consists of seven books. Much of this literature is mentioned by Fah Hian in connection with the monasteries in the Punjab, some of which could boast of eminent scholars.

The chief vehicle of Buddhist propaganda was provided by the *Jatakas*, a collection of over 500 stories. More than half of these are actually of non-Buddhist origin, but all provide insights into popular Buddhism. They also provide information on social groups and classes that do not figure in other literature. The *Milindapanha* consists of seven 'books', but only the first three seem to represent the original, the others being added after the fourth or the fifth century. This work, it is said, compares well with the dialogues of Plato. A systematic treatment of all the teachings of the Buddha is found in the *Nettipakarana* which is ascribed to Mahakachchana, a disciple of the Buddha himself. A commentary on it was written by Dhammapala in the fifth century.

Sanskrit literature took many forms. Religious orientation was given to the *Ramayana* and the *Mahabharata*. The law-books or the Dharmashastras, more popularly known as Smriti, were not entirely secular. The most important of them were associated with Manu, Yajnavalkya, Narada and Brihaspati. The well known dramatists of the period were Ashvaghosha, Bhasa, Shudraka and Kalidasa. In poetry, the name of Arya Sura can be added to those of Ashvaghosha and Kalidasa. There were prose tales for the edification of all and sundry, in collections like the *Avadanashataka* and the *Divyavadana*. Then there were works on grammar, dramaturgy, metrics, polity (*artha*), the art of love (*kama*), philosophy, medicine and astronomy. What is relevant for us to know is whether or not literature in any of these forms was produced in the Punjab, and whether or not any of it was known in the Punjab.

There cannot by any doubt that the Punjab had important links with this literary efflorescence. What is important to know is the nature and strength of the links. It has been observed that the Brahmans appropriated the Vedic texts and in their place the people accepted the Epics and the Dharmashastras, and later on the Puranas as their religious literature. Apart from religious ideas, this literature carried some social and political implications. Therefore, we may first turn to these two forms.

The *Ramayana* was given its present form in the early centuries of the Christian era. It consists of seven books of about 24,000 *shlokas*. The story of Rama as a tribal hero, now found in Books II-VI of the *Ramayana* with some interpolations, had become current before 500 BC and it was sung by professional minstrels (*sutas*). Indra was still the most important deity. After the fourth century BC and before AD 200, the first and the last book were added. Book I contains some myths and legends, and Book VII clearly identifies Rama with Vishnu. Thus, the *Ramayana* is a source not so much on the period of the original events, which took place before 700 BC, as on the period under study. The epic foretells its everlasting fame in the following words: 'As long as mountain-ranges stand, and rivers flow upon earth, so long will this Ramayana survive upon the lips of men.' It is now agreed that this epic is the most popular work of Sanskrit literature. One of its three most important recessions was prepared in the north-west. It may be safe to assume that the *Ramayana* was known to the people of the Punjab not only in the period under study but also in the centuries to come, serving among other things as the vehicle of Vaishnava ideas: Rama as the human incarnation of Vishnu, Sita as the counterpart of Shri Lakshmi, *ahimsa* in the form of vegetarianism, worship of the deity with flowers and *pranayama* (rather than sacrifice), and sanctity of the *varna* system. Ayodhya became sacred as the putative birth-place of Rama, and Sita became the ideal woman in her total devotion to him.

The events of the *Mahabharata* were earlier than those of the *Ramayana*, but the latter had been composed when the former was being elaborated. At present the *Mahabharata* contains more than 80,000 *shlokas* which make it the longest poem in the world. However, before this redaction took place by AD 200, the *Mahabharata* consisted of about 24,000 *shlokas* when it was actually known as the *Bharata*. It is suggested by some scholars that there was a still smaller version earlier, consisting of less than 10,000 *shlokas*. The extant *Mahabharata* consists of eighteen *parvas* of varying length, ranging from about 400 to 14,000 *shlokas*. The *Bhagavadgita* is a part of the epic, and the *Harivamsha* can be seen as a supplement. The kernel of the story is the eighteen-day war between the Kurus and the Pandus. In its final form, however, the epic came to incorporate several features. According to Kosambi, the *Mahabharata* began as a 'Kuru lament' and changed into a 'Pandu song of victory' before it absorbed the Naga myths and acquired fresh episodes from the Krishna saga to be 'brahmanized' by the Kashyapas and the Bhrgus.

Quite apart from the *Bhagavadgita* and the *Harivamsha*, the epic contains a number of myths, legends, fables, parables, and didactic discourses. The vast scope of its subject matter has been underlined by the saying that whatever is found here may be found elsewhere but what is not found here cannot be found anywhere else. Indeed, the epic dwells on *dharma*, *artha*, and *moksha*. Apart from the fact that a number of the 'peoples' of the Punjab are presented as participating in a war fought in the Punjab, there was a northern recension of the epic in a script that was associated with Kashmir. There can hardly be any doubt that the epic was known in the Punjab during the period under study, and in later centuries. Even more than the *Ramayana*, it underscored the validity of Vaishnava ideas and practices: Krishna as the human incarnation of Vishnu, the efficacy of *bhakti*, the emphasis on *ahimsa*, the sanctity of the *varna* system, the exaltation of the Brahman, and the authority of the husband, the father and the king.

The popularity of the *Mahabharata* ensured ready reception for the *Bhagavadgita* which itself has a great aesthetic appeal because of 'its power of expression and peculiar beauty'. Though clearly a Vaishnava text, it contains no polemic. It recognizes the validity of knowledge (*jnana*), action (*karma*) and devotion (*bhakti*) for liberation (*moksha*). It served as the middle path between renunciation and ritual. The Vedic sacrifice is discarded in the *Gita*, and the great virtue of non-killing (*ahimsa*) is repeatedly emphasized. Yet the *yajna* is seen as the generator of rain, the source of food and life. The function of *karma* in the *Gita* is 'characteristically Buddhist'. The idea of *bhakti* can be traced to an Upanishad but there is a new emphasis on this idea in the *Gita*. God, equated with Vishnu-Narayana, equated with Krishna, is the creator and the destroyer of all beings. He pervades everything. The ultimate goal of union with him is assured through an absolute faith in him.

The Vaishnava character of the *Mahabharata* was reinforced by the *Harivamsha* more even than by the *Gita*. Over 16,000 of its *shlokas* describe the history of Krishna's ancestors, his exploits as Vishnu's incarnation, and the future corruptions of the Kaliyuga. There are references to 'Puranas' in the *Harivamsha* as well as the *Mahabharata*. However, the extant Puranas have been compiled after the *Harivamsha*. The *Vishnu Purana*, the oldest of the *Vaishnava Puranas*, covers five basic themes: the 'primary creation' of the universe, 'secondary creations', genealogies of gods and patriarchs, 'reigns of various Manus', and the history of the old dynasties of kings. We may add that the Puranas continued to be composed between AD 400 and 1000. They would not remain confined to Vaishnavism. The Shaivas and Shaktas composed their own Puranas in due course to compete with the Vaishnavas.

Interest in grammar was a continuation of the developments of the earlier period. Katyayana's work was meant to explain and support, as also to amend and supplement the *sutras* of Panini. Patanjali was more extensive in explaining and correcting Panini, dealing with more than 1,700 rules in his *Mahabhashya* (Great Commentary). In the process, he gave a commentary on Katyayana's work too and provided some supplementary rules. Patanjali is associated with the north-west and his work is generally placed in the second century BC. It proved to be the last great work on Sanskrit grammar produced in the north-west during the first millennium BC.

The *Mahabhashya* refers to two dramatic representations: the 'Slaying of Kansa' (*Kansavadha*) and the 'Binding of Bali' (*Balibandha*). There were no special theatres but plays could be performed in the concert-room (*sangitashala*) of a royal palace, or the quadrangle of a temple, on the occasion of a royal marriage, a victory, or a religious festival. The oldest extant drama in Sanskrit, Ashvaghosha's *Sariputra-prakarana*, relates to the conversion of Sariputra to Buddhism. This drama for the most part follows rules which were to be embodied later in the *Natyashastra* ascribed to Bharata, written mostly in *shlokas* in the fourth century. Ashvaghosha's plays could well have been performed at religious assemblies before large audiences. His association with Kanishka and the discovery of his manuscript from Turfan in Central Asia do suggest that he was known in the north-west.

Another great name associated with Kanishka is that of Charaka who is mentioned in some Chinese sources as the official physician of the emperor. His work, the *Charaka-Samhita*, which contains later additions, came to be treated as the standard work on Ayurvedic medicine. Healing had moved, it shows, a long way from the *Atharvaveda* with its demons of disease and magical spells for cure. There is an exhaustive discussion of therapeutic medicine in the *Charaka-Samhita* which deals with eight branches of medicine relating to therapy, special diseases of the supra clavicular parts of the body, surgery, toxicology, pediatrics, virility, rejuvenation, and demonology. A large number of medicinal substances of mineral, plant and animal origin are mentioned. It was not an accident that Taxila became famous for medical studies.

Developments in the medical sciences were perhaps not unrelated to the presence of the Indo-Greeks in the north-west. Contact with other parts of the world did enrich Indian medicine during the period. Another branch of science to benefit from this contact was astronomy. Varahamihira, who is generally placed in the fifth century, reveals thorough familiarity with Greek astronomy in his *Pancha-siddhantika*. He did not belong to the north-west, but it is not unreasonable to assume that students of astronomy in the north-west were familiar with Greek astronomy. One of the subjects of study, in the *Milindapanha* is astronomy, and astronomy was not possible without mathematics.

In philosophy, a number of systems or schools were developing during this period. Philosophic ideas expressed in the Upanishads were now being systematized in the form of Sutras. Commentaries (*bhashyas*) on these Sutras were written later so that the development of the different schools of philosophy can be seen as spread over a number of centuries even after 400 AD. The *Yoga Sutras* attributed to Patanjali, the *Brahma Sutras* attributed to Baudhayana, and the *Sankhya-karika* attributed to Ishvara Krishna, appear to have been composed between the third century BC and the fifth century AD. All these three schools–Yoga, Vedanta and Sankhya–find reflection in the *Mahabharata* in which the first and the third are bracketed. In their early development, these schools were atheistic, like two other of the six best known schools of Indian philosophy, the Nyaya and Visheshka. In due course, two theistic schools were developed to meet the challenge: the Mimansa and the Vedanta. Two ideas common to all schools were the doctrine of transmigration (*samsar*) and the ideal of liberation (*moksha*). Only the Charvakas discarded these ideas to propound a thoroughly empirical and materialistic philosophy.

Whereas the philosophic Sutras informed the ideas of a few, the Dharmashastras or Smritis affected the lives of the many. Some of the Dharmasutras composed between 500 and 200 BC were given the form of Dharmashastras as expanded metrical versions, embracing not only religious rites and ceremonies but also social and legal matters. The *Vishnu Smriti*, for example, was closely connected with the *Kathaka Grhya Sutra*. Similarly, the *Yajnavalkya Dharmashastra*, consisting of a little more than 1,000 *shlokas*, was connected with the *Manava Grhya Sutra* of the *Black Yajurveda*. The oldest, the best known, the most comprehensive and the most popular *Manava Dharmashastra* or *Manu Smriti*, was based probably on the *Manava Dharma Sutra*. Given its present form between 200 BC and AD 200, and presented as of divine origin, the *Manu Smriti* relates to duties concerning the four *varnas* and the four stages (*ashramas*) of life, the duties of kings, and of husband and wife, with matters of civil and criminal law, with penances and philosophical doctrines. Of its 2,684 *shlokas*, 260 are common with the *Mahabharata*, revealing its close connection with the epic. The *Narada Smriti* of over 12,000 *shlokas* was founded chiefly on the *Manu Smriti*. The influence of the *Mahabharata* and the *Harivamsha* can be seen on the *Vishnu Smriti* too. Thus, the concerns of the redactors of the epics and the Dharmashastras were rather similar if not actually the same. Unlike the epics, however, the Dharmashastras took longer to be influential. Whereas the influence of the epics was informal, the Dharmashastras could be used for the administration of justice by the state, as for socio-political control in general.

THE SOCIAL ORDER

The Dharamshastras assign the highest status and dignity to the Brahman. His duty is to study, teach, worship, officiate at worship, make gifts and accept gifts. Next to him was the Kshatriya whose duty was to take to the profession of arms in addition to study, worship and making gifts. The duty of the Vaishya was to cultivate land, rear cattle and conduct trade in addition to study, worship and making gifts. The duty of the Shudra was to pursue arts and crafts to produce wealth and to serve 'the twice-born' that is the other three. Study, worship and making gifts was not the Shudra's privilege. In the *Manu Smriti*, the position of the Shudra is little better than that of the slave. A Brahman was to perform the same kind of penance for killing a Shudra as for killing a cat, a frog, a dog, or a crow. The four castes constituted society, according to the *Manu Smriti*. But numerous other categories are referred to in this work itself. The children of a woman two or three degrees lower than her husband formed a separate 'caste'. The intermarriage between this and the three upper castes, and further intermarriage between such 'mixed castes', led to the formation of more separate 'castes'. The offsprings of a man of lower caste and a woman of higher caste formed yet another separate 'caste', and so did they who failed to fulfil their sacred duties. In this way, the 'castes' multiplied. This was one way of admitting that the society was constituted not by four but a much larger number of 'castes'. Alternatively, there was a certain degree of confusion between *varna* and *jati*.

In the Buddhist texts the Kshatriyas head the list, followed by the Brahmans, the Vaishyas and the Shudras. Furthermore, one does not become a Brahman through inheritance but through conduct. The 'castes' other than these four do not result from any infringement of the Brahmanical norms of matrimony, but from the proliferation of occupations and the induction of new peoples into the social order. Even the Brahmans in Buddhist literature follow professions far beyond the orbit of their prescribed duties. They work as landlords and cultivators, tend cattle and pursue trade, and they act as physicians and architects, besides resorting to several other occupations. Furthermore, there were people belonging to *hina-jatis* which were regarded as lower than the four castes. Among them were fowlers, leather workers, weavers, potters, barbers, mat-makers and cart-makers. The use of the general term *mlechha* for such people implied that they were outside the pale of the 'Aryan' society. Contemporary literature reveals the existence of slaves too. It is obvious, therefore, that the social order did not conform to the *varna* order postulated by the Dharmashastras which, if rigidly enforced, would have made the society static.

Indeed, the period under consideration was marked by significant social change. Strictly speaking, the Kshatriyas of old were no longer dominant in the Punjab. Even if we look upon groups like the Yaudheyas and Kunindas as remnants of the old Kshatriyas, they were far less important than the Greeks, Shakas and Kushanas. Whereas the old Kshatriyas had to adjust to the changed circumstances, the new rulers had to find a legitimate place in the social order. Heliodorus proclaimed himself to be a Bhagavata. Even if this is looked upon as a political gesture, it indicates that a foreigner tried to become acceptable in Indian society by adopting an Indian faith. It also shows that foreigners could be admitted to Bhagavatism. Indeed, it has been suggested that Bhagavatism was largely responsible for 'the assimilation of foreigners in the society' of that time. Menander would not have been extolled so much by the Buddhists if he had not accepted their faith or championed their cause. The association of Kanishka with Buddhism and his patronage of the Buddhists is regarded as even more certain. A few other Kushana rulers also are said to have patronized Buddhism. Among the Buddhists there was no problem about admitting foreigners, because ritual ranking was not so important for them as for the Brahmans, and Buddhism did not oblige its new adherents to discard their earlier cults. It was open to *mlechhas*. It is suggested in fact that Shaivism too was much less rigid than the Vedic religion in admitting foreigners. If two of the Kushana rulers bore the name Vasudeva, some of the Shaka satraps had Shiva as a part of their names, suggesting that the Shakas were attracted to Shaivism. The coins of Vima Kadphises bear icons only of Shiva. Significantly, in the *Mahabharata*, when Indra is asked how the Yavanas, Shakas, Chinas, Kambojas, Pullindas and others could be brought into the social pale, he answers that they could be admitted if they were prepared to follow the *dharma* of the Shastras. The desire to gain social and political legitimacy induced the foreign rulers to accept Indian faiths. It is in this context that we can appreciate the Kushana patronage not only of Buddhism but also of the Sanskrit language and of Vaishnavism and Shaivism. Their example was probably followed by the members of their ruling class. Patronage of religion was a means to legitimacy.

The mercantile communities were associated with Buddhism even more closely than the ruling class or the rulers. The guilds of artisans and traders made endowments to Buddhist Sanghas. Commercial patronage and royal support enabled the latter to raise impressive monuments. Monastic establishments thrived near urban centres and in rich agricultural tracts where there was plenty to support a community of monks. The Buddhist monastery was both a retreat for meditation and an institution of action. Begging for alms and preaching the doctrine brought the monks into contact with the lay community. A distinction was made between the general run of lay followers and the *upasakas* who were specially devoted to the Sangha. The majority of these *upasakas* were affluent householders (*gahapatis*). In any case, the Sangha created a sense of community among the lay followers. Such a sense of community was the antithesis of the values of *varnashramadharma.* Whereas *varna* segregated and cordoned off groups of people, Buddhist social thought and practice cut across caste segments and appealed to a universal ethic. In contrast to the Dharmashastras which rated the artisans rather low, the Buddhist Sanghas accepted donations from them, making them socially respectable. Significantly, women gave donations for the building and adornment of stupas, not only queens and princesses but also women belonging to the families of landowners, traders and artisans. Giving donations was an act of piety but it also involved recognition of the authority of the Sangha, which in its turn meant social or political recognition for the donor. It may be added that the Buddhist monasteries served as centres of learning and education.

Wealth came to be concentrated in the hands of traders and rich landholders as well as members of the ruling class (members of the ruling family, their relatives, courtiers and counsellors, army generals and administrators at the central and provincial level). Through this change, the rich Vaishyas could become more powerful than the ordinary Kshatriyas and Brahmans. Some Shudras were more powerful than some of the erstwhile Kshatriyas. In contemporary literature there are references to two classes, *ayya* and *dasa*, or Ajja and Milakkhu, or masters and servants, indicating a conception of society as divided into the privileged and the unprivileged. The rule of foreign princes, the spread of Buddhism, and the affluence of the merchants, the artisans and the large landholders did not allow the *varna* system to take deep roots in the Punjab.

In response to the institutionalization of renunciation in Buddhism and the increasing popularity of asceticism, the compilers of the Dharmashastras incorporated the ideals of renunciation and asceticism in their conception of the four stages or *ashramas* in life. The first stage, that of the Brahmachari, was the stage of study under a chosen teacher. The second *ashrama*, that of the *grihastha*, started with marriage and involved the duties of worship (*yajna*) and making gifts (*dan*), besides setting up a home and rearing a family. In the third stage of life one was to pursue a life of restraint and denial. The fourth stage was to be marked by rigid austerities and abstention. The last two *ashramas* were based on the ideals of renunciation and asceticism. The concept of four *ashramas*, thus, sanctified the ideal but placed restrictions on its actual operation. One had to be a student and a householder first and only then a renouncer or ascetic. Women and Shudras, needless to say, were excluded from this scheme. Nevertheless, renunciation and asceticism came to be generally regarded as of great importance in Indian religious life. The renouncer became the symbol of authority, and asceticism continued to find expression in several different ways in the centuries to follow.

It is generally agreed that the position of women in the social order was worsening during this period. This is reflected in the Dharmashastras and the epics which were gaining popularity. Gender relations in the *Mahabharata* have been studied in some depth. There is clear evidence of patriarchy in the epic. The principle of integration carried the implication that 'senior men' should exercise control over 'junior men' and 'over all women'. The husband's conjugal right could be transferred to another man for the purpose of procreation through *niyog*. The only daughter's inheritance was not her own: she merely acted as the trustee of her son's inheritance. The devoted wife became the ideal: 'one who keeps smiling even when rebuked by her husband, she is true *pativrata*'; 'for women there is no god like the husband'; 'one who gets up early in the morning, cleans house, prepares food for guests and family members and after feeding them eats the leftovers, she is true sati'. The *pativrata* was to eat, drink and wear clothes according to her husband's liking. The issue of chastity was linked with the conception of the *pativrata*: the pious woman did not even glance at the sun, the moon or the trees because their names were masculine. The method of determining chastity was ordeal by fire. Celibacy among men was a measure of self-control; chastity among women was a measure essentially of social control.

A daughter had to be given in marriage. The birth of a male child was seen as a blessing; that of a female child, a source of misery. Discrimination was visible also in their bringing up. A daughter's education was confined to domestic management. A widow could not remarry and had to lead an austere life. Preferably, she should become a *sati*. A woman was revered as a mother. But to earn that reverence she had to be a *pativrata* first. Woman quo woman was sinful by nature: 'There is no creature more sinful than woman. She is a burning fire. She is the illusion that Daitya Maya created.' Unlike the male, the female slave had to perform sexual service in addition to everything else. The entire mechanism of marriage, descent, residence and inheritance minimized woman's access to resources; the cultural construction of femininity tended to place her sexuality under male control; the dichotomy between the domestic and the public confined her to the home with its inbuilt subordination. In the Buddhist Sangha, she had the option to become a nun. In the society in general, she had the option to become a dancer or a prostitute.

READING

Alan 1988; Chattopadhyaya 1968; Dani 1968; Giles 1923; Jaiswal 1967; Keith 1928; Macdonell 1990; Marshal 1975; Mukherjee 1988; Narain 1957; Parsad 1984; Rhys Davids 1890-94; Shah 1995; Sircar 1973; Thapar 1966.

5

The Proliferation of States, Agrarian Expansion and Socio-cultural Change (*c.* AD 400–1000)

The most remarkable feature of the politics of the Punjab in the fifth and sixth centuries was a contest between the Hunas and the Guptas for supremacy over the Punjab. The period as a whole was marked by the emergence of small kingdoms. The old urban centres began to decline, but agriculture began to expand. Culturally, the Punjab came to have much closer contact with the rest of northern India than with countries outside the Indian subcontinent. Buddhism gradually yielded place to Shaivism, Vaishnavism and Shaktaism. Sanskrit became more and more a monopoly of the Brahmans, and the spoken language of the people began to be used as the medium of literary expression. The works of Hiuen Tsang and Alberuni, coupled with epigraphic and archaeological evidence, provide useful insights into several aspects of the Punjab.

POLITICAL DEVELOPMENTS

In the fourth century, the Guptas of Magadha were at the height of their power, exercising suzerainty over much of the eastern Punjab. The Kidara Kushanas were ruling from Kabul over Gandhara and probably the western parts of the Punjab. In the fifth century, the Kushanas were replaced by the Hunas whose aggression against the Guptas proved to be one of the causes of their decline. The Gupta empire disintegrated by about the middle of the sixth century. It is now generally agreed that the Hunas who invaded India were different from those who invaded Europe. This distinction is indicated by the use of the term 'Epthalites' or 'the White Huns' for the Indian Hunas, a branch of the Yueh-chis. Throwing off the yoke of the Juan tribe, they had established their power in Bactria (Balkh) first and then crossed the Hindu Kush in the middle of the fifth century. Dislodging the Kidara Kushanas, they occupied Kabul and Gandhara, and perhaps the western parts of the Punjab. In the reign of Skanda Gupta (455-67) they invaded his empire but were repulsed. The supreme lord of the Epthalites in Balkh appointed his own governors or chiefs (*tegins*) in his trans-Indus territories. Tormana, a *tegin*, became independent in the early sixth century. Marching across the Punjab he occupied parts of the Gupta dominions in Uttar Pradesh and Madhya Pradesh.

Tormana was succeeded by his son Mihirakula in the second decade of the sixth century. He conquered Kashmir and invaded the Gupta empire. Narasimha Gupta Baladitya opposed him with success. Mihirakula appears to have made yet another attempt to expand his dominions in the Ganges plain, but he was defeated by Yashodharman of Malwa who had become independent of the Guptas. Mihirakula died around 530, his rule having become confined to Gandhara, Kashmir, and parts of the Punjab. His successors did not play any important role in the politics of north India but continued to rule over local kingdoms.

At Magadha the Guptas were replaced by the Later Guptas (who had actually no connection with the imperial line). Kanauj became the seat of the Maukharis who acquired power at about the same time as the Later Guptas during the Huna invasions. Their subordination to the imperial Guptas ended with the rise of the Later Guptas at Magadha. The Maukhari Ishanvarman defeated the Hunas in the third quarter of the sixth century, but his direct control did not extend even to the east Punjab where Adityavardhana was ruling from Thanesar as its third ruler. His grandfather, Maharaja Naravardhana, appears to have founded the dynasty during the time of Mihirakula. Although Pushpabhuti is mentioned by Bana as the ancestor of the Vardhanas, he remains a rather remote and a shadowy figure. Adityavarman married the sister of the Later Gupta Mahasenagupta. His son and successor, Prabhakaravardhana, adopted the title of *maharajadhiraj* to mark his independent status. He was an ambitious ruler and attacked his neighbours on all sides, except the Maukharis of Kanauj. In fact he gave his daughter, Rajyashri, in marriage to Grahavarman, a great grandson of Ishanvarman of Kanauj. Bana refers to Prabhakaravardhana as 'a lion to the Huna deer'. Probably the Hunas had encroached into his territory and had been defeated. The king of Thanesar does not appear to have extended his dominions in the Punjab before he died in the first decade of the seventh century.

Immediately after Prabhakaravardhana's death, Grahavarman of Kanauj was defeated and killed by a confederacy headed by Devagupta of eastern Malwa. Rajyashri was imprisoned. Rajyavardhana, the elder son and successor of Prabhakaravardhana, marched towards Kanauj, defeated Devagupta, and killed him. Shashanka of Bengal, an ally of Devagupta, invited Rajyavardhana to his camp and got him treacherously murdered. The Maukhari courtiers invited Harshavardhana, the younger son of Prabhakaravardhana, to rule over Kanauj. Shashanka made a strategic retreat to Bengal, leaving Harsha king of Kanauj and Thanesar. Harsha is rightly credited with the conquest of Bihar and parts of Orissa and Madhya Pradesh, but made no new conquests in the Punjab.

When Hiuen Tsang visited India in the second quarter of the seventh century, he noticed that the people of the subcontinent referred to it by different names. It consisted of five broad divisions, 'the five Indies'. The entire land was divided into 'seventy countries or so'. It is significant that Hiuen Tsang uses the word 'country' as a synonym for 'state', whether independent or dependent, or even a former kingdom. He noticed a score of kingdoms in the Punjab and its neighbourhood. The supremacy of the ruler of Kabul extended to Lamghan, Jalalabad and Gandhara. In the upper Sindh Sagar Doab, Taxila, which had formerly acknowledged the supremacy of Kabul, was now subject to Kashmir. In the Salt Range there was another kingdom with its capital at Simhapura. This too was subject to Kashmir. In the Chaj and Rachna Doabs was the kingdom of Takka, with its capital near Sakala (which had served as the capital of Mihirakula in the sixth century); this kingdom was not confined to these two Doabs, but touched the river Beas on the east and the river Indus on the west. However, it did not include the whole of the Bari Doab. In the middle of the Bari Doab was the kingdom of Patti, and in the lower Bari Doab was the kingdom of Multan. Between the Beas and the Satlej was the kingdom of Jalandhar which included the Kangra region. Beyond Kangra was the kingdom of Kulu. In the upper portions of the Satlej-Jamuna Divide there was a kingdom with its capital near Sirhind and another with its capital at Sugh. Then there was the better known kingdom of Thanesar in the lower parts of the Divide, bordering Mathura in its south-east and the kingdom of 'Paryatra' to its south-west. We know that the 'kingdom' of Thanesar was a part of the empire established by Harsha, but Hiuen

Tsang does not say anything about the status of the other kingdoms. Nor does he tell us who ruled over them. The ruler of Kashmir exercised suzerain powers over Punchh, Rajauri and Hazara as well as Taxila and Simhapura.

Early in the eighth century, the Tomara Rajputs occupied the lower parts of the Satlej-Jamuna Divide, founding the city of Dilli in 736. Dharmapala of Bengal (770–810) established his control over Kanauj. A contemporary eulogy mentions several of his tributaries in the Punjab, which suggests that he exercised suzerain power at least in the Satlej-Jamuna Divide. His successor, Devapala (810–50), is said to have exacted tribute from the whole of north India. After his death, however, Kanauj came under the control of Bhoja Pratihara, whose dominions are said to have extended to the Punjab. There is hardly any doubt that the Tomaras were still 'prosperous' in the region of Thanesar in subordination to the Pratiharas. This basic situation did not change under the Pratihara rulers Mahendrapala and Mahipala till the first quarter of the tenth century. The Tomaras appear to have become independent before the century ended. The Chauhanas of Sambhar in their south-west were hostile to them. Simharaja Chauhana defeated Salavana, a leader of the Tomaras, but the territories of the Chauhanas remained confined to Rajasthan during the tenth century.

It is not without interest that two kings of Kashmir were able to influence political developments in the Satlej-Jamuna Divide. Lalitaditya, who belonged to the Karkota dynasty (founded by Durlabhavardhana, in whose reign Kashmir was visited by Hiuen Tsang), waged a prolonged war against Yashovarman and wrested Kanauj from him. The Kashmiri invasion of the Ganges plains appears to have helped the Tomaras to come to power in the Satlej-Jamuna Divide. The second king of Kashmir who took interest in the politics of the eastern Punjab belonged to the Utpala dynasty founded by Avantivarman in the 850s. His successor, Shankaravarman, defeated the king of Takka, crossed the river Satlej and installed a prince of the Takka family as the ruler of the region around Bhatinda. But the influence of Kashmir over these kingdoms ended with the death of Shankaravarman around 900. His successors continued to rule over Kashmir till the end of the tenth century, but without any influence in the Satlej-Jamuna Divide.

Powers from outside the Indian subcontinent had begun to influence events in the western parts of the Punjab in the eighth century. The Arabs had begun to expand rapidly after the death of the Prophet of Islam in AD 632. The Umayyad Caliph al-Walid bin Abdul Malik

(705–15) appointed Hajjaj bin Yusuf Saqafi as the governor of Khurasan. Hajjaj sent an expedition against Sind under his son-in-law, Muhammad Qasim, who conquered Brahmanabad, Alor and Multan between 708 and 714. Further penetration into the Punjab was cut short by his recall and death in 714. A later Arab governor of Sind and Multan, Junaid, is said to have followed Muhammad Qasim's example and marched up to Kangra, but he lost his hold over these conquests very soon. The Abbasids, like the Umayyads, continued to appoint governors for Sind and Multan till the early ninth century, after which governorship was held by the members of one family. Sind and Multan were subjugated by the Saffarids (872–903) but after their fall, Multan became independent under a governor of its own. In the tenth century, it was occupied by a branch of the Ismailis, known as the Carmathians. They were ruling over Multan at the end of the century.

Hajjaj had imposed Arab suzerainty over the Turk Shahi rulers of Kabul. They continued to rule till the Turk Shahi king was overthrown by his Brahman minister Kallar in the second half of the ninth century to found the Hindu Shahi dynasty. If Kallar is the same person as the Lalliya Shahi of the *Rajatarangini*, he lost Kabul to the Saffarids in 870 and shifted his capital to Udabhanda on the right bank of the Indus above Attock. He successfully resisted the attack of Shankaravarman of Kashmir (883–902). Kallar was succeeded by his son Tormana but a scion of the family, named Samanta, usurped his throne. In this predicament Tormana was helped by Prabhakara, the minister of Kashmir and the lover of its queen Sugandha. Tormana was reinstalled as Kamalavarman (Alberuni's Kamalu). He was succeeded by Bhima as 'Maharajadhiraj Parameshvara Shahi Shri Bhimadeva'. Silver coins of the latter have been found in the valley of Kabul. He gave his daughter in marriage to Simharaja of Lohara and his daughter's daughter, Dida, became the queen of Kashmir in the last quarter of the tenth century. At this time the Shahi ruler at Udabhanda was Jayapala. An inscription from Swat refers to him as Paramabhattaraka Maharajadhiraj Shri Jayapaladeva. In his reign, Bharat, the ruler of the kingdom of Lahore that had been founded in the early tenth century, invaded Takeshar but was defeated and made a tributary. Jayapala annexed the kingdom of Lahore in 999. By this time he was hard-pressed by the Turks of Ghazni who were destined to extirpate the Shahi dynasty. 'This Hindu Shahiya dynasty,' observed Alberuni around 1030, 'is now extinct, and of the whole house there is no longer the slightest remnant in existence.' Alberuni also paid tribute to the Hindu Shahi rulers: 'in all their grandeur, they never slackened in the ardent desire of doing that which is good and right', and they were men of 'noble sentiment and noble bearing'.

By this time some new states had been established in the hills. The process of state formation appears to have become important during the period under consideration. The state of Chamba was founded during the second half of the sixth century. Its founder, Meru, ruled from Brahmaur. His seventh successor, Meruvarman, was ruling the state in the last quarter of the seventh century. The twentieth ruler of the state, Sahilavarman, shifted the capital to Chamba in the first half of the tenth century. The rulers of Chamba increased their territory at the cost of the rulers of Kulu, and subsequently came into conflict with other states founded later in the neighbourhood. Suket was founded in the eighth century, and Keonthal and Kashtwar in the ninth. The states of Jammu (Durgara) and Bilaspur (Kahlur) were founded in the late ninth or the early tenth century. The process was similar everywhere, an outsider becoming a Raja by subjugating the local Thakurs and Ranas. The Rajas were accompanied or followed by the priest and the trader.

POLITICIO-ECONOMIC STRUCTURE

Only some parts of the Punjab were at times directly administered by outside rulers. Thanesar formed one of the provinces (*bhuktis*) of the empire of Harsha. The provinces were generally divided into districts (*vishyas*), each consisting of a number of villages (*gramas*). The governor of the province, called Uparika, was appointed by the emperor and was responsible to him. The administrators at the district level, called Vishyapatis, were appointed either by the emperor or by the governor presumably with the approval of the emperor. They are known to have been given the titles of *maharaja*, *kumaramtya* or *ayuktaka* in the empire of Harsha. Records of land appear to have been maintained at the district level by an official known as the Pustapala. An official called the Akshapatalika dealt with the legal aspect of land transactions. The village served as the smallest unit of administration, with the Grameyaka or the *gramaadhyaksha* as its head. Assisted by the village elders, he served as the link between the village and the officials of the district. Bana and Hiuen Tsang praise Harsha's government for relative peace and mild taxation. The territories under the direct administration of the Pratiharas also appear to have been divided essentially into provinces, districts and villages, under the same kinds of functionaries as in the empire of Harsha. It is doubtful, however, that any part of the Punjab was under the direct administration of the Pratiharas.

For the most part of the period under consideration, the administration of the Punjab was under 'kings' who were either independent or subordinate to another. In the Sonepat copper-seal inscription of Harsha, the title of *maharaja* appears to have been used for his ancestors as subordinate rulers, but the title of *maharajadhiraja* is used for his father to mark his independent status. This is the title used for Harsha too. In an inscription from the Temple of Garibnath at Pehowa, the 'illustrious Bhoja' is referred to as 'the king of great kings'. There is a reference to the 'Thakkuras' also in this inscription. In another inscription from Pehowa, the Tomara chief Jaula is a *raja*. His descendants acknowledge 'the illustrious king Mahendrapala' as their overlord. The term *raja*, among several others, is used by Bana for a ruler subordinate to Harsha. The term *samanta* changed its meaning from a neighbouring cultivator, through a neighbouring king, to a subordinate ruler. Bana's *Harshacharita* refers to *samantas* gathered at the court of Harsha. By this time, the term *mahasamanta* had also come into use. It referred presumably to the subordinate king of a higher status in the hierarchy of vassals.

The suzerain maintained an army and troops to guard the frontiers, punish the refractory, and protect the palace. All the subordinate rulers were expected to assist the overlord in war. They were not to enter into any political alliance with other rulers. Some of the vassals paid personal homage to the suzerain on special occasions. A few of them entered into matrimonial relations with him. Some sent occasional gifts, while others paid regular tribute. Some of them performed services for the overlord. Most of the subordinate rulers acknowledged the overlord in their charters and grants. In one situation, a feudatory ruler could alienate the revenues of his territory without reference to the overlord, and create his own feudatories, but in another he would seek approval from the overlord for alienating land or its revenue. The suzerain-vassal polity was marked by complexities and ambiguities but, invariably, the administration of the territories of the subordinate ruler was left in his hands.

As we have already noticed, by the time of Hiuen Tsang the trans-Indus 'kingdom' had either been annexed by the rulers of Kabul to their dominions or their kings and chiefs had been made subordinate.

Similarly, the ruler of Kashmir was treating Takshashila and Simhapura as his 'tributaries'. Hiuen Tsang does not mention the political status of the kingdoms of Takka, Patti (Chinapati) and Multan. They could have been independent kingdoms. King Udita of Jalandhar was appointed by Harsha as the 'sole inspector of the affairs of religion throughout the five Indies'. On Hiuen Tsang's return from Harsha's dominions, Udita provided an escort for him. The ruler of Jalandhar may thus be said to have acknowledged Harsha as his superior. However, there is no indication that Harsha played any role in the internal affairs of Jalandhar. The status of the 'Satadru' and 'Srughna' is not mentioned by Hiuen Tsang, but there is no reference to any king either. It is not thus clear who was administering the upper Satlej-Jamuna Divide in the time of Harsha. In the later centuries, the region appears to have passed into the control of the Tomaras who remained subordinate most of the time to the Palas and the Pratiharas. The kings of Kashmir subordinated the rulers of Takka and Jalandhar, but only for short intervals of time. The Hindu Shahi rulers of Kabul occupied some of the territories formerly subordinate to Kashmir. They also had a few vassals between the Jhelam and the Ravi during the later tenth century. On the whole, it is clear that suzerain-vassal political relationship prevailed in the Punjab. Its administration was in the hands of a number of rulers, each of whom controlled a rather small territory.

Hiuen Tsang is explicit on the point that the 'governors, ministers, magistrates, and officials have each a portion of land consigned to them for their personal support'. He also talks of the private lands of the crown, which were divided into four principal parts: land for carrying out the affairs of state and providing sacrificial offerings; land for sustaining the high functionaries; land for rewarding 'men of distinguished ability'; and land to endow religious bodies. In other words, individuals of exceptional talent, religious institutions of known sanctity, and the functionaries of the state were remunerated with land. There is also the implication that all the land in the empire did not belong to the category of crownland.

Contemporary evidence indicates what exactly the king could alienate. When the king made gifts of fields, no gift of land was effected thereby; provision was made only for the maintenance of the donee. If a piece of land belonged to the king either through purchase or by right (because it did not belong to anyone else), he could gift it to anyone he thought fit. However, if land was under cultivation and belonged to someone, the king could alienate only his share from the produce in favour of the donee of his choice. The functionaries of the state were normally remunerated with the assignment of income due to the king from a certain piece of land. Hiuen Tsang mentions one-sixth of the produce from land as the king's share in the royal lands.

Harsha is known to have made generous gifts to religious institutions and individuals of known sanctity. According to his Banskhera and Madhuban inscriptions he gave 100 villages to Brahmans at the time of his first military campaign. The mention of 'ploughs' in this connection indicates that it was the revenue from land, not land itself, that was granted. After his successful campaign in Orissa, Harsha is reported to have offered the revenue of 'eighty large towns' to the Buddhist scholar Jayasena. It is a different matter that he refused to accept it. The copper plate inscriptions discovered from all over the Ganges plain leave no doubt that temples and Brahmans received a large number of grants from the rulers of the time. The earliest known copper plate grant in the Punjab comes from the second half of the tenth century and that too from the hill state of Chamba. In the first half of the tenth century, Sahilavarman of Chamba had built a number of temples and assigned lands for their support. In fact, lands are said to have been assigned for the support of temples built by Meruvarman in the late seventh century. The absence of copper plate grants, thus, does not mean that the rulers of the time did not assign lands to religious establishments. In Pehowa in the reign of Mahendrapala Pratihara, three great grandsons of Raja Jaula built three temples and assigned three villages for their support. In the reign of Bhoja Pratihara, the horse dealers at Pehowa executed a charter on behalf of all sellers and buyers to contribute a certain amount on each sale towards a fund meant for the support of several temples, including one at Pehowa. The priests of the temples were also given a small share from this collection. Temples attributed to the time of the Hindu Shahi rulers have been discovered in the Salt Range, but there is no indication whether or not any grants were given to them. Hiuen Tsang refers to a large number of Deva temples all over the Punjab. It is not difficult to visualize that these temples were built by local communities, private individuals, and persons connected with the state. The possibility of grants being given to some of them cannot be ruled out. The setting aside of revenues for the use of the Buddhist Viharas had been common in the fourth century.

For the administration of small states, there was no need to divide them into provinces, and the ruler of the state did not have to appoint any governors. In the hill states of Kulu and Chamba, the Rajas ran the administration through Thakurs and Ranas. In an inscription from Chamba, the terms *samanta* and *rajanaka* are used for the same person, making them synonymous. In another inscription the term *thakur* is used for a person in a similar position. These terms refer to the 'feudal barons' of the hills, broadly comparable to the Damaras of Kashmir. In any case, the units of administration in the hills were actually the domains of each of these feudal lords. The *kothis* in Kulu and the *parganas* in Chamba had marked at one time the domain of a Thakur or a Rana. We do not have direct information on the administrative units in the kingdoms of the Punjab plains but it may be reasonable to suggest that the Raja ran his administration through the chiefs of clans, sharing political power and social surplus with them. Thus, just as the suzerain-vassal polity introduced a certain degree of decentralization in the context of the empire, the administrative arrangements within each political unit involved a certain degree of decentralization in the context of the kingdom. The new politico-economic structure weakened the position of the king on the one hand and that of the cultivator on the other. The holders of power at the intermediate levels gained at the cost of the king and the cultivators.

Hiuen Tsang makes a brief comment on the major agricultural produce of the kingdoms of the Punjab: rice, sugar cane, and many fruit trees in Lamghan; a great quantity of fruit and cereals around Jalalabad; sugar cane, cereals and a variety of fruits around Peshawar; turmeric and an abundance of grapes and other fruits in Swat; saffron, cereals, and abundance of fruit in Kashmir; rich harvests and abundant fruits in Takshashila; abundant produce in Simhapura; rice and late-sown grain in Takka. There was a long stretch of forest between the rivers Jhelam and Ravi. The country around Patti produced abundant harvests. The land in Jalandhar was favourable for the cultivation of cereals and it produced much rice. Kulu produced a number of crops and fruits. The country around Sirhind produced cereals in abundance, and there was much fruit. The soil of Thanesar and Srughna was rich and productive, and it produced grain in abundance.

Hiuen Tsang refers to the natural and mineral resources, and the manufactures and commerce of the north-west. He talks of a variety of flowers in Swat, Kashmir, Takshashila, Jalandhar and Kulu. He talks of forests in Swat, Kashmir, Takka, Jalandhara and Kulu. He refers to medicinal plants in Kashmir and to medicinal roots in Kulu. He notices gold in Swat, Takka, Kulu and Satadru; silver in Takka, Kulu and

Satadru; iron in Swat and Takka; copper in Takka and Kulu; and precious stones in Satadru. Among the manufactured articles mentioned by Hiuen Tsang are white cotton cloth in Swat, a very shining white fabric, and red cloth in Takka, besides other kinds, and a very bright red silk in Satadru where people used to dress elegantly. Hiuen Tsang says the inhabitants of the capital of Takka were prosperous and that the houses of the people in Jalandhar were rich and well supplied. The rich families of Thanesar were given to excessive luxury. Most of the people in Thanesar were 'after worldly gain' and only a few of them gave themselves to agricultural pursuits. This comment does suggest that commerce was more important than agriculture. Indeed, Hiuen Tsang makes it quite explicit that there was 'a large accumulation here of rare and valuable merchandise from every quarter'.

Significantly, almost all the capitals mentioned by Hiuen Tsang were either cities or towns of a considerable size. If we were to go by the circuits of these urban centres, the largest among them was Peshawar with a circuit of about 11 kilometres. It was followed by Nagarahara, Sakala, Thanesar and Srughna, each with a circuit of about 6 kilometres. The capitals of Udyana, Simhapura, Chinapatti, Jalandhar, Kulu and Satadru had circuits ranging from 4 to 6 kilometres. That there were towns and cities other than the capitals is evident from the statement of Hiuen Tsang that there were four or five strong towns in Udyana. According to the *Life of Hiuen Tsang*, there was a large city on the eastern borders of Takka near the Ravi, close to the site of what was to be Lahore.

The places of importance seen by Alberuni in the Indian territories of the Ghaznavids, which in all probability were urban centres in the tenth century, were Peshawar, Waihind, Jhelam, Nandana, Sialkot, 'Lahore' and Multan, besides Kabul and Lamghan. He also refers to the city of Thanesar and to Sunam and Panipat as well known places. The context in which he mentions these centres did not require him to be exhaustive or comprehensive. Therefore, it may be reasonable to infer that the number of urban centres in the Punjab at the end of the tenth century was by no means smaller than the number of towns and cities in the time of Hiuen Tsang, who refers to desertion of towns in Gandhara. Among the old towns that virtually disappeared was Taxila.

That the cities and towns of the Punjab served as the seats of important religious institutions is evident from the records of Hiuen Tsang. It may be safe to suggest that these urban centres served as markets for the smaller towns and villages around them. Exchange of goods between the large towns of the region may also be safely assumed. Hiuen Tsang states that merchants used to pay 'a small toll' to cross rivers and barriers on roads. In some cases it is possible that the urban centres of the Punjab had trade connections with the outside world. Salt from the upper Sind Sagar Doab was sent to other parts of the Punjab and, possibly, to areas outside the Punjab. Similarly, the horses of the north-west were prized elsewhere in India. The large horse fair at Pehowa, held regularly every year in the reign of Bhoja Pratihara and probably before and after, is the only known testimony to trade in horses. The Punjab served as the market for horses from countries to its north-west. Perhaps less important but more significant was the aloewood market in Multan where merchants from different countries used to buy it from priests of the Sun-Temple who used to receive it from Kamarupa or Cambodia. Among the products of the north-west were saffron, grapes, jujube, pine and deodar wood, and skins. Another article of export was birch-bark. Alberuni's reference to the 'prosperity' of the Punjab can be appreciated in this context.

LITERATURE AND LANGUAGES

Hiuen Tsang makes no mention of the *Ramayana* in the Punjab and refers to the war at Kurukshetra in a way which suggests that he was not at all familiar with the story of the *Mahabharata*. Alberuni refers to the *Ramayana*, but generally in quotations from other works. However, he seems to have been familiar with the *Mahabharata* as a work held in veneration by the Hindus. It was said that everything which occurs in other books is found also in this book, but not all which occurs in this book is found in other books. The *Mahabharata* mentioned by Alberuni had 1,00,000 *shlokas* in eighteen *parvans*. The titles of all the *parvans* are given by him. These eighteen parts were followed by another, called *Harivamsha-Purana*, which contained stories relating to Vasudeva.

Alberuni is apologetic to his readers that he could not comprehend Sanskrit literature in all its numerous branches. He had a particular fascination for the *Panchatantra* which he wished to translate into Arabic. The book was available in Arabic and Persian–known as the book of Kalila and Dimna–as well as in Sanskrit. However, Alberuni suspected that translators had altered the text.

Alberuni takes notice of two 'auxiliary' branches of Sanskrit literature: grammar and metrics. Grammar had the first place in the estimate of the Hindus because of the importance they attached to the rules of the correctness of speech and etymology, which enabled them to acquire 'eloquent and classical style' in writing. Among the eight grammarians listed by Alberuni is Panini whose work had come to be known as *Panini*. The great grammarian was noticed by Hiuen Tsang too. He was inspired by Ishvara Deva in his work which 'contained everything known from the first till then, without exception, respecting letters and words'. Furthermore, masters of grammar had received it and handed it down in its completeness for the good of the world. The Brahmans of Panini's native town were well known for their talents; they were well informed, and had a vigorous understanding. It is interesting to note that Ugrabhuti, one of the eight grammarians listed by Alberuni, was reputedly the teacher of the Hindu Shahi Anandapala who ruled 'in our time'. His book was highly prized in Kashmir. That Panini's work was known in northern India during this period is evident from the commentaries written on it. In fact, a popular school of grammar is said to have been founded in the ninth century by Shakatayana who addressed himself primarily to Shvetambara Jains.

The science of metrics was indispensable to the Hindus because all their books were in verse. They were 'passionately fond' of their verses because they loved 'symmetry and order' which facilitated their learning by heart. The poetical works of the Hindus contained 'a great number of metres, their names differing in accordance with the number of syllables in each. The use of many metres in the same poem, in their view, made it appear 'like an embroidered piece of silk'. The smallest number of syllables in a *pada* could be four and the largest twenty-six, the range found in the Veda. The *shloka* belonged to the four-*pada* metres. Most of the works were composed in *shloka* which Alberuni wanted to use for translating some scientific works in Arabic into Sanskrit. The father of metrics was Pingala who was followed by a number of other masters. The last three centuries of the first millennium after Christ formed 'the golden age of Sanskrit poetics'; its expositions related to the theories of *rasas*, *gunas* and *alamkara*. Rajashekhara's *Kavyamimamsa*, which did not deal with these theories, was meant to serve as a practical handbook for poets.

Alberuni emphasizes the importance of the art of writing as the means of communication in space and time, and refers to the writing materials used in India. Unlike the Greeks in ancient times, the Hindus never used hides as a material for writing. Nor did they use paper which was first manufactured in China. In the south of India, the material used for writing consisted of the leaf of the tree like the cocoa-nut palm. The use of palm leaf was common in India in the time of Hiuen Tsang. The leaves with writing on them were arranged in the order required and held together by a cord going through the hole in the middle of each. In central and northern India, the bark of the *tuz* (birch) tree was used as writing material; it was called '*bhūjra*' (*bhurja-pattra*). The bark was oiled to make it hard and smooth. The single leaves marked by numbers in their proper order were fastened between two tablets of the same size, and this book, called a *pothi*, was wrapped in cloth. We know from other sources that the birch-bark manuscripts also were held together by a cord drawn through a single hole in the middle, or two holes placed some distance apart. The word *grantha* (knot) came to acquire the sense of a book. We know that there were extensive birch forests in the Himalayas, and the use of this material spread from the north-west to the other parts of India. The oldest known Sanskrit manuscript written on birch dates from the fifth century. The use of ink and a reed-pen (*kalama*) for writing had become quite common by then.

According to Hiuen Tsang, the Brahmans believed that their alphabet were 'arranged' by Brahmadeva and their 'forms' had been fixed from the beginning. Their number was forty-seven and they were combined to form words according to the object and circumstances of time or place. This alphabet had 'spread in different directions and formed diverse branches'. Hiuen Tsang appears to be referring to Brahmi and its various forms, for already in the third century before Christ two variants could be distinguished: northern and southern Brahmi. Alberuni refers to the rediscovery of the alphabet of the Hindus by Vyasa. The number of its letters (*aksharas*) was fifty. This large number could be explained partly by the fact that they express every letter by a separate sign if it is followed by a vowel, or a diphthong or a *hamza* (*visarga*), and partly by the fact that they use a larger number of consonants than any other people. Like the Greeks, the Hindus wrote from left to right: 'their ground-line is above, a straight line above every single character, and from this line the letter hangs down and is written under it'. Any sign above the line was 'nothing but a grammatical mark' to denote the pronunciation of the character above which it stood. The generally current alphabet was called *siddhamatrika*. It was used in Kashmir and Varanasi, the two places which had 'the high schools of Hindu sciences'. This script was also used in the country around Kanauj, known as the Madhyadesha, and also called

Aryavarta. The alphabet used in Malwa was called *nagara* which differed from the other only in the shape of its characters. Then there was a third alphabet, called *ardhanagari*, that is, half-*nagara*, as a compound of the other two. It was used in 'Bhatiya' and some parts of Sind. There were still other scripts: Malwari, Saindheva, Karnata, Andhri, Dirwari, Lari, Gaudi, and Bhaikshuki.

Both Hiuen Tsang and Alberuni comment on the languages of India. According to the former, Middle India preserved the original character of the language (Sanskrit) in its integrity. Here, the pronunciation was soft 'like the language of the Devas'. It was clear and pure, and 'fit as a model for all'. The people on the frontiers, however, had contracted several erroneous modes of pronunciation. The nature of their language was 'corrupt', just as their habits were licentious. Elsewhere, Hiuen Tsang makes a specific observation on the people of Takka: they were 'quick and violent' and their language was 'coarse and uncultivated'. The author of the *Life of Hiuen Tsang*, who tells us that all countries beyond Lamghan were the *mlechha* lands, makes the further observation that the common people from Lamghan to the borders of Takka differed to some degree from the people of India 'in their manners, clothing and language'. Alberuni noted that 'the language' of the Hindus was divided into 'a neglected vernacular', which was in use only among the common people, and 'a classical one', which was in use only among the upper and educated classes. This latter language was much cultivated, subject to all the rules of grammatical inflection and etymology and to all the niceties of grammar and rhetoric. Both Hiuen Tsang and Alberuni tend to assume that the literary language of India was Sanskrit. However, both of them also notice that the language used by the mass of the people, and the language in use in different parts of the country, was not the same as the literary or spoken Sanskrit.

There are indications that the language of the common people of the north-west came to be referred to as *apabhramsha* during the period under consideration. The word *apabhramsha*, taken sometimes to mean 'decadent', literally means 'corrupt'. It is important to remember, however, that the term '*apabhramsha*' was used not by those who spoke it, but by those who spoke or wrote in Sanskrit. That *apabhramsha* was looked upon as a distinct language is evident from the copper plate inscription of Guhasena of Vallabhi (AD 559–67) which praises him for his proficiency in Sanskrit, Prakrit, and Apabhramsha poetry. In the ninth century, Rudrata includes Apabhramsha in his list of six languages and says that this language had different varieties in different countries. One view is that Apabhramsha originated in the Himavant-Sindhu region. By some writers, the language of the north-west is referred to as Takki, presumably from the name of the country called Takka. If so, Takki may be regarded as the Apabhramsha of the north-west. Significantly, the writers of Apabhramsha in some parts of the subcontinent referred to their language as Deshi or 'the language of the land'.

There is hardly any doubt that Sanskrit continued to be the language of literature and exchange of thought among the educated and the learned during the entire period under consideration. This is evident not only from the prevalence of literature we have already noticed, but also from the plays like Vishakhadatta's *Mudrarakshasa* and Bana's *Harishcharita* and his epic poem *Kadambari*. Towards the end of the period we come upon the *Hanuman Nataka* which was something between an epic and a dramatic composition. There were narratives of love in prose, generally known as 'romances'. A new form to emerge before the end of the period was the *champu*. Elaborate encomia, called *prashastis*, were composed by writers who refer to themselves as *kavishvaras*. Ornate narratives in prose or verse, like the story of Nala and Damayanti, and some dictionaries were also composed during this period, starting with the *Amarakosha*. Kashmir, which at times had close contacts with the Punjab, was a centre of literature and learning. Utpala, whom Alberuni mentions among the astronomers, wrote an important work on Sanskrit metrics during the second half of the tenth century. He was preceded by Udbhata, a *sabhapati* of Jayapida, who was a representative of the *alamkara* school of poetics and was associated with several of its doctrines. His contemporary Vamana, the author of the *Kavyalamkarasutravrtti* was an exponent of the *riti* school. The new school of *dhavani*, an extension of the Rasa theory, was started by Anandavardhana through his *Dhvanyaloka* in the time of Avantivarman. Damodaragupta's didactic poem entitled *Kathanimata* was written in the reign of Jayapida. Several important epic poems (*kavya*) were written during the eighth and ninth centuries, the best known being Rajanaka Ratnakara's *Haravijaya*, depicting the demon Andhaka's death at the hands of Shiva, Shivasvamin's epic on the conversion of a king to Buddhism, and Abhinanda's *Kadambari-Kathasara*.

However, Sanskrit was becoming less and less the spoken language of the people, and Apabhramshas were becoming increasingly their literary language along with Prakrits. It is true that even Jain writers like Haribhadra had begun to make use of Sanskrit–a tendency which was to culminate in the works of Hemachandra in the twelfth century. Nevertheless, Haribhadra was a great writer of Prakrit. His *Samaraichha-kaha*, a religious tale in prose, and his *Dhutakhyana*, a secular tale in verse, were two major contributions to Prakrit literature. Uddyotanasuri, who was well versed in Prakrits, mentions eighteen provincial tongues, each with its own peculiar words. Composed in Marathi in AD 778, his work contains long passages from Apabhramshas. Rajashekara's *Karpuramanjari*, a drama in Prakrit, was composed probably in the ninth century. Svayambhu's Prakrit anthology of *Chhandas* contained the poetry of more than 50 authors who were mostly non-Jain, including two women. Svayambhudeva produced Apabhramsha versions of the *Ramayana* and the *Mahabharata*. Haribhadra wrote a long peom of high merit. Short stories were written in Apabhramsha for entertainment, or for religious and moral instruction. Quite significatly, in Apabhramsha poetry, the *doha* was the most popular metre from the sixth to the twelfth century. The metres used in Apabhramsha epic poems appear to be the forerunners of the *chaupai-doha* style of Malik Muhammad Jaisi's *Padmavat* and Tulsidasa's *Ramacharitamanasa*. References to works in Prakrit and Apabhramsha in the north-west have to be appreciated in this larger context.

ARCHITECTURE AND SCULPTURE

Hiuen Tsang talks of the wide and high walls of towns and cities, and their gates. He also talks of the *sangharamas,* constructed with 'extra-ordinary skill'. At each of the four corners of a monastery, a three-storied tower was erected. The beams of projecting heads were carved 'with great skill in different shapes'. The door, windows and low walls were painted 'profusely'. The cells of the monks were plain on the outside but ornamental on the inside. In the middle of the building was a high and wide hall. There were chambers of various storeys and turrets of different heights and shapes. The doors opened on the east, just as the royal throne faced the east. Hiuen Tsang's work contains only a few specific references to monastery buildings in the Punjab, including the Kabul valley. At one place he refers to a *sangharama* 'with a high hall and a storeyed tower made of piled up stone'. At another place he refers to an old *sangharama* 'with its double towers, connected terraces, storeyed piles and deep chambers'. All these features were supposed to reflect 'the eminence' of those illustrious monks who lived here and gained great distinction.

Many of the stupas were equally impressive. To the east of the capital of Nagarahara was a stupa, about 300 feet in height. It was a 'wonderfully constructed' stone structure, 'beautifully adorned and carved'. Within the city was a high stupa, once of 'great magnificence'. A several hundred feet high stupa in Gandhara was made of carved wood and 'veined stone'. It was the work of 'various artists'. Two other stupas in this area were of 'a considerable height and grandeur'. A stone stupa in the Simhapura area, about 200 feet high, was 'tastefully built' and was 'adorned with sculptures'. Another stupa in this area had its decorations 'much injured'. Close to yet another stupa were ten tanks, and on the walks joining them there were balustrades of different shapes and a strange character. A hundred kind of fruit trees surrounded the tanks and glistened with different shades. The trees were reflected deep down in the water. It was altogether a 'lovely spot' for a leisurely stroll. Close to another stupa and a monastery there were many fruits and flowers, 'with fountains and tanks clear as a mirror'. There were about a hundred small stupas provided with stone arches for 'movable images'. Hiuen Tsang refers to some other sculptures too. On the eastern face of a great stupa in Gandhara area two miniature stupas were carved, one 3 feet and the other 5 feet high. There were two full-sized figures of the Buddha, one 4 feet and the other 6 feet in height. In both, he was depicted seated cross-legged beneath the Bodhi tree. 'When the full rays of the sun shine on them they appear of brilliant gold colour, and as light decreases the hues of the stone seem to assume a reddish-blue colour.' To the south of the stupa was a painted figure of Buddha, about 16 feet high. Below the middle it had only one body but from the middle upwards, two bodies. To its south-west there was a figure of the Buddha in white stone, about 18 feet high. It was a standing figure, looking to the north.

According to the evidence of Hiuen Tsang, the number of *deva* temples in the Punjab was larger than the number of Buddhist monasteries and stupas. However, we do not know anything about the architecture of these temples. That these temples had images is evident from Hiuen Tsang's remark about a temple outside Purushapura, which had an 'imposing' image of the god, and from his reference to the image of Bhima Devi carved out of a bluish-green stone. Few descriptions of temples have come to light. One brief comment is found in an inscription from Sirsa of the reign of Bhoja Pratihara. The temple to

Yogeshvara there was built of burnt bricks and slabs of stone. It was 'magnificent', with a golden peak 'as high as the Kailasha mountain'. Though a Shaiva temple, it was adorned not only with the images of demons, *gandharvas*, *yakshas*, *ganas*, *kinnaras* and *siddhas* but also with the images of Vishnu and Lakshmi, and other gods. The world depicted in the sculpture emulated, as it were, 'the universal form of Vishnu'.

The sculptural pieces discovered in the Punjab generally show north Indian features, and they are not devoid of beauty. The material used for this sculpture was generally buff, brown or grey sandstone. A pillared niche from Sirsa depicts Vishnu seated on a lotus in the *padamasana*, and holding the mace and a lotus in two of his four hands. The front two hands are placed in his lap, which is appropriate for the image of Vishnu as Yoga-Narayana. A tenth century head of Vishnu in the Government Museum at Hoshiarpur shows him wearing *kirtimukuta* crown with garlands flowing from criss-cross designs. The *chakra* at the top of the crown symbolizes his supremacy over other gods. This Vishnu is aesthetically impressive. A sculpture from Pehowa depicts Vaikuntha Vishnu with three faces–the central as human but the other two as the faces of a lion and a boar. In this eight armed image of the god, he is holding objects generally associated with Vishnu: the disc (*chakra*), the conch-shell (*shankha*), the mace, the sword, the shield, the bow and arrows.

A sculpture from a village in the Ambala district shows Vishnu with his body slightly raised, lying over Shesha Naga forming with its seven heads a canopy above his head. One of his two right hands is supporting his head and the other resting on his chest. In his two left hands he is holding the disc and the conch-shell. The mace is lying near his head. His right leg is stretched and held by Lakshmi. This is a truly impressive piece. Even more attractive is the image of Lakshmi-Narayana recovered from Pinjore. Vishnu is seated on a lotus and Lakshmi is seated on his thigh. The hand holding the conch-shell encircles Lakshmi and touches her breast. The lotus seat is supported by Garuda. In a Hari-Hara image, Vishnu has his *kirtimukuta*, his disc and conch-shell, Garuda and Shridevi; the right half shows Shiva in his *jatamukuta*, with his trident and a snake curled around, Nandi and Parvati; the god is standing on a lotus pedestal, with a beautifully ornamented lotus-petalled halo.

Vishnu's incarnations represented in the sculpture are also of reasonably good quality. In an image of Varaha recovered from Pinjore, the god wears a crown, a *vanamala*, a necklace, the sacred thread, and a strap-like waistband in which a small dagger is tucked. The Vamana incarnation of Vishnu is represented in a sculpture found in a village of the Mahindragarh district. This four-armed but short-statured and still shorter-legged god is beautifully decorated with ornaments. In a very small size, Brahma and Shiva are seated on his right and left, symbolizing the supremacy of Vishnu. In a sculpture from the Bhiwani district, Vishnu's *vahana* flies independently, which gives Garuda a special significance. Though much damaged, this sculpture is suggestive of considerable beauty.

The images of Shiva are as impressive as the images of Vishnu. A *mukha-linga* from the fifth century and a dancing Shiva from the seventh century are quite beautifully sculptured. The former, discovered in the Sonepat district, shows a moustached Shiva in his *jatamukuta*, and with the third eye on his forehead. The latter, discovered near Rohtak, shows Shiva holding a trident in one of his four hands, and a snake in another. Nandi is playing the drum with its fore-legs. In an eighth or ninth century sculpture in the Government Museum at Hoshiarpur, Shiva and Parvati are shown with their right hands in the gesture of protective assurance. Shiva has matted locks, wears earrings, and a snake as a garland. Parvati has braided hair, and wears a necklace, earrings, armlets and anklets. Nandi stands behind them, with Shiva's hind right hand placed over its head. Shiva and Parvati stand in a graceful posture, with a common large nimbus behind their heads.

A tenth-century image of Shiva and Parvati is much damaged but its beauty comes through. Both of them wear necklaces. The left hand of Shiva embraces Parvati and touches her left breast, while her right hand is twined round Shiva's neck. A similar sculpture of the tenth or the eleventh century, showing Shiva and Parvati seated on Nandi, is less damaged and no less impressive. More impressive is the Uma-Maheshvara image from the Rohtak district. Shiva (Maheshvara) is seated on Nandi and Parvati (Uma) on his left thigh. His left hand is entwined round Parvati, touching her breast. Her right is round Shiva's neck. The trident and a three-headed cobra are held in two of Shiva's four hands. Ganesha and Karttikeya are shown on their right and left, close to their feet. Above them are shown the personified *trishula* and *yama*. Maheshvara's head is surrounded by a full-bloomed lotus as halo. On its two sides are seated Brahma and Vishnu.

The sons of Shiva and Parvati are represented in sculpture. An image of Ganesha, recovered from the Prachi Shiva Temple at Pehowa, shows him with a crown, a third eye on his forehead, seated on a cushioned seat. He holds a lotus, an axe, a bowl of sweets, and a flower bud or his own tooth, in his four hands. Two garlands fly from his head, near his right foot is a mouse, his mount. Another beautiful sculpture of Ganesha is placed in the Government Museum at Hoshiarpur. In a medallion on a pillar from Sirsa, Ganesha is shown holding Shakti on his lap, her right hand thrown round his neck. In the other three hands he holds a trident, a flower, and a bowl of sweets. As for Karttikeya, besides an impressive figure of him in the Government Museum at Hoshiarpur, there is a Karttikeya with six heads in an eighth century sculpture from the Rohtak district. Seated on his peacock mount, he holds a spear in his right hand and a cock in the left. He wears a *jatamukuta*, a *vanamala*, the sacred thread, a necklace, and ear ornaments..

The best images of the Goddess show her as Mahishasuramardini. In a sculpture from Sirsa she is shown with eight arms, holding a disc, a bell, a sword, a shield, and a bow and arrows. She wears a necklace, ear ornaments, armlets, bracelets, and a *dhoti* secured by a waistband. She pierces the back of the buffalo-demon with a trident in her right hand, the left holding the demon in human form that emerges from the severed head of the buffalo. Her mount, the lion, is shown on her right, ready to attack the demon. In a similar sculpture in the Government Museum at Hoshiarpur, the Goddess is holding a *patra* and the thunderbolt, which make her more ferocious. At the same time, her prominent breasts make her more feminine. The former image is assigned to the tenth century, and the latter to the tenth or eleventh. Both appear to be of a better aesthetic quality than the earlier known images of Mahishasuramardini.

Perhaps the best Surya image is the one discovered in the Rohtak district. The god stands on a lotus pedestal, holding lotus flowers in both his hands, just above the shoulders. His head is surrounded by a large lotus halo. He wears high boots and his body is covered with armour and ornaments. Brahma and Vishnu are seated on lotus flowers, close to the halo. A much damaged image of Surya from Pehowa shows him seated on a cushion in a chariot. Brahma from Pehowa is seated on a lotus pedestal, holding a book, a ladle and a *kamandalu* in three of his four hands, and wearing a garland, a pearl necklace and the sacred threads. The god has four faces. A representation of Agni from Pinjore is marked by elegance and grace, and an idol of Ishana from the same place bears a general resemblance to Agni. The identity of the former is made clear by the halo of flames behind his head and by his mount, the goat. Ishana remains close to Shiva, with his *jatamukuta*, a trident, a snake, and Nandi. Yama, on his buffalo mount, is mutilated in parts but the sculpture is none the less beautiful. An 'unfinished' Kubera appears to wear a crown of thorns and holds a cup of wine. An eighth century bronze image of the Buddha, discovered at Hansi, is graceful.

The evidence of architecture and sculpture raises the questions of patronage, availability of materials, architects, engineers, masons, sculptors in stone and metal, labourers, and the writers of encomia. On these matters, however, we have practically no information. All that is available comprises a stray reference to the farm of a monastery in the *Life of Hiuen Tsang*, references in an inscription to temples built by the descendants of Raja Jaula Tomara, a charter of horse-traders to be executed by the *goshtikas*, the names of goldsmiths in several inscriptions suggesting their association with building activity, the name of an architect, and the name of a *prashasti* writer. However, the large number and size of religious structures and the still larger number of sculptures speak of an incessant creative activity which must have involved members of many sections of the society, from the ruler down to the day-labourer.

THE SOCIAL ORDER

Many of the Puranas known to Alberuni contain some evidence of great social significance. The *Agni Purana* insists that Chandalas should be employed for the execution of criminals, they should wear the clothes of the dead, live outside the village, and not touch others. Regarding the remarriage of women, it repeats a couple of the earlier texts which permit a woman to take a second husband if the first husband dies, becomes impotent, is made an outcaste, or has become an ascetic, or has not been around for a long time. However, the *Brahma Purana* forbids the remarriage of widows under all circumstances. It also forbids the use of a number of herbs, vegetables and cereals as well as liquor by men of the twice-born castes. The *Brahmanda Purana* enjoins that one should bathe with one's clothes on if touched by a Shaiva, a Pashupata, or a Lokayatika. The *Kurma Purana* condemns a teacher who puts off instruction to pupil who has lived with him for a year. The *Aditya Purana*, does not favour long term studentship, and forbids the use of liquor by the twice-born in the Kali Age. The *Vishnudharamottara* mentions ten kinds of liquors and wines forbidden to Brahmans but allowed to Kshatriyas and Vaishyas. The *Linga Purana* describes a set of sixteen great gifts (*mahadanas*) to be distributed among Brahmans, involving large quantities of gold. The *Narada Purana* recommends perpetual studentship, and declares that marriages of twice-born men with girls of other *varnas* are forbidden. The *Varaha Purana* recommends that a Brahman who takes a stipulated fee should not be invited to a funeral repast. In fact, it gives long lists of Brahmans who must not be invited, either because of their physical appearance, or their conduct or occupation.

The *Matsya Purana* upholds the Brahman's privilege to be exempt from capital punishment for any offence whatever: he should only be banished or branded. It allows the advance payment of fee to a teacher on the argument that the just ruler would fine such a teacher if he failed to teach thereafter. It repeats Manu's injunction that the husband is entitled to beat an erring wife with a rope or a split bamboo, avoiding the head and the back. It lists the duties and rights of prostitutes, and the special clauses of the law applicable to them. It insists that the mother must never be abandoned. It also gives a long and systematic account of omens, classifying them under different heads and prescribing adequate remedies for averting their evil effects. A separate chapter is devoted to rules for propitiating the planets. The sixteen 'great gifts' to Brahmans are recommended. The Brahmans living in the *mlechha* countries such as Takka should not be invited to funeral repasts.

The sources we have invoked do not agree on every point but their differences relate to minor issues and to matters of detail. They share a general framework of *varnashramadharma* in which their statements on the privileges and duties of the Brahmans, Kshatriyas, and Vaishyas, and the obligations of the Chandalas make a lot of sense. The Brahmans were not a monolithic entity. Apart from the differences of conduct, physical appearance, religious affiliation and regional placement, there were occupational differences among them. A certain degree of distinction is sought to be made between the Brahmans on the one hand and the Kshatriyas and Vaishyas on the other. A clear distinction is made between these three *varnas* and the Shudras. The Chandalas do not belong to any *varṇa*: they are outcastes. The women are squarely placed within the patriarchal family, without any doubt about their subordination. The only profession open to them is prostitution; it is well recognized and accepted.

The normative statements of the Puranas enable us to appreciate the testimony of Hiuen Tsang. With respect to division of 'families', he says, 'there are four classifications'. The first was called Brahman who lived purely and observed the most correct principles. The second was called Kshatriya, which was 'the royal caste'. They had acted as 'the governing class' for ages. The third was called Vaishyas, 'the merchant class'. They followed profit 'at home and abroad', being engaged in commercial exchange. The fourth was called Shudra, 'the agricultural class'. Hiuen Tsang's statement about the agriculturists being Shudras is significant. It indicates the depressed status of the cultivators. Besides these four, there were many other classes. Then there were butchers, fishermen, dancers, executioners and scavengers who had their abodes outside the city. When in the city, they had to keep to the left side of the road. Thus, Hiuen Tsang refers to the hierarchy of four castes, based on ritual purity, but caste does not account for the whole society. There were 'many kinds' of other classes. And then there were the outcastes who were regarded as untouchable.

According to Hiuen Tsang, the Brahmans were particularly noted for their purity and nobility. So hallowed was their name that the other people 'generally speak of India as the country of the Brahmans'. They studied the Vedas and Shastras thoroughly and taught them well to their pupils. On completing their education at the age of thirty, the latter 'thank' their master on securing an occupation. Among the Brahmans there were some who were deeply versed in 'antiquity', devoted themselves to elegant studies, living apart from the world. The rulers appreciated them but failed to draw them to the court. The people rendered them 'universal homage'. Hiuen Tsang does not say so but the priests he noticed in the temples of 'the heretics' were Brahmans. His guide to 'the cavern of the shadow' was a Brahman. Some Brahmans acted as managers of offerings to the five sacred relics at Nagarahara. A Brahman in Takka was ploughing the field. Thus not all Brahmans were learned, nor all lived on charity.

Hiuen Tsang talks of 'the better class' and 'the lower orders' at one place. At another place he says that the high and the low took their 'proper place'. Social distinctions, it appears, were based not only on caste but also on economic position. Hiuen Tsang appears to have three categories in mind when he talks of the 'better' or the 'high' class. These classes are once mentioned together: the Kshatriyas, the Brahmans, and the rich merchants. The first two were clean and wholesome in their dress and lived in a frugal way. They were different from the kings and their great ministers, who formed a class by themselves (and who were known for their ostentatious lifestyle). The Kshatriyas and Brahmans in general wore necklaces, bracelets, and flowers in the hair. Only a few merchants wore sandals; they pierced their ears and used nose ornaments too; they bound up their hair, and their teeth were stained red or black. All the three categories of people were particular about personal cleanliness. They washed themselves before eating, and they cleansed their teeth and washed their hands and mouth after eating. They never used leftovers and did not pass dishes. Wooden and stone vessels were used only once, and then destroyed. Vessels of gold, silver, copper and iron were rubbed and polished after each meal. Each time they performed the functions of nature they washed their bodies and used perfumes of sandalwood and turmeric. Hiuen Tsang's own identification being with the 'better class', he did not take any notice of 'the lower orders' beyond the fact of their existence.

Some of the observations made by Hiuen Tsang indicate that the institution of marriage was important. In the first place, the ritual status of a person, which normally depended on birth, was affected by the caste of his spouse: it could rise or fall in accordance with the matrimonial relationship. As a rule, promiscuous marriages were discouraged. Among the classes other than the four castes, matrimony was regulated by similar rules. One rule was meant to be followed perhaps by all the higher classes: a woman once married could never take another husband.

Another social aspect in which Hiuen Tsang showed interest was the disposal of the dead. There were three methods of paying the last tribute to the dead: cremation, by water, or exposure. In the first case the body was burnt on a pyre of wood; in the second, it was thrown into deep flowing water; and in the third case, the body was abandoned in a wilderness to be devoured by beasts. No eating was allowed in a house where there had been a death, but life took its usual course after the funeral. Those who attended a funeral were considered unclean until they bathed outside the town before entering their homes. The old and infirm, near death, and those who suffered from an incurable disease, or those who wished to escape the troubles of life, were allowed to drown themselves in the Ganges amid the sounds of music. They hoped to secure birth among the *devas*. The priests were not allowed to lament or cry for the dead. The others were allowed, and they cried aloud.

About four hundred years later, Alberuni made observations on all those aspects of the society which we find noticed by Hiuen Tsang. The body of the dead had the claim upon his heirs that they should wash, embalm and wrap it in a shroud, and then burn it with wood, especially as much sandalwood as they could get. The burnt bones were thrown into the Ganges in order to ensure that the deceased went to heaven. On the spot where the body was burnt, a monument 'similar to a milestone' was raised. The bodies of children under three years were not burnt. Those who could not afford to burn their dead left them on an open field or immersed them in running water. Those who participated in the funeral rites washed themselves and their dresses for two days because they had become 'unclean' by touching the dead.

The body of a living person had the right not to be burnt. However, an exception was made in the case of a widow who chose to become a *sati*. They who were tired of life, distressed about an incurable disease, or some irremovable bodily defect, or old age and infirmity, could burn themselves. But only Vaishyas and Shudras were expected to do this in the hope of a better birth in the future, and chose auspicious days for it. Brahmans and Kshatriyas were forbidden to burn themselves. If they wished to get rid of life, they generally hired someone to drown them in the Ganges. Presumably at the time of a solar eclipse they could climb a particular tree at the confluence of the Ganges and the Jamuna and threw themselves into the water.

Alberuni thought it was strange that the Hindus took the advice of their women in all 'consultations and emergencies'. This did not mean, however, that women enjoyed any parity with men. Alberuni tells us that Hindus married at a very young age, and that parents arranged the marriage of their children. The Brahmans performed the rites of marriage and received alms. No divorce was allowed. Therefore the husband and the wife were separated only by death. A Brahman could take four wives, a Kshatriya three, a Vaishya two, and a Shudra only one. The upper limit could be maintained by a man marrying a new woman on the death of a wife. But when a wife lost her husband, she could not marry another man. She could either remain a widow or burn herself, the latter being preferable. That was why a widow was ill-treated as long as she lived. The wives of the kings had to become *sati* even against their wishes. However, an exception was made for the widow who had a son to protect her, or if she was already old.

Every man was expected to marry a woman of his own caste, or a woman of the caste or castes below his; but nobody was allowed to marry a woman of a caste superior to his own. The children were deemed to acquire the caste of the mother, that is, the lower caste. In Alberuni's time, Brahman men married only Brahman women.

During the menstrual courses, the woman was regarded as impure. The husband was not allowed to cohabit with his wife, nor even to come near her in the house. The wife was regarded as impure also when she gave birth to a child. She was not allowed to touch any vessel: the wife of a Brahman for eight days, the wife of a Kshatriya for twelve days, the wife of a Vaishya for fifteen days, and the wife of a Shudra for thirty days. No term was fixed for the people not reckoned as belonging to any caste. A Brahman performed 'a sacrifice' in the fourth month of pregnancy, and another between the birth and the moment when the mother began to nourish the child. Yet another rite was performed when a name was given to the child. It was called *namakarnam*. In the third year, the rite of the first cutting of the child's hair was performed. The child's ears were perforated in the seventh or the eighth year.

Alberuni refers to an essential feature of the patriarchal system among the Hindus: 'The chief rule of their law of inheritance is this, that women do not inherit, except the daughter.' But this exception is misleading. Alberuni goes on to explain, first, that she gets only one-fourth part of the share of a son and then, that even this fourth part was deemed to be spent on her education and dowry. After marriage, a woman had no claims on the house of her father. Alberuni makes it clear that a widow did not get any share from the property of her deceased husband. His male heir provided her food and clothing as long as she lived.

Alberuni noticed the existence of prostitutes, saying that the Hindus were 'not very severe' in punishing whoredom. He attributed this primarily to state policy. But for the fault of the kings, no Brahman or priest would have suffered in their idol-temples the women who sing, dance and play. The kings made them an attraction of their cities, a bait for people to augment state revenues, both from taxes and fines. Though referring apparently to *devadasis*, Alberuni is talking of prostitutes of all kinds.

Alberuni tended to think of the population in terms of the masses and the elite. At one place he refers to 'the educated people' and 'the common people'. Elsewhere he talks of 'those castes who are not allowed to occupy themselves with science', in contrast with 'the educated among the Hindus'. At yet another place, he refers to the views of 'the common uneducated people'. Even more interesting is his reference to 'uneducated low-class people of little understanding'. That the common, uneducated, low-class people included the mass is evident from his statement that the Vaishya and the Shudra were not allowed to hear the Veda, much less to pronounce and to recite it. If such a thing can be proved against one of them, the Brahmans drag him before the magistrate and he is punished by having his tongue cut off. The inclusion of the Vaishya in this category suggests greater exclusiveness.

Alberuni makes a rather elaborate statement of the *varnashrama* ideal, and its limitation to account for the social realities. He makes the general observation that the division of societies into classes was a common phenomenon in history. The state and religion as 'twins' had much to do with the perpetuation of a differentiated social order. The Hindus call their classes *varnas*, or 'colours'. But from a genealogical point of view they call them *jataka*, or 'births'. From the very beginning these *varnas* have been only four. The highest *varna* was that of the Brahmans who, according to their own tradition had been created from the head of God and were therefore 'the very best of mankind'. Not much below them in degree were the Kshatriyas, created from the arms of God. The Vaishya came next, created from his thigh. The Shudra were created from the feet. The difference between the last two *varnas* was not very great. Despite their differences from each other, they lived together in the same towns and villages, mixed together in the same lodgings. The four *varnas* did not account for the whole society. There were other people, below the Shudras, who did not belong to any *varna*. They were members of certain crafts or professions: the juggler, the basket and shield maker, the sailor, the fisherman, the hunter of birds and wild animals, the weaver, the fuller, and the shoemaker. These 'guilds' lived 'outside' the villages and towns. The weaver, the fuller and the shoemaker were regarded as somewhat lower than the others, who freely intermarried among themselves but not with these three. Then there were people who did not belong to either a *varna* or a 'guild'. Among them were the Hadi, Doma, Chandala and Badhatau, all regarded as one category but with different occupations. Because of their unclean work and the belief that they had descended from a Shudra father and a Brahman mother, they were treated as 'degraded outcastes'. Even they were graded. The Hadi were regarded as the best because they kept themselves free from everything unclean. Next to them were the Doma who played on the lute and sang. They were followed by the Chandalas who practised killing as a trade and inflicted judicial punishments. The worst of all were the Badhatau who devoured the flesh of dead animals.

Within each *varna*, people could follow different occupations and modes of life. Alberuni illustrates his point with reference to the Brahmans. He who stayed at home to do his work was given the general epithet of 'Brahman'. He who served one fire was called *ishtin*; he who served three fires was called *agnihotra*; if he also offered an offering to the fire, he was called *dikshita*. 'And as it is with the Brahmans, so is it also with the other castes.' Each of the four castes formed a separate group when eating together; no two men of different castes were allowed to sit together. Since it was forbidden to eat the remains of a meal, every single man had to have his own food for himself.

One view among the Hindus was that only Brahmans and Kshatriyas were capable of attaining to liberation for the others could not learn the Vedas. However, according to the Hindu philosophers, liberation was common to all castes, and to the whole human race, provided the intention was perfect. On this point, Alberuni quotes the well known lines of Vasudeva-Krishna addressed to Arjuna: 'God distributes recompense without injustice and without impartiality. He reckons the good as bad if people in doing good forget Him; he reckons the bad as good if people in doing bad remember Him and do not forget Him, whether those people be Vaishya or Shudra, or women. How much more will this be the case when they are Brahmana or Kshatriya.' This quotation admits the woman, the Shudra, and the Vaishya rather condescendingly, and it does not move out of the four *varnas*. Alberuni himself knew that there were a number of 'guilds' and a whole world of people beyond the four castes.

The Brahman alone could teach the Veda, he alone could perform 'sacrifice' (*hom*), and he alone could receive alms. Alberuni gives some detail of the daily life of a Brahman. Five vegetables were forbidden to Brahmans, including onion and garlic. For eating his meal, a Brahman prepared his 'table-cloth' in the shape of a square by pouring water over a spot and plastering it with the dung of cows. A Brahman was not expected to leave the country. The *ashramas*, according to Alberuni, were meant only for the Brahmans. He gives details of what a Brahman was supposed to do at each of the four stages. After education as the first stage, he became a householder when he could set himself as a teacher, act as a *purohita*, or live on state charity. As a recluse in the third stage, he does not take shelter under a roof but sleeps on the ground, nourishes himself with fruit, vegetables and roots, and lets his hair grow. In the fourth stage he wears a red garment, gives himself to meditation, and cultivates complete detachment. 'He has no other business but that of caring for the path which leads to salvation, and for reaching *moksha*, whence there is no return to this world.' If a Brahman died without an heir, the king had no right to meddle with his inheritance; it was given away in alms.

Like the Brahman, the Kshatriya was expected to study the Veda. But, unlike the Brahman, he could not teach it. His duty was to rule the people and to defend them. The duty of the Vaishya was to practise agriculture, to tend cattle, and to tend the needs of the Brahmans. All the three were 'twice-born' but their ritual status was indicated by the kind of sacred thread each one was to wear. The Shudra was like a servant to the Brahman, taking care of his affairs and serving him. The Vaishyas and Shudras could not study or recite the Veda. However, meditation on God, works of piety, and alms-giving were not forbidden to them. In theory, the occupations of the four *varnas* were fixed. A man who took to an occupation that was not allowed to his caste was supposed to have committed a crime, no less serious than the crime of theft. According to this norm, a Brahman could not take to trade, and a Shudra could not take to agriculture. Alberuni quotes a tradition in which Rama killed a Chandala for performing worship and self-mortification.

Though generally appreciative of the Hindu philosophers, Alberuni appears to have held the view that they tended to accommodate if not really to exploit the ignorance of the masses. In one chapter he talks explicitly of the Hindu sciences which 'prey on the ignorance of the people'. One of these was alchemy, which claimed to transmute silver into gold. The Hindu 'scientists' appeared to use the method for gilding silver. A science similar to alchemy was *rasayana*. It claimed to restore the health of those who were ill beyond hope, to restore youth to the old, to change white hair into black, to restore the sharpness of senses and juvenile agility, to increase the capacity for cohabitation, and to prolong the life of a person. Alberuni did not believe that such things were possible. Therefore, he favours the idea that this 'science' should be banished from the world. Alberuni places charms and incantations in the same category. One cause of the weaknesses of Hindu astronomy in his view was the way in which the Hindus mixed up scientific questions with religious traditions. The notion of auspicious and inauspicious times also had no scientific validity. Belief in lucky and unlucky planets had little to do with science. Augury from the flight of birds was no better.

According to Alberuni, the killing of sheep, goats, gazelles, hares, rhinoceroses, fish and buffaloes for meat was allowed, like the killing of such birds as sparrows, doves and peacocks. It was forbidden to kill cows, horses, mules, asses, camels, elephants, crows, parrots and nightingales. Some Hindus were of the view that the meat of cows was allowed before the Bharata War. In fact many things which were now forbidden were allowed before the coming of Vasudeva, and one such thing was the flesh of cows. Alberuni expresses his view that the cow serves man in carrying his load, in ploughing and sowing, and by yielding milk. Even its dung was used by man. That was why it was forbidden to kill the cow for meat. Alberuni makes the general observation that the injunction to abstain from the killing of animals was 'only a special part of the general order to abstain from doing anything hurtful'. Liquor was allowed only to a Shudra, but he could not sell it.

Alberuni observed that a notion of Kaliyuga was prevalent among the Hindus. In the Kaliyuga, the dignity of the Brahmans would diminish to such a degree that a Shudra would be impudent to them. The castes would be in uproar against each other, the genealogies would become confused, the four castes would be abolished, and there would be many religions and sects. Finally, when evil would have reached its highest pitch, Kalki would come to destroy evil and to cleanse the earth of all impurity. A new age would begin. The futuristic comment was partly a comment on the past and the present.

According to Alberuni, the Hindus were extremely proud of their polity, culture, and country. They believed that 'there is no country but theirs, no kings like theirs, no religion like theirs, no science like theirs'. According to their belief 'there is no other country on earth but theirs, no other race of men but theirs, and no created beings besides them have any knowledge or science whatsoever'. They looked upon all foreigners as *mlechha*, or impure, and forbade any connection with them, 'be it by intermarriage or any other kind of relationship, or by sitting, eating or drinking with them'. The Hindus did not receive anybody who did not belong to them even if he was inclined to their religion. In the prevalent systems of religion in India there was no provision for 'conversion' or 'reconversion'. One of the reasons for the general attitude of the Hindus towards the people of the Western countries was the invasions of Mahmud which 'utterly ruined the prosperity of the country'. Alberuni says further that 'Hindu sciences have retired away from those parts of the country conquered by us'; they fled to Kashmir, Banaras, and other places which had not yet been conquered by Muslims. The implication is clear: these sciences were cultivated in the Punjab until the Turkish invasions.

Alberuni notices a large volume of literature on astronomy, starting with the five *Siddhantas* of Lata, Vishnuchandra, Paulisa (the Greek), Srishena (Roman), and Brahmagupta. The *Pancha*-Siddhantika of Varahamihira underlined the fact of the number of the *Siddhantas* rather than their contents, and much less their essence. Alberuni was able to procure two Siddhantas for translation into Arabic: the *Paulisa-Siddhanta* and the *Brahman-Siddhanta.* He gives the contents of twenty-four chapters of the latter which indicate the vast scope of astronomy. Most of the subjects mentioned in this work are actually discussed by Alberuni in a number of the later chapters of his book. One chapter in the *Brahma-Siddhanta* was on the solution of problems not by mathematical calculation but by speculation. Alberuni's own view was that no problem of astronomy could be solved 'by anything save by mathematics'. The works which did not reach the standard of the *Siddhanta* were called Tantras or Karanas. A famous Tantra was written by Aryabhata (the first), and another by Balabhadra who was a native of Multan. Brahmagupta had written a Karana under the title *Karana-Khanda-Khandyaka*, which contained the ideas of Aryabhata. Another work was written by Brahmagupta, called *Uttara-Khanda-Khandyaka.* In Alberuni's view, the *Khanda-Khandyaka-tippa* was authored by Balabhadra. Utpala of Kashmir had written *Rahunrakarana.* Indeed, such books were 'innumerable'.

The 'science of astronomy', says Alberuni, was 'the most famous' among the Hindus because 'the affairs of their religion' were in various ways connected with it. Therefore, if a man wanted to gain the title of an astronomer he had to know not only scientific or mathematical astronomy but also astrology. A number of authors, including Balabhadra of Multan, had produced Samhitas of astrology. These dealt with prophecies about dynasties, the knowledge of lucky and unlucky things, forewarnings relating to a journey derived from meteorological occurrences, auguries from the flight or cries of birds, prophesying from the lines of the hand, and the interpretation of dreams. These works treated also of meteorology and cosmology. A number of authors had written books on nativities, known as *Jatakas*. Varahamihira had written two *Jatakas*, a small and a large one. The former was translated into Arabic by Alberuni and the latter was explained by Balabhadra. There were separate volumes of astrology regarding travel, marriage, and architecture. Alberuni observed that the Puranas, which guided the people in fulfilling the rites of their religion, contained ideas which were opposed by the scientific truth known to the Hindu astronomers themselves. But the astronomers accepted their popular notions as truth. 'This is the reason why the two theories, the vulgar and the scientific, have become intermingled in the course of time.'

Alberuni gives primacy to astronomy, but does mention some other sciences. Closest to mathematical astronomy as a science was medicine. The best of the Hindu literature on medicine was the book attributed to Charaka and known also as the *Charaka*. It had been translated into Arabic, and Alberuni refers to this translation. According to the Hindu belief, the first elements had been received by certain Rishis from Indra who had received them from Ashvin, and Ashvin had received it from Prajapati or Brahma, the first father. The Hindus cultivated numerous other branches of science, but Alberuni could not study them all. Nevertheless, he talks about arithmetic and underlines the fact that the Hindus alone had names of the orders of numbers up to eighteen. He had written a treatise to show how far the Hindus were possibly ahead of others in this subject. Alberuni talks of weights and measures, directions (involving the idea of *ashtadikapalas*), and geography in his work.

BUDDHISM AND ITS DECLINE

At the beginning of the fifth century, Buddhism was flourishing in many parts of India. The sages of Hinayana Buddhism were elucidating their doctrines and elaborating their rituals and ceremonies, and two schools had emerged in the process. One of these was the Sautrantika based on the Sutras or Sutrantas. Its founder was Kumaralabdha, a native of Takshashila, who came to be regarded as one of the 'four suns' of India. The three others were Ashvaghosha, Nagarjuna and Aryadeva. The second school, known as the Vaibhashika, gave greater importance to commentaries (*vibhasha*) on Katyayanputra's *Jnanaprasthanasutra*, the principal Abhidharma text of Sarvastivadin Hinayana. The Sanskrit Vibhasha was attributed to Ashvaghosha. Among the eminent teachers of the school were Dharmatrata, Vasumitra, Buddhadeva, Dharmottara, and Ghoshaka. One of the classic texts of Buddhism was produced by Vasubandhu, a native of Gandhara, who studied the Vibhashas in Kashmir and wrote his *Abhidharmakosha* and its *Bhashya*.

The Mahayana form of Buddhism had become more prevalent than the Hinayana. The two forms did not differ so much in the rules of monastic life as in doctrine and the modes of worship. The Mahayanists regarded the Buddha as eternal and beyond description. They advocated complete detachment, even from the monk's robe, and absolute renunciation even of the desire for *nirvana*. Self-effacement was to be sought not for one's own *nirvana* but for the service of others, in not one but several lives. This altruistic ideal was the hallmark of Mahayanism. The Mahayanist monk had to pursue six 'perfections' (*paramitas*): liberality (*dana*), morality (*shila*), forbearance (*kshanti*), mental strength (*virya*), mental concentration (*dhyana*), and knowledge of the truth (*prajna*). These 'perfections' had to be relentlessly pursued in a number of 'births', leading to the state of *bodhi-chitta* who after many lives of altruistic service as Bodhisattva was destined to attain *nirvana* and to become Buddha. Two schools of thought arose in Mahayanism too: the Madhyamika, with Nagarjuna as its accredited founder, and the Yogachara, with Ashvaghosha as its putative founder. Maitreya's *Abhisamayalankara-Kartika* was an authoritative text of the Yogacharas. Among the luminaries of this school were Asangha of Ayodhya and his younger brother Vasubandhu of Nalanda, both natives of Gandhara.

Tantric elements had begun to enter Buddhism before the end of the eighth century. Dharnis, though only a part of the Mahayana Sutras, became increasingly important. The ritual of the worship of the Buddhas and the Bodhisattvas was elaborated, including repetition of *mantras* on days regarded as auspicious throughout the year. Tara came to be associated with Avalokiteshvara. In Tantric Buddhism, known as Vajrayana, Truth came to be equated with the phenomenal world and with the Buddha. Great importance was attached to *mantras* and directions were formulated for drawing pictures of Buddhas, Bodhisattvas, Tara and other deities; rites and ceremonies of worship were elaborated. There were two schools of Vajrayana: the Madhyamika and the Yogachara. In the latter, *mudras*, *mandalas*, *mantras*, *yoga* and *hathayoga* became increasingly important. Tara came to be treated as the Shakti of the Adi Buddha. The ritual of eating meat and indulging in sexual intercourse became a feature of Tantric Buddhism.

Hiuen Tsang makes some general observations on the character of Buddhism in India. The protagonists of the Mahayana and the Hinayana lived apart. There were eighteen schools in all, each claiming pre-eminence for itself. They were at variance with one another, and 'their contending utterances rise like the angry waves of the sea'. Hiuen Tsang indicates that the attitude of the Brahmans towards the Buddhists was hostile. The monks were governed according to the distinctive rules of each fraternity. They had three kinds of robes. Facilities given in a monastery to the monk depended upon his proficiency in Buddhist literature. At the lowest level was the one who could explain one class of literature; he was exempted from manual labour (*karmadan*). The monk of the highest status was the one who could explain six classes of books; he could ride an elephant and have an escort. The one who distinguished himself in a public debate by 'refined language, subtle investigation, deep penetration, and severe logic' was mounted on an elephant covered with precious ornaments, and escorted by many to the gates of the monastery.

Hiuen Tsang provides a vivid picture of the state of Buddhism from Nagarahara to Mathura. The people of Nagarahara cultivated the religion of the Buddha, and few believed in other doctrines. The monasteries were many but not the monks; the stupas were 'desolate and ruined'. To the east of the capital was a stupa said to have been built by Ashoka, commemorating the meeting of Sakya as a Bodhisattva with Dipankara Buddha, when the former covered the muddy road with his deer skin and his hair let loose for the Buddha to pass. He was assured of Buddhahood. On fast days all sorts of flowers rained down here and excited a religious frame of mind in the people.

In the city itself there were the ruins of a great stupa which at one time had contained a tooth of the Buddha. By its side was a small stupa which, it was believed, had fallen from heaven and placed itself there. To the south-west of the city was a stupa built by the people out of reverence for the spot where Tathagata had alighted for the sake of converting men. He had come from mid-India passing through the air. To the east was a stupa on the spot where Sakya as a Bodhisattva had met Dipankara Buddha and bought flowers from a girl who sold them on the condition that she should always be born as his wife. This belief provided a motif for the sculptors of the Punjab. About 6 kilometres from the city was a monastery with 'a storeyed tower' but it had no monks. In its centre was a stupa believed to have been built by Ashoka.

Close to this monastery was a waterfall, and the mountain side had a great cavern regarded as the abode of the Naga Gopala. There used to be a shadow of the Buddha here in former times, 'bright as the true form, with all its characteristic marks'. Now it appeared only in a feeble likeness. 'But whoever prays with fervent faith, he is mysteriously endowed, and he sees it clearly before him, though not for long'. According to the *Life of Hiuen Tsang*, he prayed here fervently and saw the shadow. Hiuen Tsang relates the legend in which Gopala, a shepherd, is made a great dragon to destroy the people and Tathagata takes pity on the people. By his spiritual power he comes from mid-India and the dragon accepts his precept against killing. Tathagata accepts his request to leave his shadow in the cavern. Outside the gate of the cavern of the shadow there were two square stones: on each was the impression of the foot of Tathagata. To the north-west of the cavern there was a stupa where the Buddha had walked up and down. Beside this was another stupa containing some of the hair and the nail-parings of Tathagata. In yet another stupa nearby, Tathagata had manifested the secret principles of his true doctrine. To the west of the cavern was a rock on which Tathagata had spread out his robe after washing: 'the marks of the tissue still exist'.

A stupa in the town of Hidda contained a bone relic of the Buddha, enclosed in a precious casket and placed in the middle of the stupa. People pressed a paste of scented earth on to the bone for 'lucky or unlucky presages'. Close to this stupa was another with a similar precious casket containing a similar relic. Yet another stupa contained his eyeball. It was as large as an *amra* fruit and 'bright and clear throughout'. There was also his *sanghati* robe, made of fine cotton of a yellow-red colour. Contained in another case was his sandalwood staff, with its rings of tin. These five sacred objects 'often work miracles'. The king of Kapisa had appointed five Brahmans to offer scents and flowers to these objects. The people who wished to see the relics had to pay a gold piece; those who wished to take an impression had to pay five pieces. Prices were similarly fixed for the other relics. The worshippers were 'numerous' despite the heavy charges.

In Gandhara most of the people belonged to 'heretical schools' and a few believed in 'the true law'. This 'borderland of India' had produced many scholars, Narayanadeva, Asangha Bhodisattva, Vasubandhu Bodhisattva, Dharmatrata, Manorhita, and the noble Parsva, for example. There were about a thousand monasteries in Gandhara but 'deserted and in ruins', 'filled with wild shrubs, and solitary to the last degree'. The stupas too were mostly decayed. The precious tower of the bowl (*patra*) of the Buddha was nothing more than the foundations. Outside the royal city there was a *pipal* tree about 30 metres high: the four past Buddhas had sat under it and their 'sitting figures' were still there. It was believed that the remaining 996 Buddhas would also sit here during the Bhadra Kalpa. As foretold by Sakya Tathagata, Kanishka built a stupa to the south of this tree, over relics of the Buddha. People burnt incense and offered flowers, and paid their devotions with a sincere faith for cure in serious sickness: 'In many cases a remedy is found'. There were two figures of the Buddha, sitting cross-legged under the Bodhi tree. One of these was nearly 2 metres high. On the southern steps of the great stupa, there was a painted statue of the Buddha about 5 metres high, with two bodies from the middle upwards. Another representation of the Buddha in white stone was about 6 metres high. Different musical sounds were at times heard here. This was the work of the sages of the past who 'at times are seen, walking around the stupas'. An old monastery to the west of the great stupa was somewhat decayed. The few monks there studied the Little Vehicle (Hinayana). Many authors of Shastras had lived here and attained Arhatship. Among them was the honourable Parsvika who had embraced Buddhism at the age of eighty. To the east of his chamber was a building where Vasubandhu prepared his *Abhidharmakosha Shastra*. To the south of his house was the pavilion in which Manorhita composed his *Vibhasha Shastra*.

To the east of the city of Pushkalavati was a stupa believed to have been built by Ashoka. Here the four former Buddhas had preached the law. Vasumitra had composed his *Abhidharma Prakarana-pada* here. To the north of the city was a monastery, its halls deserted. There were very few monks, and they followed the Hinayana. Dharmatrata had composed his *Samyuktabhidharma Shastra* in this monastery. By its side was a stupa attributed to Ashoka. Sakya had been born in this country a thousand times as king and had given his eyes as an offering in each birth as a Bodhisattva before becoming the Buddha.

Not far from this monastery were two stupas, one believed to have been built by Brahma and the other by Indra. These structures were in ruins. About 16 kilometres to their north-west was another stupa where Tathagata had converted the mother of the demons so that she refrained from hurting people. The common folk of this country made sacrifices to her in order to obtain children. About 16 kilometres to the north of the stupa was another, where Samaka Bodhisattva had nourished his blind father and mother as a boy (Sarwan of Punjabi folklore). About 64 kilometres to the south-east of this stupa, there was another which was associated with a prince who had given his father's great elephant in charity to Brahmans and had been banished. Close to it was a monastery with about fifty Hinayanist monks. Here Ishvara had composed a Shastra. Not far from here was another monastery with about fifty Hinayanist monks. Two stupas in this area were attributed to Ashoka. About 32 kilometres away was a monastery with a few Mahayanist monks. Here too a stupa was attributed to

Ashoka. In Salatura, the birth place of Panini, there was a stupa commemorating the conversion of a disciple of Panini at the hands of an Arhat.

The people of Taxila honoured the three gems: the Buddha, the Dhamma and the Sangha. They all studied the Mahayana. About 24 kilometres to the north-west of the capital, was the tank of Nagaraja Elapatra, associated with a *bhikshu* who in the time of Kashyapa Buddha had destroyed an Elapatra tree. The people of the country used to go to the side of the tank with the monks to pray for rain or for fine weather, and their prayers were answered. About 8 kilometres to the south-east of the tank, there was a stupa attributed to Ashoka. Sakya Tathagata had predicted that one of the four great gem treasures which were to appear of themselves on the appearance of Maitreya should be in this land. The spot on which stood the stupa remained perfectly still whenever there was an earthquake. But if men try to dig the earth here for the treasure, the earth shakes and they are thrown down headlong. By the side of this stupa was a monastery in ruins: there was no monk. A stupa attributed to Ashoka was about 2.5 miles to the north of the city. On feast days it glowed with light, and divine flowers fell around it, and heavenly music was heard. This was the spot where Tathagata as the king of the country had cut off his head in a thousand successive births for acquiring Buddhahood. By the side of this stupa was a monastery with its courts deserted, but there were still a few monks. This was the monastery where Kumara-labdha had composed several treatises of the school of Sautrantikas.

To the south-west of Takshashila was a stupa believed to have been built by Ashoka in memory of his son Kunala who had been unjustly accused by his stepmother and blinded. 'When the blind pray to it with fervent faith, many of them recover their sight.' Hiuen Tsang relates the story of Kunala. In its broad outline, this story is similar to that of Puran Bhagat in the folklore of the Punjab.

To the south of the capital city of Simhapura was a stupa attributed to Ashoka. Its decorations were 'much injured'. Spiritual wonders were 'continually connected with it'. The monastery by its side was deserted and had no monks. About 15 kilometres to the south-east of the city was another stupa attributed to Ashoka. There were ten tanks and a monastery without any monk. In the monastery at Manikyala, however, there were about a hundred monks, all given to the study of the Mahayana. A stupa near this monastery commemorated the sacrifice of Mahasattva as a prince to revive a hungry cub with his blood. 'On this account all the earth and the plants of this place are dyed with a blood colour'. Another stupa nearby was attributed to Ashoka. Spiritual 'indications' appeared here from time to time. 'Whatever sick there are who can circumambulate it are mostly restored to health.' About 16 kilometres to the east of the stupa, there was a monastery with about 200 Mahayana monks. By its side was a stupa on a spot where Tathagata had restrained a wicked *yaksha* from eating flesh.

Not many people in the Takka country believed in the Buddha. In former times there were many charitable houses (*punyasalas*) in this country to provide food, clothing and medicine to the poor and to travellers. There were about ten monasteries extant. The one in the capital (near the present-day Sialkot) had about a hundred Hinayana monks. Vasubandhu had compressed his *Paramarthasatya Shastra* in this monastery. By its side was a stupa. The four past Buddhas had preached the law here; the traces of their feet could still be seen. Over a kilometre from this place was a stupa attributed to Ashoka. Tathagata had stopped here on his northward journey for propagating the Dhamma. In a great city on the eastern border of Takka (close to the present-day Lahore), Hiuen Tsang stayed for a month to study the Sutras, the *Shata-shastra* and the *Shata-shastra Vaipulyam*. The author of the last work, Deva Bodhisattva, was a disciple of Nagarjuna.

In Chinapatti there were ten monasteries. The capital and the country derived its name from the fact that Kanishka had kept some Chinese hostages here. Its monastery could boast of a scholar like Vinitaprabha who had mastered the three *Pitakas* and composed a commentary on the *Panchas-khanda Shastra* and the *Vidyamitra Siddhi-tridasha Shastra*. Hiuen Tsang stayed here for more than a year to study the *Abhidharma Shastra*, the *Abhidharma-prakarna-sasana Shastra*, and the *Nyayadvara-taraka Shastra*, among others. Presumably in the kingdom of Chinapatti, the monastery of Tamasavana (the dark forest) had about 300 monks 'of conspicuous virtue and pure life'. They were deeply versed in Hinayana, and studied the doctrine of the Sarvastivada school. 'The 1000 Buddhas of the Bhadarakalpa will explain, in this country, to the assembly of the Devas the principle of the excellent law.' This was the monastery in which the master of Shastras, Katyayana, had composed his *Abhidharmajnana-prasthana Shastra*. A stupa was attributed to Ashoka. By its side were the traces of the four past Buddhas, where they sat and walked. Many *arhats* had attained *nirvana* here. 'Their teeth and bones still remain.'

In Jalandhar, there were about fifty monasteries, with about 2,000 monks. They studied both the Mahayana and the Hinayana. Udhita, the king of this country, met an Arhat and heard the law and was converted to Buddhism. Formerly, he had shown great partiality to the heretics, but now he built a number of monasteries and stupas throughout 'the five Indies' wherever there were traces of the Buddha. He showed open respect for the virtuous and reputable monks and punished the disorderly ones. In the Nagaradhana monastery of the royal city of Jalandhar there was Chandravarma who was thoroughly acquainted with the *Tripitaka*. Hiuen Tsang stayed here for four months to study the *Prakarana-pada-vibhasha Shastra.*

In Kulu there were about twenty monasteries and about a thousand Mahayanist monks. There were only a few followers of the other schools (*nikayas*). Tathagata was believed to have come to this country 'to preach the law and to save men'. A stupa in the middle of the country, attributed to Ashoka, was meant to commemorate Tathagata's visit.

The people of the Satudra sincerely believed in the law of the Buddha and showed great respect for it. Within and outside the capital city (near the present-day Sirhind) were ten monasteries; the halls were now 'deserted and cold', and there were but few monks. Over a kilometre from the city there was a stupa attributed to Ashoka, 'where the four past Buddhas sat or walked'.

In Thanesar, there were three monasteries and about 700 monks who studied the Hinayana. Over a kilometre to the north-west of the city was a stupa attributed to Ashoka. Brilliant light was frequently emitted from it and 'many spiritual prodigies' were exhibited.

In Srughna (Sugh), there were five monasteries, with about 1,000 monks. Most of them studied the Hinayana. They had the reputation of being learned and polite in debates and discourses. Men from different regions came here to get their doubts clarified. Close to the capital city there was a monastery and a stupa, attributed to Ashoka, to mark the place where Tathagata preached the law. In another stupa nearby there were his hair and nails. Around this were the stupas of Sariputra and Maudgalyayana, and a large number of other Arhats. Jayagupta, a monk of this kingdom, was renowned for his study of the *Tripitaka*. Hiuen Tsang stayed here 'one winter and half the spring season' to study the Vibhasha according to the school of Sautrantikas.

In Mathura there were about twenty monasteries with 2,000 monks. They studied equally the Mahayana and the Hinayana. Three stupas were attributed to Ashoka. There were 'very many traces' of the four past Buddhas. There were stupas of the holy followers of Tathagata:

Sariputra, Mudgalaputra, Purnamaitrayaniputra, Upali, Ananda, Rahula, and Manjushri. Every year during the months in which long fasts are observed, and during the six fast days of each month, the monks went there with offerings. Those who studied the Abhidharma honoured Sariputra; those who practised meditation honoured Mudgalaputra; those who recited the Sutras honoured Purnamaitrayaniputra; those who studied the Vinaya did reverence to Upali; the *bhikshunis* honoured Ananda; the young novices who were not yet fully ordained honoured Rahula; and those who studied the Mahayana did reverence to the Bodhisattvas. The king of the country and his ministers applied themselves to these religious duties with zeal. Jewelled banners were spread out, rich parasols were displayed, the smoke of incense rose to the clouds, and flowers were scattered in every direction; the sun and the moon were concealed as by clouds hanging over the moist valleys.

The picture of Buddhism that emerges from this evidence shows the existence of a large number of monasteries and stupas in the Punjab. Many of them were associated with the Buddha, Bodhisattvas, and Ashoka. They presented a beautiful spectacle, but many of them were either totally abandoned or on the decline. The number of monks was decreasing. Several rulers were still well disposed towards Buddhism but only Harsha and Udhita were keen to promote it. Like the great Buddhist structures, great Buddhist works had been produced in the past, and there were still some well known scholars in some of the monasteries. Their creativity, however, was confined to commentaries. It is not insignificant that Hiuen Tsang stayed in the Punjab for over three years to study various branches of Buddhist literature. Relatively speaking, the Mahayana was dominant in the Doabs and the Hinayana in the Satlej-Jamuna Divide. Three Buddhas had appeared in the universe before Sakya, and 996 more were to come. Each Buddhahood was the culmination of a large number of lives of Bodhisattvahood and this process was to continue for a number of cosmic cycles (*kalpas*). The supreme aim of life was to attain *nirvana* and thereby to end the transmigratory cycle, the source of sorrow and suffering. Meditation and asceticism were believed to lead one along the right path. Emphasis was laid on compassion and non-injury to living beings. Buddhist ritual was marked by the worship of idols and sacred relics by incantations, the burning of incense, and offerings (precious articles as well as flowers). At places, rates were fixed for the earning of different degrees of religious merit. Belief in the supernatural was common. Prayers were believed to affect the behaviour of nature. Boons could result from ritual, and the sick could be healed. Brahmanical gods like Indra and Brahma were introduced to the Buddhist world of the *devas*, and male and female demons were yoked to the cause of Buddhism.

Just as Ashoka and Kanishka were looked upon as the promoters of Buddhism in the past, Mihirakula was seen as its destroyer. According to Hiuen Tsang, Mihirakula was offended by the indifference of certain monks to his inclination towards Buddhism. He issued an edict to destroy all the monks throughout 'the five Indies', to overthrow the law of the Buddha, and to leave nothing remaining. He destroyed 1,600 stupas and monasteries in Gandhara alone. Thousands of people were slain or enslaved. Mihirakula withered away like a falling leaf at last.

Modern scholars hold different views on the destructive role of the Hunas. Marshall attributes the destruction of monasteries at Taxila to the predecessors of Toramana and Mihirakula. Dani discounts destruction at the hands of the Epthalites. There is no doubt that state patronage or persecution could affect the fortunes of Buddhism, but state policy alone would account neither for its earlier popularity nor for its later disappearance. No rulers seem to have tried to promote Buddhism after Harsha and Udhita, and no guilds of traders or artisans appear to have been associated with monasteries. Divided among themselves, the monks were compromising with popular beliefs and practices or turning monasteries into ivory towers. The exponents of other faiths, especially the Brahmans, appear to have become more active. As an outpost of the Hindu Shahis, Taxila shows no signs of Buddhism. Survivals of Buddhism in the Satlej-Jamuna Divide are indicated by a bronze image of the Buddha from Hansi, and a few sandstone heads of the Buddha from the districts of Ambala and Rohtak, ascribed to the ninth and tenth centuries. Buddhism had virtually disappeared from the Punjab by the end of the first millennium AD. Alberuni, who was seriously interested in Buddhism and wanted to know about it, was unable to find any Buddhist scholar or a Buddhist work in the Punjab.

ASCENDANCY OF VAISHNAVISM, SHAIVISM AND SHAKTAISM

The religious systems which largely replaced Buddhism by the end of the tenth century were the Vaishnava, Shaiva and the Shakta. All over the subcontinent, Lakshmi came to be associated with Vishnu as his consort, and the images of Vishnu and Lakshmi became an essential feature of Vaishnava temples. The incarnations of Vishnu became increasingly popular. In Vedic literature, Vamana (dwarf) is associated with Vishnu; Varaha (boar), Matsya (fish) and Kurma (tortoise) are mentioned independently; Narasimha (man-lion) is alluded to. In the *Mahabharata*, Vishnu has four *avatars,* the Dwarf, Boar, Man-Lion, and Man (Vasudeva-Krishna); elsewhere in the text, Rama Bhargava and Rama Dasharatha are also mentioned; and at yet another place Matsya, Kurma, Hamsa and Kalki are mentioned. The *Harivamsha* and the *Matsya Purana* each has a list of ten *avatars* of Vishnu, but the two lists are only partially common. The epigraphic records of the fourth to the eighth centuries contain evidence of the worship of the incarnations of Vishnu. There is an elaborate mythology of Vishnu, and there is abundant sculptural evidence in support of this mythology.

Shaivism flourished side by side with Vaishnavism and became probably more important than Vaishnavism in the eighth, ninth and tenth centuries. Shaiva Agamas became as important as the Vaishnava Samhitas, and Shaivism found increasing representation in Puranic literature. Architectural and sculptural evidence from all over India leaves no doubt about the popularity of Shaivism. Uma or Parvati came to be associated with Shiva as his consort; the marriage of Shiva and Parvati became a popular motif in sculpture; Ganesha and Karttikeya became associated with them. Ganga's descent from the matted locks of Shiva became an important myth. Shiva was symbolized by the *linga* as the god of fertility and his Trimurti image symbolized his superiority over Brahma and Vishnu. He is also shown in sculpture as the master of dancing, musical instruments, Shastras, and Yoga. Equally popular were images in which he is depicted standing side by side with Uma or sitting with her near or on Nandi. Parvati sitting on his thigh in the Uma-Maheshvara images was perhaps more popular at the end of the period under consideration.

The Shaktas, or the worshippers of the goddess under various names, were next in importance only to the Shaivas and Vaishnavas. The Samkhya philosophy with its concepts of Prusha and Prakriti made the association of Shakti with a male god rather easy. We have noticed the association of the Buddhist Tara with Avalokiteshvara. What raised goddess to the position of the supreme deity was perhaps the popularity of her exploits described in the *Devimahatmya* chapters of the *Markandeya Purana* in which the goddess destroys Mahishasura, Raktavija, Shambha and Nishambha, and Chunda and Munda. The importance attached to these exploits is reflected in the images of the goddess, especially as Mahishasuramardini with eight or ten arms. The easy association of the goddess with 'the mother' (Amba) and the subordination of the 'seven mothers' or 'eight mothers' to her, combined her benign aspect with the fierce and ferocious, assimilating Devi or Durga with Shiva. Ganesha and Karttikeya gained greater importance with the emergence of Devi. The climax came with her revelation of the Tantras which, as claimed by the Shaktas, superseded all previous systems of religious belief and practice for the Kali Age. The Shakta Tantras, thus, became comparable with Shaiva Agamas and Vaishnava Samhitas. In theory, the Shakta cult was open to women and Shudras. To the Tantric Buddhist ritual of eating meat and indulging in sexual intercourse was added the use of liquor, fish and grains in rites which were practised secretly or openly.

In the face of the rising tide of the Shaiva, Shakta and Vaishnava faiths, only Surya of the Vedic gods appears to have retained some importance, if we were to go by the evidence of temples and sculptures. The iconic representation of Surya became more elaborate, and he was shown sometimes jointly with Narayana or Shiva or in combination with the gods of the Trimurti of Brahma, Shiva and Vishnu. Brahma became less important as the supreme deity in his own right. Sarasvati came to be associated with him. As the creator of the Vedas he could not become wholly extinct but very often he was shown in a position subordinate to that of Shiva or Vishnu; or a niche was found for him in both Shaiva and Vaishnava temples. Some of the other Vedic gods survived as the guardians of different quarters: Indra of the east, Varuna of the west, and Yama of the south. For the north, however, there was the new god Kubera. Agni was associated with the south-east, and Nirriti with the south-west. Whereas Vayu was associated with the north-west, the guardian of the north-east was a new god, Ishana. In many of the Vaishnava and Shaiva temples in different parts of India, these eight guardians (*ashta-dikpalas*) were found carved on various parts of the outside wall. While Shiva and Vishnu were Vedic gods only in name, and the non-Vedic Mother Goddess had come to share the stage with them, the other Vedic deities became peripheral.

The period under consideration was marked by the emergence of Puranic literature. In the Brahmanas, the term *purana* was used to designate 'cosmogonic inquiries'. In the *Mahabharata* it came to be used for 'ancient legendary lore'. Furthermore, the epic refers to eighteen Puranas as literary works. However, the extant Puranas were composed later than the *Mahabharata*. Many of them draw upon the epic and the *Harivamsha* but they contain much other matter, both old and new. Collectively, they deal with cosmology, descriptions of the earth, cosmic ages, exploits of gods and heroes, accounts of the *avatars* of Vishnu, the genealogies of the solar and lunar dynasties, the thousand names of Vishnu and Shiva, rites and customs, for example. Smriti material relating to rites which formed the subject matter of the Smriti of Manu and of Yajnavalkya was added to some of the Puranas in the fifth and sixth centuries. Later on, new matter was added, relating to gifts, the glorification of holy places, the consecration of images, sacrifices to the planets and their appeasement, popular worship (*puja*) and vows (*vrata*). Some of the Puranas tend to be rather encyclopaedic in terms of their contents.

The *Vishnu Purana* and the *Bhagavata Purana* were the Vaishnava texts *par excellence*, glorifying Vishnu and the exploits of Krishna as his incarnation. In the former, the myths of Prahlad, Dhruva, and the churning of the ocean are related, and Kaliyuga is forecast in detail. In the latter, Buddha and Kapila appear as the incarnations of Vishnu. The *Brahma Purana*, known also as the *Adi Purana*, dwells on the rewards of Vishnu's worship, the legends of Krishna and sacred places; it emphasizes the importance of the *shraddhas* and the duties of *varnas* and *ashramas*. The *Padma Purana* contains among other things the story of Rama, based not only on the *Ramayana* but also on Kalidasa's *Raghuvamsha*. The *Adhyatma Ramayana* is considered to be a part of the *Brahmanda Purana* which talks of devotion to Rama as the sure path to salvation, and glorifies sacred places. The *Narada Purana* is professedly 'sectarian' in favour of Vishnu. The creator of the world in the *Brahmavaivarta Purana* is Brahma, but its last book describes the life of Krishna; Ganesha is regarded as Krishna's incarnation; and Prakriti resolves itself into five goddesses–Durga, Lakshmi, Sarasvati, Savitri and Radha. The *Garuda Purana* is very comprehensive in its scope, retailing the contents of the *Ramayana*, the *Mahabharata* and the *Harivamsha*, and dealing with cosmology, astronomy, astrology, medicine, metrics, grammar, polity, chiromancy, omens and portents, and the 'science' of precious stones.

All these Puranas leave the impression that Vaishnavism was coming to the fore on the religious scene. But this is only one side of the picture. The *Agni Purana* is essentially a Shaiva work, dealing with Ganesha, Durga and the Linga, and it includes a variety of other subjects: astronomy, astrology, polity, law, medicine, metrics, grammar and the rites of marriage and death. The *Vayu Purana* contains many legends which glorify Shiva. Indeed, an alternative name for it is *Shiva Purana*. The worship of Shiva, especially in the form of *linga*, is sought to be propagated in the *Linga Purana*. The *Skanda Purana* is said to have consisted of six Samhitas which emphasized the worship of Shiva. Its Kashi-Khanda underlines the sanctity of Banaras as a sacred place. The extant *Vamana Purana* has a considerable portion on *linga* worship and, among other things, deals with many legends about Shiva and Uma, Ganesha, and Karttikeya. The extant *Bhavishya Purana* describes the Brahmanical rites and duties of the *varnas*, but the original Purana is said to have contained much of the matter now incorporated in the *Vayu*, *Matsya* and *Brahmanda Puranas*. The least 'sectarian' of all is the *Markandeya Purana*, dealing with Indra, Agni and Surya as well as Vishnu and Shiva. As we noticed earlier, it deals also with the goddess in its *Devimahatmya* portion which glorifies her exploits, including the episode of the Mahishasura-mardini. The idea that Brahma, Vishnu and Shiva are only one being is emphasized in the *Markandeya Purana*, though it is found in the *Harivamsha* and the *Padma Purana* as well.

It is maintained that the Puranas afford us great insight into all aspects and phases of Hinduism, its mythology and philosophy, idol-worship, love of God, and superstitions. Festivals and ceremonies are described. It is important for us, therefore, to remember that most of the Puranas were known in the Punjab by the end of the tenth century. Alberuni gives a list of eighteen Puranas on the basis of his investigations in the Punjab. This list does not tally with the one given by Alberuni from the *Vishnu Purana*. In fact, only twelve titles are common to the two lists. In other words, Alberuni's evidence suggests the existence of twenty-four Puranas. Three of these were studied by him more thoroughly: the *Vayu*, the *Matsya*, and the *Aditya*. There are also texts called Upapuranas and their number too is conventionally stated to be eighteen. At least one of these is often quoted by Alberuni as the *Vishnudharma* (*Vishnudharmottara*) which he attributed to Markandeya.

For philosophic as well as religious ideas Alberuni quotes Kapila and Patanjali as often as the *Gita*. The book associated with Patanjali is not named but two works are attributed to Kapila: the *Samkhya* and the *Nyayabhasha*. Alberuni refers also to the *Mimamsa* of Jaimini, the *Laukayata* of Brihaspati, and the *Agastyamata* of Agastya. There is hardly any doubt that philosophic Shastras were known in the Punjab.

The Samkhya system, on which Buddhism and Jainism were based, was as important as the Vedanta on which much of the later developments in thought and religion in India came to be based. Kapila was a pre-Buddhist figure but his name remained associated with the Samkhya system. Panchashikha's Sutras were superseded by Ishvara-Krshna's *Samkhya-Karika* at the beginning of the period under consideration. A commentary on this work was composed by Gaudapada in the late seventh or the early eighth century. Alberuni refers to a work of Gauda known after his name. Matter (*prakriti*) and individual souls (*purushas*) in the Samkhya are without beginning and end. The idea of a god who creates and governs the universe is redundant in this context. His existence is denied. The world itself is real, its diversity explained by the three qualities (*gunas*) of matter: *sattvas*, *rajas* and *tamas*. The soul itself possesses no qualities. Salvation consists in its absolute isolation from matter.

Closely related to the Samkhya was the Yoga school of philosophy, believed to have been expounded by Patanjali. A commentary on his work was written by Vyas in the seventh century. The idea of a personal god is present in the *Yoga Sutras* but this does not affect the basic philosophy. The individual souls are not derived from God as the 'special soul' but are without a beginning. The final aim of life is represented as the isolation of the soul from matter and not union with or absorption in God. By mental concentration on a particular object, one could acquire supernatural powers and attain salvation. One of the four chapters of the *Yoga Sutras* deals with miraculous powers (*vibhutis*) and another with the isolation of the redeemed soul; the two other chapters relate to deep meditation (*samadhi*) and its means (*sadhana*). In the later commentaries, mental concentration is referred to as *raja-yoga* and the external expedients as *kriya-yoga*. A more intense form of the latter is called *hatha-yoga* in which a number of sitting postures (*asanas*) and contortions of the limbs (*mudras*) are recommended.

Opposed to the dualistic and atheistic schools of Samkhya and Yoga there were two schools of theistic philosophy, both known as the *Mimamsa*. The *Purva Mimamsa* was set forth by Jaimini in his *Karma-Mimamsa Sutras*. Also known as *Karma-Mimamsa* or simply as *Mimamsa*, this system emphasizes the importance of the sacred ceremonies and the rewards which result from them. Holding the Veda to be eternal, it lays stress on the proposition that articulate sounds are eternal. Therefore the connection of a word with its sense is by nature inherent in the word itself. The *Bhashya* of Shabara Svamin is a commentary on the *Mimamsa Sutras*. In the seventh century, Kumarila wrote commentaries on Shabara Svamin's own commentary in his *Tantra-Varttika* and his *Shloka-Varttika* (actually a metrical paraphrase of Shabara's exposition of the first aphorism of Patanjali). Kumarila laid great stress on the ritual side of the Vedas, especially the Brahmanas. He attacked the Buddhist and Jain logicians with zeal.

In the *Uttara Mimamsa*, usually called Vedanta, the stress is laid on the philosophy of the Upanishads, interpreted in terms of idealistic monism (*advaita-vada*) which denies existence to everything other than Brahman. The empirical world is an illusion (*maya*). Under the influence of desire (*trishna*), appropriately called 'deer-thirst' (*mriga-trishna*), the soul perceives the illusion as reality (just as the deer perceives water in the desert). This illusion is the result of innate ignorance (*avidya*). It vanishes with the acquisition of true knowledge. The semblance of any distinction between soul and God disappears, resulting in liberation (*moksha*), which is the primary aim of human life. Brahma, as the Lord of the Universe, is an illusory form of the only real Brahman or the Ultimate Reality. This attempt to make the Vedanta theistic remains unconvincing. As a system of philosophy, the Vedanta needs no personal God. The doctrines of this system were set forth by Badarayana in his *Brahma Sutras* which become clear only with the help of Shankaracharya's commentary in his *Bhashya*. With its exposition by Shankara, the Vedanta made a bid for supremacy over all other systems, including the *Purva Mimamsa* which regarded *karma* (ritual) as the essence of the Vedas against the Vedanta's virtually exclusive stress on *jnana* (knowledge).

Shankara is said to have created such an extraordinary position for Vedanta that writers belonging to both Shaivism and Vaishnavism began to utilize it as the philosophical basis of their own creeds. This could be done by identifying Vishnu or Shiva with Brahman, making the deity immanent and transcendant at one and the same time. In the religious phenomenon known as Kashmir Shaivism, the individual soul and the world are essentially identical with Shiva. Its beginnings are traced to the *Shiva Sutras* of Vasugupta who lived in the late eighth-early ninth century. He was followed by Kallata and Somananda, to be followed by Utpala, Ramakantha and Abhinavagupta. The last named, a contemporary of Alberuni, was the author of the Advaita work *Paramarthasara*. Shiva or Shambhu, the Supreme God, is the Ultimate Reality; *atman* is the immutable and perfect self of all beings. Salvation consists in the soul's recognition of its identity with Shiva. *Moksha* is a return to the original state of perfection and purity of consciousness. According to Abhinavagupta, when the imagined duality has vanished and one has surmounted the illusion of *maya*, one is merged in Brahman 'as water in water, as milk in milk'. No grief or delusion can befall him 'who surveys the universe as *brahman*'.

Despite his preoccupation with Buddhism, Hiuen Tsang noticed the importance of Brahmans in India. He refers to their dedication to the study of the Vedas. He refers to a hundred *deva* temples in Gandhara and to over three hundred in the area between the Chenab and the Jamuna. But that is all. The meagre information he provides on non-Buddhist faiths in the Punjab is none the less precious. Outside the western gate of Pushkalavati there was a *deva* temple with which were associated 'constant miracles'. At another place in Gandhara, on a high mountain, there was a temple dedicated to Bhima Devi, wife of Ishvara Deva.

> It has the reputation of working numerous miracles, and therefore is venerated by all, so that from every part of India men came to pay their vows and seek prosperity thereby. Both poor and rich assemble here from every part, near and distant. Those who wish to see the form of the divine spirit, being filled with faith and free from doubt, after fasting seven days are privileged to behold it, and obtain for the most part their prayers.

Below the mountain was the temple of Mahesvara Deva. The 'heretics' who came here to offer sacrifice covered themselves with ashes. Many people in Takka offered sacrifice to Devas and heavenly spirits in some hundreds of temples. According to the *Life of Hiuen Tsang*, in a city on the eastern border of Takka (near the present-day Lahore) an old Brahman was an authority on the Vedas and other books. The majority of the people of this city of several thousand dwellings were 'heretics': they did not believe in the Buddha. In Jalandhar, all the 'heretics' were cinder-sprinkled Pashupatas.

Hiuen Tsang observed that within a circuit of about 64 kilometres of Thanesar was an area locally known as 'the land of religious merit'. Here a great battle was fought in a very remote period of time on the assumption that death on this battlefield led to 'heavenly joys'. Obedient grandchildren and pious children who assisted their aged parents in walking about this land reaped happiness without bounds. Rewards for all acts in this land were out of all proportion to their intrinsic merit. That was why it was called 'the field of religious merit' (*dharmakshetra*). By the fifth century the sanctity of Kurukshetra as a place of pilgrimage had come to be recognized by the Brahmanical world. In a stone inscription from Laos, Kurukshetra is regarded as 'the most distinguished in all the three worlds'. Here all sins were washed away. The merit of pilgrimage to Kurukshetra was equal to the merit gained from a thousand horse sacrifices, a hundred *vajapeya* sacrifices, and the gift of a hundred thousand cows. In an inscription from Pehowa, Kurukshetra is invoked to remove the taint of all sins.

The field of religious merit was matched by the river of religious merit, the river Ganges which could wash away countless sins. 'Those who are weary of life, if they end their days in it, are borne to heaven and receive happiness which a man dies and his bones are cast into the river, he can not fall into an evil way; whilst he is carried by its waters and forgotten by men, his soul is preserved in safety in the other world.' Hiuen Tsang relates an anecdote in which Deva Bodhisattva tries to demonstrate to the people that the water of the Ganges cannot reach their dead ancestors. In the *Life of Hiuen Tsang* it is stated further that in popular belief those who drink water of the Ganges, or even rinse their mouth therefrom, 'escape from all danger and calamities, and when they die are born in heaven, and enjoy happiness'. A number of beliefs were thus associated with the Ganges by the common people in the early seventh century. As for the Saraswati, in an inscription from Pehowa, it is invoked to cut the bonds of misery from all sides, and to serve as a boat for crossing the ocean of mundane existence.

Hiuen Tsang noticed the presence of Jains in the Punjab. In Simhapura, a particular place was associated with the original teacher of 'the white-robed heretics'. Here, he had arrived at the knowledge of the principles he sought, and first preached the law. Presumably there was a Jain temple here. 'The persons who frequent it subject themselves to austerities; day and night they use constant diligence without relaxation. The laws of their founder are mostly fetched from the principles of the books of Buddha. These men are of different classes and select their rules and frame their precepts accordingly. The great ones are called, Bhikshus; the younger are called Sramaneras.' In their ceremonies and modes of life the Jains greatly resembled the Buddhist monks. But they went naked, or wore white clothes. They classed the figure of their sacred master with that of Tathagata, differing only in point of clothing. Hiuen Tsang saw some basic similarities between the Jains and the Buddhists. Sharing perhaps the view of his Buddhist hosts, he looked upon the Jains as deliberate imitators of the Buddhists. Jainism survived in a small way throughout the period under consideration. A typically Jain sculpture, popularly called *chaumukhi*, or four-faced, has been discovered in a village 16 kilometres east of Faridkot. Carved in schist on a square shaft, this image shows four Jina figures in *dhyana-mudra* on lion thrones. Another *chaumukhi* is preserved in the Museum at Hoshiarpur.

Translating Alberuni's *India*, Edward Sachau got the impression that India was Vaishnava rather than Shaiva. Indeed, Vishnu or Narayana is the first god in the pantheon of Alberuni's 'Hindu informants and literary authorities'. Shiva is mentioned but only incidentally and not always in a favourable manner. This was remarkable, thought Sachau, because the Hindu Shahi rulers of the Punjab were worshippers of Shiva; their coins were adorned with the image of Nandi, the vehicle of Shiva. Sachau's impression of Vaishnava dominance in the Punjab can be explained by the fact that the works collected by Alberuni were largely Vaishnava.

The religious system of the Hindus, according to Alberuni, was professedly based on the Vedas coming from God and promulgated by the mouth of Brahma. However, the Brahmans recited the Vedas without understanding its meaning; they learnt it by heart. Only a few knew its meaning and a fewer still had mastered it. The Vedas were not committed to writing. The Smriti was derived from the Vedas. Next to the Vedas were the Puranas, composed by *rishis* and, therefore, of human origin. Then there were the epics which were held in great veneration, especially the *Mahabharata*. From Alberuni's notices it appears that the majority of the people were influenced by the epics and the Puranas. This leaves the impression that the Punjab was Vaishnava rather than Shaiva. We shall see later that this was not the whole truth.

In Hindu philosophy God is one, eternal, without beginning and end, acting by free-will, almighty, all-wise, living, giving life, ruling, preserving; his sovereignty is unique, he is beyond all likeness and unlikeness, and he does not resemble anything, nor does anything resemble him; he is called Ishvara, that is, self-sufficing and beneficent; his existence alone is real; nothing else really exists. The common people, however, thought of God in human terms and went to the extent of speaking of 'wife, son, daughter, of the rendering pregnant and other physical processes' in connection with God. Such people were numerous but 'nobody minds these classes and their theories'. What the Brahmans thought and believed was important because 'they are specially trained for preserving and maintaining their religion'.

Alberuni underscores the importance of the idea of transmigration among the Hindus. As the shiboleth of Islam was 'There is no god but God, Muhammad is his prophet', of Christianity it was the trinity, and of Judaism it was the Sabbath, so the shiboleth of the Hindu religion was metempsychosis. According to this doctrine, imperishable souls wander about in perishable bodies in accordance with their actions. Ignorance was the cause of the soul's bond with bodies and knowledge was the means of liberation leading to union with God.

Alberuni refers to the trinity of Brahma the creator, Vishnu the preserver, and Shiva the destroyer. As he puts it, there were three primary forces dynamically at work in the universe. The first was called Brahma, or Prajapati, who was identical with nature insofar as it was active. The creation of the world, was attributed to Brahma. The second force was Narayana. Nature, insofar it had reached the end of its action, was now striving to preserve what had been produced. Narayana strives so to arrange the world that it should endure. The third force was called Mahadeva or Shankara but his best known name was Rudra. His work was destruction and annihilation. Alberuni sees an analogy between these three forces and the trinity of 'Father, Son and Holy Ghost' in Christianity, which infringed the unity of God.

Significantly, the common source of all the three forces for Alberuni's Hindus was Vishnu, 'a name which more properly designates the middle force'. Vishnu, thus, becomes synonymous with the Supreme Deity equated with Narayana. He was also 'a supernatural power' which prevented evil from dominating over good. For this purpose Narayana appeared in the world from time to time to restore the balance in favour of good. He kept himself occupied thus in each Age. A quotation from the *Vishnu Purana* refers to four incarnations of Vishnu in the first three *yugas*: Kapila, Rama, Vyasa and Vasudeva. A separate chapter is devoted to Vasudeva by Alberuni, underlining his connection with the Bharata War. At the end of the Kaliyuga, Vishnu would appear as Kali (Kalki).

Concerning idol-worship, Alberuni makes a distinction between 'the common uneducated people' and the learned among the Hindus. Those who marched on the path of liberation or studied philosophy and theology, and who desired abstract truth, were 'entirely free from worshipping anything but God alone'. They could never dream of worshipping an image manufactured to represent him. Nevertheless, others had been making idols of various kinds for worship. The famous idol of Multan, dedicated to the sun, was called Aditya. It was made of wood and covered with red Cordovan leather; in its two eyes were two red rubies. It was believed to be the cause of the flourishing state of the city and its accumulated treasures: pilgrims from 'all sides' came to visit it. The idol at Thanesar was called Chakraswami, the owner of the *chakra* (Vishnu). It was made of bronze, nearly the size of a man.

Alberuni quotes Varahamihira's *Samhita* on the construction of the idols of various deities. The priests who ministered to the idols belonged to different classes: the Bhagavatas were devoted to Vishnu, the Magians were devoted to the Sun, the ascetics with long hair who covered their bodies with ashes were devoted to Mahadeva, the Shamanians were devoted to the Buddha, the naked monks were devoted to Arhant, and the Brahmans in general were devoted to the Eight Mothers. Here, Alberuni refers not only to Buddhists, Jains, and the worshippers of the Sun, but also to Vaishnavas, Shaivas and Shaktas.

According to Alberuni, pilgrimages were not 'obligatory' but 'meritorious'. A holy river, a holy region or a much venerated idol was generally the object of the pilgrim who offered worship, presents, and prayers, observed fasts and gave alms to Brahmans and others on such occasions. At places of special holiness, the Hindus constructed ponds for ablution. They had attained a high degree of art in the building of tanks. The basic idea was to obviate crowding by pilgrims. This was ensured by building terraces and a circumambulatory road all around the tank. Two such tanks were at Multan and Thanesar or Kurukshetra, the theatre of the exploits of Vasudeva in the wars of Bharata. Another sacred place was Mathura where Vasudeva was born and brought up. The most sacred river for the Hindus was the Ganges, associated with Mahadeva. People threw the ashes of their dead into this river. For the Shaiva ascetics, Banaras was of great importance as a place of pilgrimage, but they also went to Kashmir and to the Himalayas.

Fasting, like pilgrimage, was not obligatory for the Hindus but it was generally regarded as meritorious. Abstention from food and remembrance of that being whose benevolence one wished to gain--a god, angel, or some other being--were the two basic conditions of fasting. There were several modes of fasting. The reward of fasting depended also on the month in which it was observed: wealth, happiness, lordship, favour with women, wisdom, health, victory, honour, reputation, or birth in a beautiful and fertile country. He who fasts during all the months, breaking the fast only twelve times, resides in paradise for 10,000 years and is reborn in a noble family. The eleventh day of the white half of every month was specially holy to Vasudeva. There were several other days holy to him. There were particular days similarly holy to other deities. There were fasts meant only for women.

Many festivals were celebrated by only women or children. There were festivals to commemorate secular events or to celebrate seasonal changes. An interesting festival in this connection was that of the vernal equinox, called Vasanta. But there were also festivals held in honour of deities and in commemoration of events deemed to be connected with them–Vasudeva, Lakshmi, Bhagvati, Gauri, the Sun, for example. The last was held at Multan. Most of the festivals were associated with Vaishnavism and Shaivism in general and with Vasudeva and Gauri in particular. On the eighth of Assuj, holy to Mahanavami, a festival was held in honour of Bhagvati (Durga) to whom children were sacrificed. The festival of Diwali on the new moon day of Kattik was associated with Lakshmi as the wife of Vasudeva (and not yet with Rama). On the night of the sixteenth of Phagun, the festival of Shivaratri was celebrated in honour of Mahadeva, when his devotees remained awake all the night and offered perfumes and flowers to him.

The evidence of Hiuen Tsang and Alberuni begins to make a lot of sense when combined with inscriptional and sculptural evidence from the Punjab. The inscription on the Sonepat copper seal of Harsha refers to one of his ancestors, as 'the most devout worshipper of the Sun'. This was true also of Adityavardhana and Prabhakaravardhana. In the inscription from the temple of Garibnath at Pehowa, the horse traders in the reign of Bhoja Pratihara offer their donation to a temple dedicated to the boar incarnation of Vishnu. The Pehowa inscription of the reign of Mahendrapala Pratihara invokes Madhava (Vishnu), 'the holder of the *saranga*-bow' for protection He is the protector of all the three worlds. He continues to exist when the Sun and the Moon are there no more, when human beings have disintegrated, and when the stars have tumbled down. Lakshmi is associated with Vishnu. In another inscription three descendants of Raja Jaula Tomara build at Pehowa three temples to Vishnu in their desire to cross the dreadful ocean of mundane existence. An inscription on the Hissar pillar refers to 'the worshipper of Bhagavat'. Three inscriptions from the Gurgaon district refer to Vishnu and his worshippers. A reservoir in the Rohtak district was dedicated to Vishnu by his devotee Somatrata, an 'Acharya of the Yoga philosophy'.

A stone inscription from Sirsa of the reign of Shri Bhojadeva refers to Ratnarasi, a leader of the Pashupatas. He has conquered *kama* and is resplendent like Shiva himself. Associated with Shiva is Parvati, daughter of the Himalaya. Ratnarasi's commands were carried out with devotion by the multitude of kings with folded hands. Nilakantha, presumably a disciple, built a temple of Yogishvara. Devotion to *yoga* is stated to destroy all ill omens, and enlightens the adept with knowledge. He knows that earthly joys vanish like the waves in water, that youth is short-lived, and that human existence is like a stormy ocean that one has to cross.

Sculptures related to the religious phenomena in the Punjab have already been noticed. There is more evidence of this kind on Vaishnavism, Shaivism, and Shaktaism coming from the Bhima Devi Temple at Pinjore and the Prachi Shiva Temple at Pehowa, from the places like Hansi, Kaithal, Kapalmochan, Jaintipur-Muradnagar, Sirsa, Dholbaha and Zahura, and from the districts like Gurgaon, Sonepat, Rohtak, Mahendragarh, Bhiwani, Hissar, and Hoshiarpur. This evidence relates to Vishnu in association with Shesha Naga, his incarnations as Varaha, Vamana and Narasimha, his *vahana* Garuda, and to Vishnu in association with Shiva as Hari-Hara; it relates also to Shiva in the dancing posture, his *linga*, and his consort Uma or Parvati as Uma-Maheshwara and Shiva-Parvati; Ganesh and Karttikeya, and Ganesh with his *shakti*, are also represented; the Goddess is represented as Chamunda, Kali, and Mahishasuramardini.

Deities not related to Vaishnava, Shaiva or Shakta faiths were also represented in the Punjab during this period. We have already referred to the Sun temple of Multan which was a popular centre of pilgrimage for people from all over the country. Before the end of the tenth century, this Sun temple was destroyed by the Carmathians. The temple of Martand in Kashmir was built in honour of Surya. The god is represented in a number of sculptures. Perhaps the best of these is the one recovered from village Beri in district Rohtak. A sandstone image of Surya found at Pehowa shows him seated on a cushioned seat in a chariot. The sculpture is severely damaged. Only three of the usual seven horses remain now. The lame charioteer, Aruna, is also missing.

Brahma is represented in a sandstone sculpture of the ninth century found from the Prachi Shiva Temple at Pehowa. Seated in a lotus pedestal, he has four faces, only three of which can be seen. In three of his four hands, he has a ladle, a book and a *kamandalu*. Close to his right leg is his mount, the swan. Behind the upper two hands are two altars with three flames. He wears a garland, a pearl necklace, and the sacred thread. In a sandstone sculpture of the tenth-eleventh century recovered from district Sonepat, Brahma is shown jointly with Vishnu as Hari-Pitamha, the two gods standing back to back, with a common halo. Brahma here has three faces; the central face is bearded, and has an ornamented *jatamukuta*.

A sculpture of Agni was found from the Bhima Devi Temple at Pinjore. Standing with a long knotted beard, he wears a necklace, the sacred thread, a *vanamala*, armlets and bracelets. His *dhoti*-like lower garment is supported by a waistband. In his four hands he holds an *akshamala*, a spear, a flower and a *kamandalu*. His halo of flames is behind his head. Near his right foot is his mount, the goat. One of the two female attendants in pillared niches on either side of the god is turned backwards and holds a child in her left arm. Agni was no longer a god who commanded worship; he adorned the walls of temples dedicated to new gods, or goddesses. A statue of Yama in buff sandstone, collected from Sirsa, shows him standing in a pillared niche. His mount, the buffalo, is standing at the back. With a crown over his head, the god has *kundalas* in his ears and wears a necklace, the sacred thread, armlets and a waistband. In his right hand is *khatvang*. Kubera, found from Sirsa in a seated posture, wears a necklace, earrings and a crown of thorns (*karanda mukuta*). He has an ornamental halo over his head and wine-cup in his right hand. This god of wealth has no mount. An image of Ishana, obtained from the Bhima Devi Temple at Pinjore, bears a general resemblance to the image of Agni, but the Ishana image shows a trident, a snake, *jatamukuta* and Nandi, which bring the god close to Shiva.

In the Punjab hills, the evidence of inscriptions, temples and sculptures indicates the greater popularity of the Shakta faith than that of Vaishnavism. Meruvarman of Chamba built a temple of Lakshana Devi at Brahmaur and a temple of Shakti Devi at Chhatrari. The temple of Naina Devi was erected by the founder of the Bilaspur state in the ninth or tenth century. At Kangra, there was a temple of Bhima Devi, in addition to the temple of the goddess at Jwalamukhi. Only in the tenth century was a temple of Lakshmi-Narayana built in Chamba by Sahilavarman who is also said to have sent elephants for charitable distribution at Kurukshetra at the time of a solar eclipse. A temple of Narasimha was built at Brahmaur by a successor of Sahilavarman. Much of the evidence from Chamba relates to Shaivism. The temple of Mani Mahesha was built by Meruvarman who also dedicated a temple to Ganesha. In a tenth century Shiva Temple at Chamba there is an image of Ganapati in addition to the three faced image of Shiva. Before the end of the tenth century, a temple of Gauri Shankar was built at Chamba. We have noticed the rise of Shaivism in Kashmir. Already, in the early seventh century, Hiuen Tsang had regretted that the kingdom of Kashmir was no longer much given to Buddhism: 'the temples of the heretics were their sole thought'.

The religious literature of the period, the observations made by Hiuen Tsang and Alberuni, the epigraphic evidence of the period, and its sculpture indicate a variety of religious beliefs and practices in the Punjab. Many of the Vedic gods survived into the period but only as subordinate entities. Buddhism was certainly on the verge of disappearance and Jainism was not important. The cult of the goddess was dominant in the hills and known in the plains. The most important systems of religious belief and practice were Vaishnava and Shaiva. It is difficult to say which of these two was more important.

READING

Beal 1963; Charak 1977; Chattopadhyaya 1994; Devahuti 1970; Handa 1989; Niyogi 1962; Pushalkar 1955; Sachau 1989; Sharma 1965, 1987; Thapar 1966; Vogel 1990; Watters 1973; Wilson 1864-70.

Bibliography

Agarwal, D.P., *The Copper Bronze Age in India*. Delhi, 1971.

Agarwal, V.S., *India as Known to Panini*. Varanasi, 1963.

Alam, Humera, *Gandhara Sculptures in Lahore Museum*. Lahore, 1988.

Allan, J.A., *Catalogue of the Coins of Ancient India*. London, 1967.

Allchin, Bridget and Raymond, *Rise of Civilization in India and Pakistan*. Delhi, 1983.

Apte, V.M., *Social and Religious Life in the Grihya Sutra*. Bombay, 1954.

Banerji, S.C., *Dharma-Sutras, A Study in their Origin and Development*. Calcutta, 1962.

Bary, Wm Theodore de et al., *Sources of Indian Tradition*. New York, 1958.

Basham, A.L., *The Wonder That Was India*. New York, 1959.

Beal, Samuel (tr), *Chinese Accounts of India* (Translated from the Chinese of Hiuen Tsang). 4 vols. Calcutta, 1963.

Bhardwaj, H.C., *Aspects of Ancient Indian Technology*. Delhi, 1979.

Bogard, Levin C., *Mauryan India*. Delhi, 1985.

Bohtlingk, D. (tr), *Chandogya Upanishad*. Leipzig, 1889.

Buddha Prakash, *Political and Social Movements in Ancient Panjab* (From the Vedic Age up to the Mauryan Period). Delhi, 1964.

——, *Glimpses of Ancient Panjab*. Patiala, 1966.

——, *Evolution of Heroic Tradition in Ancient Panjab*. Patiala, 1971.

Buhler, G. (tr), *Apastamba Dharmasutra*. Oxford University Press, 1879. (Reprinted by Motilal Banarsidass in 1965 in *The Sacred Law of Aryas*).

—— (tr), *Gautama Dharma-Sutra*. Oxford, 1897.

—— G. (tr), *Budhayana Dharma-Sutra*. Oxford, 1882. (Reprinted in *The Sacred Law of the Aryas in 1965* by Motilal Banarsidass).

——, *On the Origin of the Indian Brahmi Alphabet*. Strassburg, 1898.

Burrow, T., *The Sanskrit Language*. London, 1965.

Caland, W. (tr), *Pancha Vimsha Brahmana*. Calcutta, 1931.

—— (tr), *Shankhayana Shrauta Sutra*. Delhi, 1980.

Chakravarti, U., *The Social Dimensions of Early Buddhism*. Delhi, 1987.

Chanana, D.R., *Slavery in Ancient India as Depicted in Pali and Sanskrit Texts*. Delhi, 1960.

Charak, Sukhdev Singh (tr), *Gulabnama of Diwan Kirpa Ram*. Delhi, 1977.

Chattopadhyaya, B.D., *The Making of Early Medieval India*. Delhi, 1994.

Chattopadhyaya, D.P., *Lokayata: A Study in Ancient Indian Materialism*. Delhi, 1959.

Chattopadhyaya, D.P., *History of Science and Technology in Ancient India–The Beginning*. Calcutta, 1986.

Chattopadhyaya, S., *The Achaemenians and India*. Delhi, 1974.

Chattopadhyaya, Sudhakar, *Early History of North India*. Calcutta, 1968.

Chaudhuri, U., *Indra and Varuna in Indian Mythology*. Delhi, 1981.

Childe, V. Gordon, *New Light on the Most Ancient East*. London, 1958.

——, *What Happened in History*. Harmondsworth, Penguin Books, 1967.

Chowdhuri, K.A., *Ancient Agriculture and Forestry in Northern India*. Bombay, 1977.

Cowell, E. (ed), *Buddhacharita*. Oxford, 1893.

Cunningham, A., *Ancient Geography of India*. Calcutta, 1924.

Dandamaev, M.A. and V.G. Lokonin, *The Culture and Social Institutions of Ancient Iran*. Cambridge, 1989.

Dani, A.H., *Indian Paleography*. Oxford, 1963.

——, *The Historic City of Taxila*. Paris and Tokyo, UNESCO, 1968.

——, *Recent Archaeological Discoveries in Pakistan*. Paris, 1986.

Devahuti, D., *Harsha: A Political Study*. Oxford, 1970.

Dikshit, M.G., *History of Indian Glass*. Bombay, 1969.

Dutt, M.N. (tr), *Bhagvata Purana*. Calcutta, 1895.

Eggeling, J. (tr), *Satpatha Brahmana*. Oxford 1882 (Reprinted in 1963 from Delhi by Motilal Banarsidass in five volumes).

Fairservis Jr., Walter A., *The Roots of Ancient India*. London, 1971.

Fleet, S.J.F., *Inscriptions of the Early Gupta Kings and Their Successors*. Varanasi, 1970.

Frauwallner, E., *The Earliest Vinaya and the Beginnings of Buddhist Literature*. Rome, 1956.

Geigir, W. (tr), *Mahavamsha*. London, 1912.

Gharpure, G.R. (tr), *Yajnavalkya Smriti*. Bombay, 1936.

Ghosh, A., *Archaeological Remains, Monuments and Museums*. Delhi, 1964.

——, *The City in Early Historical India*. Shimla, 1990.

Giles, H.A. (tr), *Travels of Faheien*. Cambridge, 1923.

Goldman, R.P., *Gods, Priests and Warriors: The Bhrigus of the Mahabharata*. New York, 1977.

Gonda, J., *Vedic Literature*. Wiesbaden, 1975.

Gopal, L., *Aspects of History of Agriculture in Ancient India*. Varanasi, 1980.

Goshal, U.N., *A History of Indian Political Ideas*. London, 1966.

Griffith, Ralph T.H. (tr), *The Hymns of the Rigveda: Translated with a Popular Commentary*. Delhi, 1976.

Griswold, H.D., *The Religion of the Rigveda*. Delhi, 1973.

Gupta, Parmanand, *Geographical Names in Ancient Indian Inscriptions*. Delhi, 1977.

Handa, Devendra, *Heritage of Haryana*, 2 vols. Chandigarh, 1989.

Hare, F.L. (tr), *The Book of Gradual Saying*. London, 1932–6.

Held, G.J., *The Mahabharata: An Ethnological Study*. Amsterdam, 1935.
Herodotus, *The Histories*. Tr. Aubrey de Selincourt. Harmondsworth, 1955.
Horner, I.B. (tr), *The Middle Length Saying*. London, 1954.
Hutchison, J. and J. Ph. Vogel, *History of the Panjab Hill States*, 2 vols. Shimla, 1982.
Jacobi, H., *Samaraicca Kaha: A Jaina Prakrit Work*. Calcutta, 1926.
Jaiswal, Suvira, *The Origin and Development of Vaishnavism (200 B.C.–A.D. 500)*. Delhi, 1967.
Jha, D.N., *Revenue System in Post-Maurya and Gupta Times*. Calcutta, 1967.
——, *Ancient India: An Introductory Outline*. Delhi, 1977.
Jolly, J. (tr), *Narada Smrti*. Oxford, 1889.
Joshi, L.M. (ed), *History of the Panjab from Prehistoric Times to the Age of Ashoka*. Patiala, 1977.
Kangle, R.P., *The Kautilya Arthashastra*. Bombay, 1965.
Keith, A.B., *The Aitareya Aranyaka*. Oxford, 1909.
——, *The Taittiriya Samhita*. Cambridge, 1914.
——, *The Rigveda Brahmanas*. Cambridge, 1920.
—— (tr), *Aitareya Brahmana*. Cambridge (Mass), 1920.
——, *Religion and Philosophy of the Vedas and the Upanishads*. Cambridge, 1925.
——, *History of Sanskrit Literature*. Oxford, 1928.
Kosambi, D.D., *Myth and Reality: Studies in the Formation of Indian Culture*. Bombay, 1962.
——, *The Culture and Civilization of Ancient India in Historical Outline*. Delhi, 1982.
Kuiper, F.B.J., *Aryans in the Rigveda*. Amsterdam, 1991.
Lakshman Sarup, *Nighantu Tatha Nirukta*. Delhi, 1967.
Macdonell, A.A., *A History of Sanskrit Literature*. Delhi, 1990.
Maity, Sachindra Kumar, *Economic Life in Northarn India in the Gupta Period (A.D. 300–550)*. Delhi, 1970.
——, *The Imperial Guptas and Their Times*. Delhi, 1975.
Makhan Lal, *Settlement History and Rise of Civilization in the Ganga-Yamuna Doab*. Delhi, 1984.
Malik, S.C. (ed), *Indian Civilization, The First Phase*. Simla, 1971.
Marshall, Sir John, *Taxila: An Illustrated Account of Archaeological Excavations*, 3 vols. Delhi, 1975.
McCrindle, J.W., *Ancient India as Described by Magasthenes and Arrian*. London, 1877.
——, *The Invasion of India by Alexander the Great*. London, 1896.
Mitchiner, M., *The Origins of Indian Coinage*. London, 1973.
Mookerji, Radha Kumud, *Hindu Civilization*. Bombay, 1977.
Mukherjee, B.N., *The Rise and Fall of the Kushana Empire*. Calcutta, 1988.
Narain, A.K., *The Indo-Greeks*. Oxford, 1957.

Nikam, K.A. and R. Mekeon, *The Edicts of Ashoka*. Chicago, 1949.
Niyogi, Pushpa, *Contributions to the Economic History of Northern India*. Calcutta, 1962.
Oldenberg, H. (tr), *Gobhila Grhya Sutra*. Oxford, 1892.
—— (tr), *Hiranyakesin Grhya Sutra*. Oxford, 1892.
—— (tr), *Dipavamsha*. London, 1979.
Pande, G.C., *Studies in the Origins of Buddhism*. Allahabad, 1957.
Patel, M. (tr), *The Danastutis of the Rigveda*. Vallabha Vidyanagar, 1961.
Pathak, S. and S. Chitrao, *Panini-Sutra*. Poona, 1935.
Patil, D.R., *Cultural History from the Vayu Purana*. Delhi, 1973.
Pigott, Stuart, *Prehistoric India*. Penguin Books, 1961.
Prasad, Beni, *The State in Ancient India*. Allahabad, 1974.
Prasad, Kameshwar, *Cities, Crafts and Commerce under the Kushanas*. Delhi, 1984.
Pushalkar, A.D., *Studies in the Epics and the Puranas*. Bombay, 1955.
Radhakrishnan, S. (tr), *The Principal Upanishads*. London, 1953.
Ram Gopal, *India of the Vedic Kalpa Sutras*. Delhi, 1983.
Ratnagar, Shereen, *Understanding Harappa: Civilization in the Greater Indus Valley*. Delhi, 2001 (paperback).
Raychaudhuri, Hemchandra, *Political History of Ancient India*. Calcutta, 1972.
Rhys Davids, T.W., *Buddhism in India*. London, 1903.
—— (tr), *Malindapanho*. Oxford, 1890–4.
—— (tr), *Digha Nikaya*. London, 1899, 1910, 1921.
Rhys Davids, T.W. and H. Oldenberg (trs), *Vinaya Pitaka*. Oxford, 1881–5.
Rhys Davids, Mrs (tr), *Dhammapada*. London, 1931.
Rhys Davids, Mrs. and F.L. Woodward (trs), *Book of Kindred Sayings*. London, 1913.
Roy, Kumkum, *The Emergence of Monarchy in North India, Eighth-Fourth Centuries B.C.* Delhi, 1994.
Sachau, Edward C. (tr), *Alberuni's India*. Delhi, 1989.
Sankalia, H.D., *Ramayana: Myth or Reality*. New Delhi, 1973.
——, *Prehistory and Protohistory of India and Pakistan*. Poona, 1974.
Shafer, R., *Ethnography of Ancient India*. Wiesbaden, 1954.
Shah, Shalini, *The Making of Womanhood: Gender Relations in the Mahabharata*. Delhi, 1995.
Shamasastry, R. (tr), *Kautilya's Arthashastra*. Bangalore, 1915.
—— (tr), *Arthashastra*. Mysore, 1956.
Sharma, J.P., *Republics in Ancient India*. Leiden, 1968.
Sharma, R.S., *Indian Feudalism*, Calcutta, 1965.
——, *Shudras in Ancient India*. Delhi, 1980.
——, *Social Change in Early Medieval India*. Delhi, 1981.
——, *Perspectives in Social and Economic History of Early India*. Delhi, 1983.
——, *Urban Decay in India (c 300–c 1000)*. Delhi, 1987.
——, *Origin of the State in India*. Bombay, 1989.

Sharma, R.S., *Aspects of Political Ideas and Institutions in Ancient India*. Delhi, 1991.
——, *The State and Varna Formation in the Mid-Ganga Plains: An Ethno-archaelogical View*. Delhi, 1996.
Shastri, A., *India as Seen in the Kattani-Mata of Damodara Gupta*. Delhi, 1975.
Shastri, A.M., *India as Seen in the Brhatsamhita of Varahamihira*. Delhi, 1969.
Sircar, D.C., *Inscriptions of Ashoka*. Delhi, 1957.
——, *Indian Epigraphy*. Delhi, 1965.
——, *Landlordism and Tenancy in Ancient and Medieval India as Revealed by Epigraphical Records*. Lucknow, 1969.
——, *Iranians and Greeks in Ancient Punjab*. Patiala, 1973.
Srinivasan, D., *Concept of Cow in the Rigveda*. Delhi, 1979.
Srivastava, K.M., *Community Movements in Protohistoric India*. Delhi, 1979.
Syed, A.J. (ed), *D.D. Kosambi on History and Society: Problems of Interpretation*. Bombay, 1985.
Thapar, Romila, *A History of India*. Penguin Books, 1966.
——, *Ashoka and the Decline of the Mauryas*. Delhi, 1973.
——, *The Past and Prejudice*. Delhi, 1975.
——, *Exile and the Kingdom: Some Thoughts on the Ramayana*. Bangalore, 1978.
——, *The Mauryas Revisited*. Calcutta, 1987.
——, *Clan, Caste and Origin Myths in Early India*. Shimla, 1992.
——, *Interpreting Early India*. Delhi, 1994.
——, *Cultural Transactions in Early India: Tradition and Patronage*. Delhi, 1994.
——, *From Lineages to State*. Delhi, 1995.
——, *Time as a Metaphor of History: Early India*. Delhi, 1996.
Thaplayal, K.K., *Studies in Ancient Indian Seals*. Lucknow, 1972.
Trautmann, T.R., *Kautilya and the Arthashastra*. London, 1971.
Tripathi, T.M. (ed), *Kuttani-Matam or Shambhali-Matam*. Bombay, 1924.
Tripathi, V., *The Painted Grey Ware, An Iron Age Culture of Northern India*. Delhi, 1976.
Upasak, C.S., *The History of Palaeography of Mauryan Brahmi Script*. Nalanda, 1960.
Varma, T.P., *The Palaeography of Brahmi Script in North India*. Varanasi, 1971.
Vasu, S.C. (ed), (Panini's) *Ashtadhyayi*. Delhi, 1962.
Vogel, J. Ph., *Catalogue of the Bhuri Singh Museum at Chamba*. Calcutta, 1990.
Wagle, N., *Society at the Time of Buddha*. Bombay, 1966.
Watters, T. (tr), *On Yuan Chwang's Travels in India*. Delhi, 1973.
Wheeler, R.E.M., *Early India and Pakistan*. London, 1960.
——, *Civilizations of the Indus Valley and Beyond*. London, 1966.
——, *The Indus Civilization*. Cambridge, 1968.
Whitney, W.D. (tr), *Atharvaveda Samhita*. Delhi, 1971.
Wilson, H.H. (tr), *Vishnu Purana*. 5 vols. London, 1864–70.

Index